Praise for previous editions of

QUICK ESCAPES®
PACIFIC NORTHWEST

"The Quick Escapes series is one of the nation's top sources for day-trip or short vacation planning. . . . Hop in the car with this book and marvel at just how wonderful your own area is."

—*Stateman-Journal* (Salem, Oregon)

"This guide is full of tips on what to see and do on weekend trips around Seattle, Portland, and Vancouver, British Columbia."

—*Los Angeles Daily News*

"As an idea book, this one is hard to beat."

—*Spokane Chronicle*

"A valuable guide for travelers whose time is tight. *Quick Escapes* covers both the big name attractions and lesser known spots that locals love. . . . *Quick Escapes* takes the work out of wandering."

—Vickie Nelson, senior editor, *Northwest Travel*

Help Us Keep This Guide Up to Date

Every effort has been made by the authors and editors to make this guide as accurate and useful as possible. However, many things can change after a guide is published—establishments close, phone numbers change, facilities come under new management, etc.

We would love to hear from you concerning your experiences with this guide and how you feel it could be improved and be kept up to date. Though we may not be able to respond to all comments and suggestions, we'll take them to heart, and we'll also make certain to share them with the author. Please send your comments and suggestions to the following address:

The Globe Pequot Press
Reader Response/Editorial Department
P.O. Box 480
Guilford, CT 06437

Or you may e-mail us at:
editorial@globe-pequot.com

Thanks for your input, and happy travels!

QUICK ESCAPES® SERIES

QUICK ESCAPES®
PACIFIC NORTHWEST

Fourth Edition

32 WEEKEND TRIPS FROM
PORTLAND, SEATTLE, AND VANCOUVER, B.C.

BY

MARILYN McFARLANE

EDITED BY

CHRISTINE CUNNINGHAM

The Globe Pequot Press

GUILFORD, CONNECTICUT

Photo Credits: pages 1, 14, 65, 203, and 219 courtesy Micky Jones; pages 111, 186, 229, 247, and 278 courtesy Marilyn McFarlane; page 40 courtesy Dick Powers; page 76 courtesy Washington County Visitors Association; page 94 courtesy McKenzie River Rafting Company; page 103 courtesy Gary Brettnacher; page 138 courtesy John Parkhurst; page 150 courtesy George White/Salish Lodge; page 168 courtesy North Cascades National Park Service.

Cover photo by William D. McKinney/SuperStock, Inc.
Cover design by Laura Augustine
Interior design by Nancy Freeborn
Maps by Maryann Dubé

Quick Escapes is a registered trademark of The Globe Pequot Press.

Library of Congress Cataloging-in-Publication Data
McFarlane, Marilyn.
    Quick escapes Pacific Northwest : 32 weekend trips from Portland, Seattle, and Vancouver,
    B.C. / by Marilyn McFarlane : edited by Christine Cunningham. — 4th ed.
        p.   cm. — (Quick escapes series)
    Includes index.
    ISBN 0-7627-0468-3
    1. Northwest, Pacific—Tours. I. Cunningham, Christine. II. Title. III. Series.
E852.3.M379 1999
917.9504'43—DC21   99-24575
                                                                                                      CIP

Manufactured in the United States of America
Fourth Edition/First Printing

CONTENTS

Introduction xi

PORTLAND ESCAPES 1

1. Hell's Canyon 2
2. Seaside to Lincoln City 11
3. Eugene-Florence-Newport 23
4. Mount Hood Loop. 34
5. Around Mount St. Helens 43
6. Astoria and Long Beach Water Pleasures 52
7. Columbia River Gorge: Oregon. 62
8. Oregon Wine Country 71
9. John Day Fossil Beds to Shaniko. 81
10. McKenzie River Highway 91
11. Central Oregon 100

SEATTLE ESCAPES 111

1. By Train to Vancouver, Canada 112
2. San Juan and Orcas Islands 121
3. Strait of Juan de Fuca 131
4. The Hoh River Valley, Olympic Peninsula 142
5. Snoqualmie Falls and Fall City 148
6. Leavenworth to Ellensburg. 155
7. North Cascades 166
8. Mount Rainier Loop. 175
9. North Kitsap Peninsula 183
10. Skagit County 190
11. Gig Harbor 197

continued

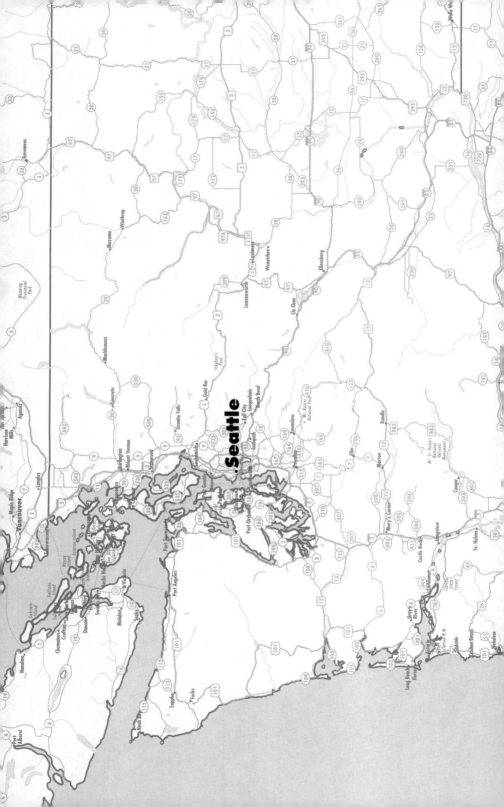

VANCOUVER ESCAPES. 203

1. Explore the Fraser Valley 204
2. Mountain/Canyon Circle. 214
3. Vancouver Island: West Shore 225
4. South Vancouver Island 235
5. The Gulf Islands 243
6. Langdale to Lund 254
7. Salt Spring Island 265
8. The Okanagan 273
9. Southeast Vancouver Island. 285
10. Vancouver Island: Northeast Coast 297

Index. 309
About the Author and the Editor 323

The prices and rates listed in this guidebook were confirmed at
press time. We recommend, however, that you call establishments
before traveling to obtain current information.

Maps provided for each escape are for general reference only
and should be used in conjunction with a regional road map. Distances indicated are also approximate.

INTRODUCTION

This guide to brief getaways from Portland, Seattle, and Vancouver is intended for longtime residents, newcomers to the Pacific Northwest, and visitors passing through—anyone who's eager to explore the recreational wonderland that lies beyond the three major cities of the region.

When you want to travel scenic byways and discover their hidden treasures, take this book with you. It will lead you to well-known spots that no tourist should miss and will uncover hideaways that only the local folk know.

The guide provides fully detailed itineraries, much like a customized, organized tour. But they are suggestions only! Don't try to do everything listed on each trip, or you'll feel too rushed to enjoy yourself. Pick and choose among the activities, and plan to return for those you missed.

At the end of each chapter, **There's More** provides more reasons to come back. **Special Events** lists regional events and holiday activities. **Other Recommended Restaurants and Lodgings** gives concise descriptions of good places to eat and stay other than those included in the itinerary. Finally, **For More Information** tells you who to contact to obtain maps and learn about the area you're visiting.

The itineraries are designed as auto tours, but public transport, walking, and bicycling are viable alternatives in many cases. I recommend using them whenever you can.

Consider traveling in the off-season, rather than the high-use summer months. The weather is mild in spring and fall, though rains are frequent. Winter has its own appeal, with the crowds gone and the landscape spare or clad in white.

Facilities for the handicapped are mentioned where appropriate.

Rates and fees are not specifically stated, as they often change, but you may assume that most costs are reasonable. If a place seemed unusually expensive (or amazingly inexpensive), I have so indicated. Museums usually charge a nominal admission fee or request a donation.

Distances are approximate and are expressed in miles (and in kilometers in the Vancouver, British Columbia, section). American standard spelling is used throughout, except for Canadian place-names.

Make reservations in advance at hotels and inns whenever possible. Some are very small, and rooms fill quickly, especially during the busy season.

The following is a list of standard equipment you'll probably need on your escapes:

Raingear (in the Northwest, the weather is unpredictable)
Jacket
Sturdy walking shoes
Daypack
Water bottle
Insect repellent
Camera
Binoculars
Travel-size umbrella
Regional maps

A great deal of effort has gone into making this book as accurate as possible, but places do change. If you wish to suggest a correction or a special find that should be included in a future edition, please let me know. I'll be glad to investigate. Meanwhile, enjoy your mini-vacations—all thirty-two of them.

Marilyn McFarlane
Portland, Oregon

PORTLAND
ESCAPES

Hell's Canyon

JET-BOATING THROUGH HELL'S CANYON

2 NIGHTS

Jet-boating • Raging river • Mile-deep canyon • Petroglyphs
Wilderness lodge • Historic ruins • Mail boat • Three states

Jet boats carry modern travelers, young and old, over the riffles and rapids of the Snake River and through Hell's Canyon, the deepest canyon in North America. The Snake cuts through high desert plateaus of Washington and Oregon, and the craggy mountains of Idaho, before plunging between the narrow walls of the canyon.

Native Americans took refuge here. Miners, ranchers, and steamboaters tried to tame the canyon, but the only permanent residents who survive are a few stubborn ranchers. Some ride 8 miles on horseback to collect their weekly mail.

Beamers Hell's Canyon Tours and Excursions, which offers one- to four-day trips, is the largest of several riverboat companies. You can ride the historic mail boat on its weekly Wednesday run. Otherwise, follow the two-day, one-night Copper Creek Overnight tour that leaves Beamer's Landing in Clarkston, Washington, across the river from Lewiston, Idaho, daily, bucks furious water for 70 miles upriver to its overnight stop at Copper Creek Lodge, and returns the following day.

Boats that ride like bucking broncos on the high raging waters of spring offer a gentler swinging ride in summer and fall. Spring and fall are recommended tour times, when crowds are few and temperatures moderate.

An impending National Forest Service plan might restrict the number of tours that go to the end of navigation, but it probably won't affect this tour to Copper Creek Lodge and back.

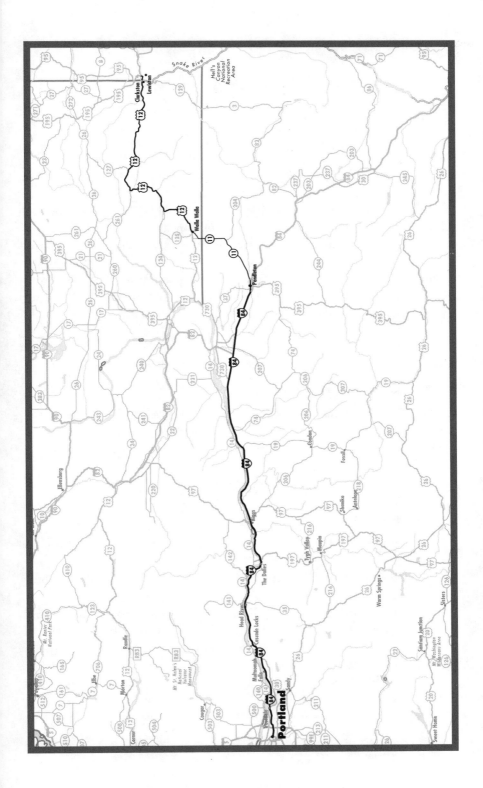

DAY 1

Morning

It is worth the time and money to fly from Portland to Lewiston, Idaho, for this Escape, although it is a pleasant and scenic 345-mile drive. If you drive, leave early and follow I–84 down the Oregon side of the **Columbia River** and have lunch 208 miles east in **Pendleton,** Oregon.

From Pendleton, follow State Route 11 to **Walla Walla,** Washington, and U.S. 12 to **Clarkston,** Washington, population about 7,000. Clarkston is Washington's most inland seaport, 450 miles up the Columbia and Snake rivers. A bridge connects Clarkston with its sister city of **Lewiston,** Idaho, with a population of about 28,000, across the **Snake River.** The towns were named after William Clark and Meriwether Lewis, the noted explorers of the Lewis and Clark expedition, who camped here at the confluence of the Snake and Clearwater Rivers in 1805 and again in 1806.

Afternoon

DINNER: Quality Inn—Clarkston, overlooking the river.

LODGING: Quality Inn—Clarkston, 700 Port Drive. (509) 758–9500. The two-story motor inn has a heated swimming pool and easy access to the dock where your jet boat leaves in the morning.

DAY 2

Morning

Walk behind the Quality Inn to Beamers Hell's Canyon Tours and Excursions at 700 Port Drive (800–522–6966). You should have a reservation on one of Beamer's eight covered aluminum jet boats, each 30 to 40 feet long. The boat leaves at 7:00 A.M.

You will be sitting, or, more accurately, bouncing on a padded seat aboard the *Hell's Canyon Rose* or maybe the *Spirit of Copper Creek*. Dress warmly and comfortably, with shoes appropriate to riverside docks and rustic pathways. Plan to get a little river water on your face when you open and close the sliding glass windows for a better view! These are regular tour boats, not river rafts, but you will be bouncing up and down on your seat, so sit at the rear of the boat if you have back trouble.

A few jokes from the captain, and you are under the interstate bridge that crosses between Idaho and Washington. One thrust of the jet engines and the boat moves from float speed to full engine. For a few moments the rooftops of the town climb the grassy hills and steep ridges, but you are soon between high, green flat-topped hills, scored and folded as they rise straight up to plateau pastures high above the river.

Captain Tim Stuart will probably be at the helm, describing the river and the history that is visible to those who know where to look. Civilization ends when you pass the houses and gas stations of **Asotin,** once a wintering place for the Nez Percé, now the last town on our journey. Its name means "a place of eel"; freshwater eels were once caught there.

A rusty old paddle wheel steamer, the **Steamboat Jean,** is snugged against the shore. Its black-and-red stacks are a memorial to the days when gold miners braved the river. As the old wreck recedes behind your boat, the rocky outcroppings dominate the view. The sumac that climbs the steep hills on both sides is green in spring but turns the landscape red in autumn.

The essence of these deep river valleys is, of course, water. In spring, the water partially submerges the riverside trees. The jet boat rides high and hard above the angry river in May; it rides on much shallower water in September.

"We're passing through **Buffalo Eddy,**" the captain says. "The water here can be 120 feet deep."

He steers to the far bank of the river and slows so that you can see **petroglyphs** carved by ancient Nez Percé natives. Nobody knows how long ago these figures were made, but the Nez Percé have been in this area for 7,200 years.

The Snake River begins to churn and boil, but this is just the approach to Hell's Canyon, so you are not yet in wild rapids. The first stop of the day is at **Heller Bar,** homesteaded by Cecil Heller.

BREAKFAST: Beamer's Heller Bar Lodge, where a light continental breakfast is served amid guidebooks and postcards.

A high green hill seems to block the river beyond Heller Bar. This is where the **Grand Ronde River** joins the Snake. Excitement mounts as the boat passes a clutter of houses at the base of a hill and turns left at **Lime Point.** The National Geological Society and the United States Army Corps of Engineers designate this point as the entrance to **Hell's Canyon.**

"We are now at river mile 170, 170 miles from the confluence of the Columbia River and the Snake River at Pasco, Idaho. You can see three states from here," the captain says. "Idaho is to your left, Washington to your right, and Oregon straight ahead. Those cabins clinging to shelves of rock are on original land grants and can be accessed only by water."

Outcroppings pull the mountains up steeply in dark ridges of rock and grass. The river narrows and the water churns as you move into 652,977-acre **Hell's Canyon National Recreation Area,** created under the Wild and Scenic Rivers Act in 1975 to preserve the natural flow of the Snake River. Some private land remains on the Idaho bank, but all the land on the Oregon side is administered by the Forest Service from here to the end of navigation.

The jet boat twists and turns through **Deer Head Rapids** and **Wild Goose Rapids** on the way to **Geneva Bar** and the **Salmon River.** As you ride the wild rapids, you won't be surprised to learn that the explorers abandoned Hell's Canyon as a transportation route. Green hills give way to steep rocky mountains fringed with green. A sheep rancher's cabin sits alone on the draw now, but there was a time when wool was stacked beside the river waiting for the mail boat.

The 429-mile-long Salmon River, which begins and ends in Idaho, is one of the last free-flowing fishing rivers in the West. The 1,000-mile-long Snake River can rise and fall 6 or 7 feet in a day because it is controlled by dams, but the Salmon, which has no dams, can fluctuate 20 to 30 feet in depth over the seasons.

Travel this river in fall, and you will have a swinging water ride, with endangered elk on either bank. Go in the high water of spring, and it is more like a wild roller coaster that crashes on every wave. As the boat is launched out of the water—and you are launched out of your seat—on your way past **High Mountain Sheep Rapids,** think about the steamboats that braved this river at the turn of the century. Prospectors came because the canyon was full of mineral wealth, but they didn't last long.

A regularly scheduled stern-wheeler, the *Imnaha,* made its way between Lewiston and Eureka by being winched over those rapids by cables anchored to rocks, until the day in 1906 when the cable failed. By some miracle, everybody got out alive, but the steamboating era was over.

By the time you pass the *Imnaha,* the river is at full boil. "Look up that hill and you'll see the foundation of the old hotel at **Eureka Bar,**" the captain says. The town was a tiny version of the Klondike, but these prospectors were looking for that valuable 3-foot vein of copper claimed by the Eureka Mining Company and funded by Eastern investors. The copper mine went 580 feet through the ridge to the Imnaha River, but now all that remains are a few visible mining ruins and the laughter of the Imnaha Rapids.

The mail boat still comes up this wild river canyon every Wednesday. You can ride aboard as a passenger. From your bouncing transportation you can see the mailbox hanging over the riverbank of a ranch leased by the Forest Service at **Dug Bar,** also known as **Nez Percé Crossing.** Chief Joseph crossed here with his tribe and his horses. If you think this ride is interesting, imagine being among the women and children pulled on rafts across the river by horses.

There are only a few signs of life in the canyon wilderness today, but many human dramas have been played here. At **Deep Creek,** thirty-two Chinese gold miners were robbed and killed by seven horse thieves in 1887. Deep Creek is at river mile 201.

LUNCH: Picnic at **Kirkwood Ranch,** a working ranch maintained by the Forest Service as a museum.

Afternoon

Navigation ends upriver at river mile 232, 17 miles below Hell's Canyon Dam. As the jet boat turns back downriver, you will look straight up for 1½ miles to the top of **He Devil Mountain.**

The captain pulls out of the wild river to a dock at river mile 208. You are home for the night, at **Beamers Copper Creek Lodge,** first homesteaded by Billy Rankin, who prospected for gold and copper in 1903.

Deer wander away as you climb the slight slope to a complex of buildings overlooking the river. If you have ever been to summer camp, you recognize the layout: dining hall, cabins scattered along the path. Couples and families may choose cabins with hotel-style beds and private bathrooms; others choose bunk beds.

The sun goes down. Deer drink from the shore. Stars leap out of the skies in the clear air. After all that "water exercise" and fresh air, guests go to bed early.

DINNER: Copper Creek Lodge, where you eat a hearty meal around large tables in the dining hall.

LODGING: Copper Creek Lodge.

DAY 3

Morning

BREAKFAST: Copper Creek Lodge, which serves an old-fashioned rancher's breakfast.

You can relax at the lodge, or repeat the upriver portion of yesterday's journey to Kirkwood Ranch and the end of navigation.

LUNCH: Picnic at Kirkwood Ranch or lunch at Copper Creek Lodge.

Afternoon

Your jet boat leaves mid-afternoon for its wild ride downriver, with the captain shouting "Hold on!" as you round every curve at 35 miles an hour.

During the brief steamship period at the turn of the century, it took five days for an intrepid steam-powered stern-wheeler to go upriver and three-and-a-half hours for it to go back downriver. Nowadays, it only takes about four hours of bucking-bronco jet-boating to go upstream to Copper Creek Lodge, and two or three hours to come down.

By the time they have stopped once more at Heller Bar and made the last long run back to the dock at Clarkston, most passengers have had enough river.

If you flew, you have probably reserved a late afternoon flight out of Lewiston Airport. If you drove, you may want to drive two hours to Walla Walla, Washington, or another hour to Pendleton, Oregon, before you stop for the night.

THERE'S MORE

Asotin County Historical Museum, Third and Filmore, Asotin. (509) 243–4659. An 1882 log cabin, and an exhibit of branding irons and carriages in a nearby pole barn. Open Tuesday through Saturday.

Chief Looking Glass Park, 5 miles south of Clarkston, offers boat launch ramps to the Snake, as well as docks, moorage, and picnic tables. From there, you can follow the 16-mile wheelchair-accessible Clearwater and Snake River National Recreation Trail to historic sites and attractions in Hellsgate State Park, Swallows Nest Rock, and West Pond.

Chief Timothy State Park, 8 miles west of Clarkston off State Route 12, sits on an island in the middle of the Snake River. The Alpowai Interpretive Center offers audiovisual programs and exhibits.

Hell's Canyon Adventures, P.O. Box 159, Oxbow, OR 97840. (800) 422–3568. Offers white-water rafting as well as jet-boat tours.

SPECIAL EVENTS

Clarkston

Late April. Asotin County Fair, Clarkston. Features rodeo, stock show and sale.

Late April to mid-May. Dogwood Festival, Lewiston. Includes garden tours and crafts fair.

Late April to mid-May. Dogwood Festival of the Lewis Clark Valley. Includes garden tours and crafts fair.

June. I Made the Grade, Clarkston. Thirteen-mile bicycle ride that climbs 1,000 feet.

Mid-July. Lewis and Clark Air Festival, Lewiston.

September. Thunder on the Snake hydroplane races, Lewiston.

September. Nez Percé County Fair, Lewiston. Includes agricultural, live-stock, and homemaking competitions, carnival and midway, and commercial booths.

Mid-September. Lewiston Roundup, Lewiston.

Mid-December. Reflections on the Confluence, Clarkston. Lighted boat parade on the Snake River near Swallows Nest Park.

OTHER RECOMMENDED RESTAURANTS AND LODGINGS

Clarkston

Best Western Rivertree Inn, 1257 Bridge Street. (509) 758–9551. Outdoor swimming pool, fitness room, sauna, and hot tub.

Lewiston

Red Lion Inn, 621 Twenty-first Street. (208) 799–1000. Full-service motor inn.

Sacajawea Select Inn, 1824 Main Street. (208) 746–1393 or (800) 333–1393. Near scenic river walkway and bike trail.

FOR MORE INFORMATION

Clarkston Chamber of Commerce, 502 Bridge Street, Clarkston, WA 99403.
(509) 758–7712.

Lewiston Airport is served by three airlines. Call the American Automobile
Association in Portland, (503) 222–6734, or Global Travel in Lewiston,
(800) 574–9949.

Seaside to Lincoln City
A COASTAL PANORAMA

2 OR 3 NIGHTS

Rural countryside • Sandy beaches • Ocean views
Hiking • Kite flying • Fishing • Boutiques • Art galleries
Fine dining • Fresh seafood

More visitors come to the northern Oregon coast than to any other part of the state. Yet despite the strollers, kite flyers, picnickers, surfers, and driftwood collectors, it seldom feels crowded. In the off-season, yours may be the only footprints on a wide, smooth, sandy beach, and the only sounds you hear will be the hiss of the surf and the cries of gulls.

This getaway covers the stretch of coastline from Seaside to Lincoln City and encompasses a variety of shoreline pleasures.

DAY 1

Morning

Drive northwest on U.S. Route 26, which cuts through a valley of rich farmland before rising into the forests of the coastal mountain range.

At **Camp 18,** west of Elsie (about 55 miles from Portland), stop for coffee or, if you've skipped breakfast, a whopping "Logger's Breakfast." The hand-built log restaurant-museum was constructed in the early 1970s by Gordon Smith as a monument to loggers. The ridge pole in the Camp 18 dining room is 85 feet long and weighs 25 tons. The 500-pound doors are hand carved; ax handles form door pulls. Carved figures include an eagle, a logger, Smokey the Bear, and Big Foot.

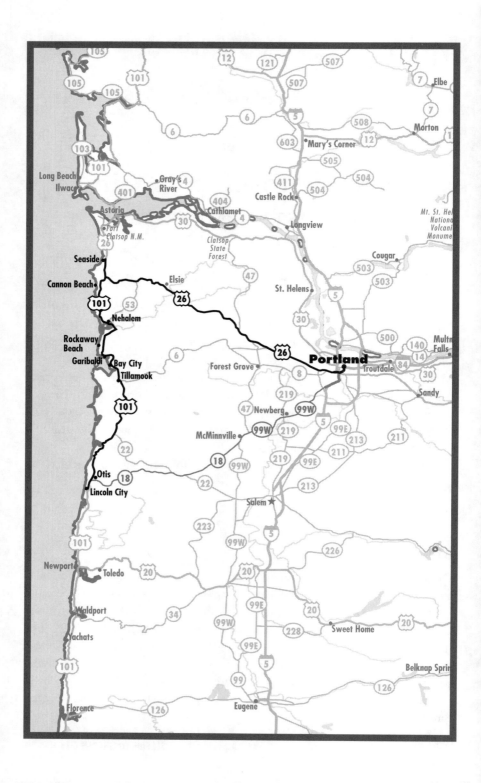

A few miles farther, watch for a sign on the right to the **largest Sitka spruce tree** in the United States. The giant tree is a short distance off the highway.

Continue on Route 26 to **Seaside** (80 miles from Portland), a resort town that bustles with conventions, tourist traffic, souvenir shops, and arcades. It has secluded, quiet corners as well.

To get your bearings and an impression of both town and shore, stroll the 2-mile-long **Promenade** that borders the beach. You'll see kites flying, children building castles, volleyball games on the sand, and surf waders—unless the weather is stormy. In that case, everyone will be indoors reading by the fire, watching the wind whip waves high and the spindrift fly. Or they'll be downtown shopping.

Seaside's main thoroughfare, Broadway, has been spruced up and is occasionally closed to vehicles and now boasts dozens of thriving shops and a lively atmosphere. **Seaside Guild of Artists,** in Heritage Square, displays works of local artists.

LUNCH: Dooger's, 505 Broadway, Seaside. (503) 738–3773. Justifiably famous for its rich, flavorsome clam chowder. Top off your lunch with a slice of German chocolate cake at **Harrison's Bakery.**

Afternoon

Drive Highway 101 south 6 miles to **Cannon Beach,** a festive little community with a gorgeous setting. Cannon Beach gets its name from the cannon that swept ashore after a shipwreck in 1846. Replicas of the cannon stand sentinel at either end of town.

There are several access points to the beach, and parking is free in public lots and on the street. Stairs descend from the bluff to the shore. This is a near-perfect, 7-mile stretch of sand for strolling, building castles, playing ball games, and wading in the surf. **Haystack Rock,** a 235-foot-high monolith that is a wildlife refuge, looms just offshore, surrounded by other rock formations. Waves billow and crash against them, tossing great plumes of white spray.

At low tide, you may find **nature interpreters** at Haystack, telling visitors about intertidal life and nesting birds in the wildlife refuge. The interpreters supply binoculars and spotting scopes and explain what to look for.

If you want to swim, check the colored flags by the lifeguard tower. Red means a dangerous surf; yellow urges caution. A lifeguard is on duty during the summer.

Haystack Rock at Cannon Beach is one of the world's largest monoliths.

More than any other coastal community, Cannon Beach is known for its **art galleries and shops,** which sell a happy combination of fine art, T-shirts, handicrafts, souvenirs, cards, kites, natural-fiber clothing, and good books. Most are on Hemlock, the main street, with others lining the side streets.

Look for top-quality artworks in White Bird, Haystack Gallery, and Hannen Stained Glass. Buy Amish folk art at Country Shores and European woolens and lace at Aagensen's Imports. Gepetto's sells intriguing toys, and El Mundo has a wide selection of stylish clothing and hats.

Midafternoon, stop in **Cannon Beach Cookie Company,** 239 North Hemlock, for coffee and an oversize cookie.

Step into **The Wine Shack** to taste domestic and imported wines (tastings on Saturdays, 1:00 to 5:00 P.M.).

DINNER: Cafe de la Mer, 1287 South Hemlock Street, Cannon Beach. (503) 436–1179. Globally influenced Northwest cuisine. Expensive, and not open every night, but check because the food is superb, the service prompt, and the atmosphere congenial. A good alternative is **The Wayfarer,** Ocean Front and Gower, Cannon Beach. (503) 436–1108.

If you choose to dine elsewhere, less extravagantly, reserve part of the evening for the **Coaster Theater,** at 108 North Hemlock. Professional performances include plays, concerts, ballet and modern dance, and musical revues.

LODGING: The Waves, P.O. Box 3, Cannon Beach, OR 97110. (503) 436–2205 or (800) 822–2468. Thirty-five-unit complex above the beach, in the heart of town and close to everything. Various styles of rooms; some have kitchens, fireplaces, and views.

DAY 2

Morning

BREAKFAST: Cook for yourself, or eat at **Lazy Susan Cafe,** 126 North Hemlock Street, Cannon Beach. (503) 436–2816. A cheery cafe on two levels, in a brick courtyard off the main street. Rich coffee, crisp waffles, and generous omelets. A popular, usually crowded spot.

Drive south from Cannon Beach on U.S. Highway 101, along the wooded coastline to **Arch Cape** and **Oswald West State Park.** Park in the lot and walk the ½-mile path that leads through groves of fir and cedar trees to a protected beach with tide pools. Next to it is **Cape Falcon,** a headland honeycombed with trails that wind through salal and wild roses out to rocky cliffs. Cormorants fly above the waves that hurl against this rugged shore.

Farther south, Highway 101 rises and curves around the west side of **Neahkahnie Mountain.** The views are stunning. From high on the mountainside you can see for miles down the undulating coast, where forested headlands meet wide beaches and the constant surf. A trail leads to even more panoramic viewing points at the summit of Neahkahnie, 1,600 feet high. Legend has it that the mountain hides buried treasure from a seventeenth-century Spanish shipwreck.

Continuing on Highway 101, you'll come to the turnoff to **Manzanita,** a quiet community on the ocean with a nine-hole golf course, numerous summer homes, and a couple of excellent restaurants.

From Manzanita, the highway turns slightly inland as you drive south to **Nehalem,** a hillside village above the **Nehalem River.** The low-key fishing community, where fading cabins line the banks of the river, has in recent years gained a reputation as an **art and antiques center.**

At Shepherd Gallery you can purchase pottery, paintings, and handcrafted gold jewelry, or you can find furniture at Pete's Antiques. More than forty dealers have shops in Nehalem Antique Mall and in Nehalem Trading Post. Three Village Gallery has fine-quality artworks: Robert Bateman's wildlife paintings, hand-carved decoys, and Southwestern Indian blankets and jewelry are examples.

Enjoy a cup of cappuccino and buy a bottle of Oregon wine at **The Waterway** in Wheeler, on Nehalem Bay. Then continue south on 101, passing through the village, which is home to retirees and a favored headquarters for fishing and crabbing.

Rockaway Beach, a few miles south, is a resort town with an emphasis on family recreation. There are volleyball nets on the beach (balls can be rented at the minimarket), a kite shop, and an arcade with video games, pizza, and popcorn. Bowling and miniature golf are available. **Spring Lake Park,** on the south end of town, offers paddleboats, bumper boats, hot tubs at the edge of the lake, and RV spaces.

Rockaway has retained its character in places like **True Value Hardware,** on Main Street. Once a pool hall and house of ill repute run by "Redhead Ruby," it became the Sea Hag Tavern in the 1930s. Old-timers say a stream ran under the building and a person could fish for trout through a hole in the floor. Since the 1940s the place has been a hardware store, now including gift items and souvenirs.

Don't miss **Flamingo Jim's** (in fact, it's almost impossible to miss) for its amazing array of lawn decorations—deer, seagulls, frogs, ducks, owls, gnomes, and raccoons are just a few.

From Rockaway, drive 3 miles south to **Garibaldi.** The little town tucked against the northern curve of Tillamook Bay is known for its deep-sea fishing charters and fresh seafood outlets.

Follow the shore of **Tillamook Bay** south to **Bay City.** Stop here at **Hayes Oysters** for fresh oysters; then continue for 5 more miles on Highway 101, which turns inland toward Tillamook.

Tillamook is dairy country, where cows graze in lush pastures along the roadside. Dairy farms were established here in the mid-1800s by Swiss settlers, who began the milk and cheese heritage that continues today.

The small town of 4,000 people lies 8 miles inland from the ocean, south of Tillamook Bay. It was named for a large tribe of Salish Indians, the Killamooks (one of many spellings).

LUNCH: Blue Heron French Cheese Company, 2001 Blue Heron Drive. (503) 842–8281. Blue-and-white former dairy barn north of Tillamook, off Highway 101. Deli sells soups and sandwiches; try the Blue Heron Classic, with smoked turkey and brie.

Afternoon

At the Blue Heron Cheese Company, taste Oregon wines and Blue Heron's own brie, as well as other cheeses and regional products, and buy top-quality items in the gift shop.

The nearby **Tillamook Cheese Factory** is one of Oregon's most visited sites. There's a self-guided tour that takes you through the plant, which produces 45 million pounds of cheese a year. The tour ends in a gift shop, deli, and ice cream counter.

You can learn about local history at the **Pioneer Museum,** 2106 Second Street, located in Tillamook's former courthouse, built in 1905. The engrossing museum has three well-lighted floors of exhibits showing life as it was a century ago on the Oregon coast. There are pioneer tools and clothing; a replica of the treehouse lived in by Joe Champion, the area's first white settler; a collection of carriages; and dozens of animals and birds of the region. The natural history display reaches far afield, showing mounted rhino horns, a leopard, elephant tusks, and an ashtray made from a rhino's foot—curious trophies from a former day, when few considered the fate of endangered species.

Leaving Tillamook, drive south toward the quiet resort community of **Neskowin.** Here the land rises to form **Cascade Head,** one of Oregon's great treasures of nature.

To climb the Head's wooded, grassy trails, which are maintained by the Nature Conservancy, is to experience the best the coast has to offer. Misty in rain and fog, shadow-dappled in sun, the forests of spruce, hemlock, and alder open to wide meadows covered with Queen Anne's lace and wild cucumber vines in spring. From the meadows, 700 feet above the foamy surf, you can hear barking sea lions and see the mouth of the Salmon River as it joins the sea. The Pacific is a blue panorama to the horizon.

South of Cascade Head is **Lincoln City,** a long sprawl of commercial development on a slope beside a beautiful beach. Spend the rest of the afternoon strolling the beach, flying a kite, or browsing in the shops of this major resort town. Sip cappuccino while you read at **Cafe Roma,** a combined coffee shop and bookstore.

Lincoln City is becoming a center for antique dealers; numerous **antiques shops** line the highway. Check Rocking Horse Mall, in a historic building, and the displays in Abbington's Antiques, where a white Persian cat reigns.

At the intersection of Highway 101 and East Devils Lake Road is a $13-million development of forty-five factory outlet stores. This complex, **Factory Stores at Lincoln City,** sells name brand goods at discount prices.

The **Naval Air Museum,** 6030 Hangar Road, (503) 842–1130, exhibits World War II memorabilia and planes in a blimp hangar said to be the largest freestanding wooden structure in the world. It's south of Tillamook on Highway 101.

DINNER: Bay House, 5911 Southwest Highway 101, Lincoln City. (541) 996–3222. Fine continental dining south of town, with a view of Siletz Bay. Expensive for this area, but one of the best on the coast.

LODGING: The Hideaway, 810 Southwest Tenth, Lincoln City, OR 97367. (541) 994–8874. Quiet, cottage-style lodgings on a bluff above the beach. Kitchens, ocean views, some sundecks and fireplaces. Pet friendly.

DAY 3

Morning

BREAKFAST: In your own dining nook at The Hideaway (groceries available at several nearby stores).

After a morning beach walk, drive south ½ mile to Drift Creek Road and follow it to the end. Turn right, and go ¼ mile farther to the **Drift Creek Covered Bridge**—the oldest covered bridge in Oregon (1914).

Return to Highway 101 and drive for a mile to Immonen Road, and turn left. Down this shady, wooded road you'll find two studios tucked among the ferns. First is **Mossy Creek,** a shop carrying the wares of local potters. Farther on is quaint **Alder House,** where you can watch glassblowers at work and buy exquisite pieces of glass workmanship.

Return to Lincoln City and head north on Route 101 to the junction with Route 18 at **Otis.** The fields around this tiny community are dotted with yellow in spring, when the skunk cabbage and daffodils bloom.

LUNCH: Otis Cafe, Route 18 in Otis. (541) 994-2813. A cozy, casual eatery famed for its down-home atmosphere and good cooking. Hamburgers and pies are sensational. Famous breakfast includes potatoes *Country American* magazine called "best around." Even the *New York Times* likes the Otis Cafe.

Afternoon

Take Route 18 east through the forests of the Coast Range and the Van Duzer Corridor to the open country of the Willamette Valley. Red-winged blackbirds flash by as you pass nurseries and orchards, fields and vineyards, on your way to join Highway 99W, which will take you into Portland.

THERE'S MORE

Bear Creek Artichokes. Eleven miles south of Tillamook on Highway 101, this roadside stand offers, in season, plentiful herbs, fresh produce, artichoke plants, honey, and flowers. (503) 398–5411.

Fishing. Fish for steelhead, chinook, and trout in the Kilchis, Wilson, Trask, Nestucca, and Salmon Rivers. Catch trout, perch, and bass in Devils Lake. Find perch, crab, and flounder in Siletz Bay. Surf-fish for perch, or arrange a deep-sea charter. Check with local tackle stores.

Golf. Hawk Creek Golf, Neskowin (nine holes) (503) 392–4120. Neskowin Beach Golf, Neskowin (nine holes) (503) 392–3377. Alderbrook Golf Course, Tillamook (eighteen holes) (503) 842–6413. Bay Breeze Golf Course and Driving Range (503) 842–1166. (Closed November through February.)

Morning Star II, on the grounds of the Tillamook Cheese Factory. This vessel is a replica of a schooner that was built in 1854 to transport goods when road travel was hazardous or nonexistent in this area.

Munson Creek Falls. The highest falls (266 feet) in the Coast Range are 9 miles south of Tillamook and 2 miles east of Highway 101. Trails lead to upper and lower falls.

Salt Cairn, Seaside. Replica of salt cairn used by the Lewis and Clark expedition to extract salt from seawater.

Three Capes Scenic Drive. From Tillamook, a coastal road leads to headlands with hiking trails, a wildlife refuge, the village of Oceanside, state parks, and a lighthouse.

Whale watching. Any bluff along the coast provides a vantage point for sighting gray whales on their migratory journeys. Cascade Head and Road's End Wayside, north of Lincoln City, are favorite spots. Whales are spotted all year long, but November to April are the likeliest months, and January, when about thirty whales per hour move along the coast, is the peak. The best views are usually seen in the early morning, when the sea is calm and there is no glare from the sun.

SPECIAL EVENTS

Early May. Spring Kite Festival, Lincoln City. Kite-flying extravaganza and contest. Awards for most unusual, most amusing, best children's, and best stunt kites, among others.

June. Sandcastle Days, Cannon Beach. Granddaddy of sand-sculpture contests, with international entries and cash prizes.

June. Dairy Parade and Rodeo, Tillamook. Band marches, Swiss polkas, clowns, food booths, golf tournament, music.

Mid-July. Nehalem Arts Festival, Nehalem. Outdoor exhibition of arts and crafts by artists from around the West. Food booths, strolling musicians.

July and August. Robert Gray Historical Pageant, Tillamook. Celebrates first American landing on Pacific Coast. Captain Robert Gray arrived on the site of Tillamook County in 1788.

Mid-August. Tillamook County Fair. Dairy show, livestock exhibitions, carnival, horse racing, grandstand shows.

OTHER RECOMMENDED RESTAURANTS AND LODGINGS

Cannon Beach

Cannon Beach Hotel, 1116 South Hemlock. (503) 436–1392. Attractive European-style hotel with nine rooms. Gracious furnishings, phones, television, fireplace in lobby. Light breakfast included. Short walk to beach.

Cloverdale

Sandlake Country Inn, 8505 Galloway Road. (503) 965–6745. Restored historic farmhouse 16 miles southwest of Tillamook (in Sandlake). The ultimate in bed-and-breakfast country charm. Full breakfast served and delivered to room.

Hebo

Hogie Jo's, Route 22. (503) 392–3355. Casual cafe with excellent Mexican food on weekends.

Lincoln City

Kyllo's, 1110 Northwest First Court. (541) 994–3179. Bright, festive beach-side restaurant at D River Wayside. Imaginative decor, ocean views, good seafood, very popular.

Lighthouse Restaurant and Brewery, Lighthouse Square. (541) 994–7238. Brewery tours, chowder, chili, and sandwiches in a two-story, fern-filled restaurant with atrium.

Inlet Garden, 646 Northwest Inlet. (541) 994–7932. Light, bright, contemporary inn with three guest rooms, one with ocean view and fireplace. One block to beach.

Spyglass Inn, 2510 Southwest Dune Avenue. (541) 994–2785. Hilltop home with spectacular ocean views, balconies, books, privacy. Full breakfast.

Manzanita

Arbors in Manzanita, 78 Idaho. (503) 368–7566. Charming, English-style cottage a block from the beach. Two guest rooms, flower gardens, full breakfast.

Inn at Manzanita, 67 Laneda. (503) 368–6754. Luxury inn a short walk from the sea. Some ocean views. Stylish pastels, natural wood, light and airy. All units have two-person spas.

Blue Sky Cafe, 154 Laneda. (503) 368–5712. Fresh seafood, pasta, beef, chicken, all prepared with savory herbs and sauces.

Jarboe's, 137 Laneda. (503) 368–5113. Noted for innovative and superb cuisine.

Netarts Bay

Terimore Motel, 5105 Crab Avenue. (503) 842–4623. Ocean- and bay-view units with kitchens and fireplaces. Housekeeping cottages with one or two bedrooms.

Wee Willie's, 6060 Whiskey Creek Road. (503) 842–6869. Cafe overlooking bay. Noted for its health-conscious menu. Fish-and-chips, burgers, crab sandwiches, blackberry pie.

Seaside

Shilo Inn, 30 North Promenade. (503) 738–9571 or (800) 222–2244. Large, well-run motel facing the beach. Restaurant, swimming pool.

Tillamook

Shilo Inn, 2515 North Main. (503) 842–7971 or (800) 222–2244. A 101-unit motel south of cheese factory on Highway 101. Pool, sauna, laundromat, kitchenettes. Wheelchair accessible. Hot complimentary breakfast.

Blue Haven Inn, 3025 Gienger Road. (503) 842–2265. Gracious bed-and-breakfast home south of Tillamook. Attractive gardens, three guest rooms. Full breakfast in formal dining room.

Wheeler

Nina's Italian Restaurant and Lounge, Highway 101. (503) 368–6592. Italian dishes, pastas, seafood, excellent pizza. Lounge and view of the bay. State of Oregon Lottery Service Center available.

FOR MORE INFORMATION

Cannon Beach Chamber of Commerce, 207 North Spruce, P.O. Box 64, Cannon Beach, OR 97110. (503) 436–0434.

Cannon Beach Visitors Bureau, 207 North Spruce. (503) 436–2623.

Lincoln City Visitors and Convention Bureau, 801 Southwest Highway 101, Lincoln City, OR 97367. (541) 994–8378 or (800) 452–2151.

Seaside Chamber of Commerce, 7 North Roosevelt, P.O. Box 7, Seaside, OR 97138. (503) 738–6391 or (800) 444–6740.

Seaside Visitors Bureau, 989 Boradway, Seaside, OR 97138-6825. (888) 306–2326 or (503) 738–3097.

Tillamook Chamber of Commerce, 3705 Highway 101 North, Tillamook, OR 97141. (503) 842–7525.

Eugene–Florence–Newport

CITY CULTURE AND COASTAL BEAUTY

2 NIGHTS

College campus • Wineries • Rugged coastline
Fine dining • Sand dunes • Marine life
Rhododendrons • Ocean views • Aquarium

This three-day tour gives you a sampling of some of the best that an Oregon city and the Oregon coastline have to offer visitors. From the restaurants, shopping, and cultural events of Eugene to the rocky coast where waves crash and spray, the variety is exhilarating.

DAY 1

Morning

Travel south on I–5 100 miles to **Eugene,** and stop at the Convention and Visitors Association of Lane County Oregon, 115 West Eighth Street, Suite 190, for maps and brochures. Check the calendar for concerts and events taking place at the **Hult Center for the Performing Arts;** if the evening's attraction appeals, call for reservations. The Hult Center hosts top artists from around the world in its 2,500-seat, acoustically ideal concert hall. The Eugene-Springfield symphony, ballet, and opera perform on this stage. In June and July the internationally renowned Oregon Bach Festival takes place. Plan on an early dinner if you're attending the theater.

Next, drive north on Lincoln Street to **Skinner Butte Park** and go to the top of the butte. On a clear day, you'll have panoramic views of the city, the Willamette River flowing through town, the surrounding green hills and

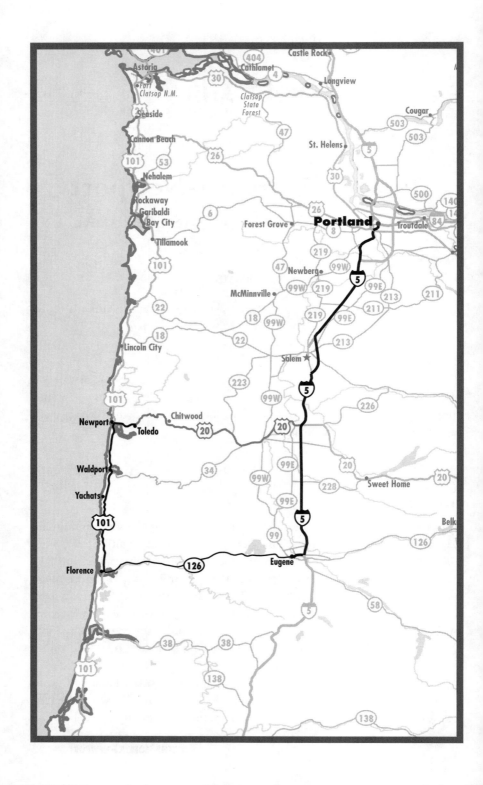

fields, and the mountain on the horizon. Walk through the rose garden and along tree-shaded paths in this grassy park, which was named for the first homesteader in the area; then head back downtown to the **Market District.**

There are dozens of shops to browse through in the district, but the main complex is **Fifth Street Public Market.** Once a feed mill, it's now a collection of interesting specialty stores selling clothing, gift items, kitchenware, arts and crafts, and foods from around the world. **Casablanca,** a good lunch spot, has Middle Eastern dishes, and **Terry's Diner** serves hamburgers and malteds in a 1950s atmosphere.

LUNCH: Mekala's, Fifth Street Public Market. (541) 342–4872. Good Thai food, hot and spicy or not, as you request, and homemade coconut ice cream. Windows overlook the flower-filled courtyard of the market.

Afternoon

A short distance from downtown Eugene, the **University of Oregon** covers 250 acres and is an arboretum with more than 2,000 varieties of trees. The university, the city's largest employer, enrolls about 20,000 students. Its lovely grounds are graced with nineteenth-century and modern buildings and outdoor sculpture.

Next to the library, on Fourteenth and Kincaid Streets, is the **University of Oregon Museum of Art.** Its highly respected collection of Asian art is well worth a tour. There are other exhibits and a gift shop as well. (Open year-round, noon to 5:00 P.M.) Also on campus is the **University of Oregon Museum of Natural History,** which displays fossils and animals and artifacts from prehistoric Oregon.

If there is time, take a stroll through **Hendricks Park,** 2 miles southeast of the campus. Don't miss it in the spring, when the rhododendron displays are magnificent. Thousands of the colorful plants bloom in this park, which also has paths, secluded benches, and picnic areas.

DINNER: Cafe Zenon, 898 Pearl Street. (541) 343–3005. Controlled hubbub in a busy slice of Eugene life. Outdoor tables when weather permits. Variety of ethnic cuisines, always interesting.

LODGING: Campus Cottage, 1136 East Nineteenth. (541) 342–5346. Bed-and-breakfast in a 1920s home near University of Oregon campus. Four well-furnished rooms with private baths, hospitable innkeeper, good conversation.

DAY 2

Morning

BREAKFAST: Early morning coffee and then full breakfast at Campus Cottage. Fresh-baked scones with jam, fruit, juice, and an egg dish.

Head west on Highway 126. In 12 miles you'll reach **Fern Ridge Lake,** a 4.5-mile-long reservoir that is popular for sailing, power boating, jet skiing, and water skiing. Shortly after the lake and Peninsula Park, you'll come to a **wildlife viewing area.** The wetlands and marshes here provide shelter to a variety of birds and animals.

Continue on to Territorial Highway and turn left toward the Veneta business district and **Hinman Vineyards,** 27012 Briggs Hill Road. Hinman, established in 1979 in the foothills of the Coast Range, is a brick winery with graceful arches and a tower. Tastings are offered, and a picnic area on the landscaped grounds is available.

If you turn right instead of left on Territorial Highway, you'll be headed for Elmira and **LaVelle Vineyards,** 89697 Sheffler Road. This small, family-owned winery is next to groves of fir trees at the end of a mile-long lane.

Continuing on Highway 126 you'll drive through Noti, a timber town where piles of logs are stacked higher than the buildings. The road winds up into the Coast Range, through dense forest where the tree trunks seem to be made of moss, they're so velvety green. In spring, the dogwood blossoms float creamy white against the dark firs, and in fall the maples and alders show yellow, brown, and red.

At the confluence of the Siuslaw River and Wild Cat Creek, watch for a **covered bridge** that was built in 1925. The pretty white bridge, a charming addition to the landscape, is easy to miss in summer because it's hidden behind the foliage. Take a sharp right at Whittaker Creek turnoff, pass under Highway 126, and you will see the bridge.

Continue on 126 to **Florence,** at the mouth of the Siuslaw River, and follow the signs to **Old Town.** The historic bayfront here offers quaint shops, boutiques, and restaurants by the harbor, home of a small fishing fleet. It won't take long to look around the area. Check the kite shop, buy a souvenir, have a cappuccino, and head for the dunes.

The **Oregon Dunes National Recreation Area** is a 47-mile stretch of sand dunes, encompassing some 32,000 acres. Walking in these undulating, desert-like hills is an experience not to be missed. South of Florence is **Jesse**

M. Honeyman State Park, with convenient access to the dunes. Here a high hill, a favorite spot for climbing and sliding on the sand, meets the edge of a watery gem, Cleawox Lake.

About 10 miles south of Honeyman is the **Oregon Dunes Overlook,** where you can see the dunes from boardwalks and viewing platforms. A short trail leads into the dunes, and interpretive signs explain the natural features such as evergreen islands, beach grass, wildlife, and little lakes. The overlook is wheelchair accessible.

LUNCH: Traveler's Cove Restaurant and Imports, 1362 Bay Street, (541) 997–6845. Riverfront favorite serving coastal classics from chowder to crabby Caesar salads. Dine on deck (sunglasses provided).

Afternoon

Leaving Florence, drive north on U.S. Highway 101 to **Darlingtonia Wayside.** Walk the boardwalk here to see the exotic-looking cobra lilies growing in the marsh. These plants are carnivorous, luring insects down a tube lined with nectar.

Continue north for 10 miles to **Sea Lion Caves,** and take the elevator down to the caves where Steller sea lions dwell (there is an admission fee). You can get a close look at the only wild breeding colony of the sea lions on the coast, as well as postcard views of **Heceta Head lighthouse** to the north. Pigeon guillemots and Brandt's cormorants nest by the thousands in the area and can be seen from a path along the cliff.

As you drive north on 101 along the coast, you'll pass miles of smooth, uncrowded beach. Stop at any parking area to explore the shoreline; all the beaches are open to the public by state law. A park with a sandy cove, lawns, and picnic tables lies at the base of the cliff where the picturesque Heceta Head lighthouse stands (open for tours in summer).

Along the way are landmarks such as Devil's Elbow, Devil's Churn, Muriel O. Ponsler Memorial Wayside, and Captain Cook's Chasm. At **Cape Perpetua,** you can enjoy panoramic views up and down the coast. Check at Cape Perpetua Visitors' Center for exhibits and information. Walk the trails on this massive basaltic headland to see old-growth forest, tide pools, shell mounds, and chasms of turbulent foam.

When you reach **Yachats** (Ya-hots), you're in a charming seaside town nestled between the Coast Range forests and the Pacific Ocean—the perfect spot for a quiet getaway. Visit the **Little Log Church,** a tiny church built in 1927 and now open as a historical museum.

DINNER: La Serre, Second and Beach Streets, Yachats. (541) 547–3420. Greenery, windows, and skylights give this highly rated restaurant a garden atmosphere. Fresh seafood, tasty salads.

LODGING: Shamrock Lodgettes, Highway 101, Yachats. (541) 547–3312 or (800) 845–5028; (541) 547–3843 (fax). Log cabins on sloping lawns above the beach at the mouth of the Yachats River.

DAY 3

Morning

BREAKFAST: New Morning Coffeehouse, Fourth Street, Highway 101, Yachats. (541) 547–3706. Warm, light-filled, inexpensive eatery serving good pastries and coffee. Outdoor terrace, light lunches.

Drive north on Highway 101 to **Waldport** and stop at the **Alsea Bay Bridge Interpretive Center.** Once the bay was spanned by a classic 1937 bridge; it was replaced in 1991 and the interpretive center was opened to provide information and displays on bridge history, early road development, and the settlement of the Alsea Bay area.

A few miles north of Waldport, as you approach Seal Rock, you'll see a sign for Art on the Rocks. Stop here for a look at the works of local and international artists in jewelry, paintings, and photography. Semiprecious stones are sold as well.

The heart of the Seal Rock community is a collection of shops clustered near the **General Store.** Near here is **Granny's Country Store,** which is filled with antiques and collectibles—lots of nice glass and china. Next door is another intriguing shop called Antiques, etc.

Don't miss a browse through **Trade Bead Gallery,** which has an outstanding collection of ancient and modern beads from all over the world. Even if you're not excited about beads, you'll be fascinated by the information provided on the displays of rare trade beads.

Choose something sweet at Fudge, which sells ice cream and luscious, handmade candies, and see the carved items at Seal Rock Wood Works. Tour Sea Gulch, if you're interested in chainsaw sculpture. This is a western-and-hillbilly theme park, with some 400 red-cedar carvings.

At **Ona Beach State Park,** on the estuary of Beaver Creek, there are picnic tables on the well-landscaped, wooded grounds.

Paved paths curve to a bridge that crosses the creek and leads to a wide, sandy beach with driftwood. Rest rooms in the park have wheelchair access.

Continuing north, before crossing the high bridge over Yaquina Bay into **Newport,** stop at the new **Oregon Coast Aquarium,** home to Keiko, the orca whale that starred in the movie *Free Willy.* The state-of-the-art facility replicates the dunes, rocky pools, cliffs, and caves of coastal Oregon. Marine creatures native to the area live in pools and tanks that resemble their wild habitat. You'll see octopi, tufted puffins, seals, sea otters, and a tank of lavender-pink jellyfish floating through the water in elegant dance. There's also a touch tank of starfish and other tidepool creatures. (Open daily except Christmas.)

The **Mark O. Hatfield Marine Science Center** is nearby, with more displays of Northwest sea life. The Center is part of Oregon State University's educational and research program and offers classes, workshops, and field trips.

LUNCH: Canyon Way Restaurant and Bookstore, 1216 Canyon Way SW. (541) 265–8319. Imaginative entrees, seafood, salads. Deli with soups, salads, sandwiches to go, espresso. Open 10:00 A.M. to 4:00 P.M. Dining room with full lunch and dinner. Lunch 11:00 A.M. to 3:00 P.M. Monday through Sunday and dinner 5:00 P.M. until closing Tuesday through Sunday. Outdoor terrace, gift shop, and bookstore.

Afternoon

Tour the **Old Bay Front,** where you can watch the fishing boats come and go, buy souvenirs, and, if tourist attractions appeal, see the Wax Works, Undersea Gardens, and Ripley's Believe It Or Not. Alternatively, you might take a two-and-a-half-hour **whale-watching trip** or go crabbing in the bay with Newport Tradewinds (541–265–2101). The company also offers longer trips for deep-sea fishing.

Turn east on U.S. 20, a byway that follows Elk Creek to **Toledo.** If you have the time, stop at the Michael Gibbons Gallery and Studio to view the noted artist's landscape paintings. The gallery is in a former church rectory at 40 Northeast Alder, (541) 336–2797.

Continue on Route 20 to Chitwood, where you'll see an old-fashioned **covered bridge,** and on through the wooded hills and farmlands of the Willamette Valley to I–5. Turn north to take the freeway to Portland.

THERE'S MORE

Dorris Ranch, 220 South Second Street and Dorris Avenue, Springfield. (541) 726–2748. The nation's first filbert orchard, now a living history farm on 250 acres. Tours every second and fourth Saturday, April through November. Nominal admission fee.

Drift Creek Wilderness, Waldport. Pocket wilderness in Siuslaw National Forest, contains some of the last of the coastal old-growth forest. Maps ($2.00) available at Waldport Ranger Station, (541) 563–3211.

Golf. Oakway Golf Course, Eugene. (541) 484–1927. Executive eighteen-hole course, no tee times required. Florence Golf Club, Florence. (541) 997–3232. Nine-hole course by the sand dunes, "Oregon's biggest sand trap." Sandpines Golf Course, Florence. (541) 997–1937. Eighteen-hole course, one of Lane County's largest, built on sand dunes. Open year-round.

Gwynn Creek Trail, Cape Perpetua. Easily accessible and beautiful walk from Cape Perpetua Visitors' Center. Climbs Gwynn Creek Canyon, through old-growth stands of Douglas fir and Sitka spruce. Full loop, 6.5 miles.

Hiking, running, canoeing, white-water rafting. All are available in or near Eugene and Springfield. Check with the Association of Lane County, Oregon, for specific places and arrangements.

Lane County Ice, Lane County Fairgrounds, Eugene. (541) 687–3615. Full-size arena ice rink, open daily.

Lively Park Swim Center, 6100 Thurston Road, Springfield. (541) 747–9283. Indoor water fun in surf of 4-foot waves, 136-foot open flume water slide. Spa, kiddy pool.

Saturday Market, High Street, Eugene. Near the Market District, an outdoor array of booths—a great place to stroll and shop on a Saturday between April and late December.

Siuslaw River cruises aboard the *Westward Ho!,* a half-scale replica of a stern-wheeler that once plied the Columbia River. Frontier theme, costumes, entertainment, dinner cruises. (541) 268–4017. One-hour tours depart from Old Town dock in Florence.

SPECIAL EVENTS

Late February. Seafood and Wine Festival, Newport.

March. Dune Mushers Mail Run, Horsfall Beach to Florence. Dog sled teams run 72 miles through sand dunes.

June/July. Oregon Bach Festival, Eugene. Two weeks of music by world-famous performers. Concerts, workshops, lectures, dance.

Mid-July. Oregon Country Fair, Veneta. Arts and crafts in the woods near Eugene. Food, music.

Summer. Oregon Festival of American Music, Hult Center for the Performing Arts and Cuthbert Ampitheater, Eugene. (541) 345–0028. Regional performances of American classic music.

Mid-September. Florence Fall Festival, Florence. "Fabulous fifties" theme for a clam chowder cook-off, mushroom hunt, dances, entertainment, and arts-and-crafts fair.

October. Newport Microbrew Festival. Northwest brewers showcase beer, crafts, entertainment, food.

OTHER RECOMMENDED RESTAURANTS AND LODGINGS

Elmira

McGillivray's Log Home Bed and Breakfast, 88680 Evers Road. (541) 935–3564. Oversize log home in the country with two spacious guest rooms. Full breakfast, private baths.

Eugene

(See Portland Escape Ten for more Eugene recommendations.)

Oregon Electric Station, 27 East Fifth. (541) 485–4444. Red-brick restaurant in Market District. Lunch, dinner, and Sunday brunch in antique railroad car, three lounges, live jazz.

Pookie's Bed 'n' Breakfast, 2013 Charnelton Street. (541) 343–0383. Two guest rooms in nicely restored 1918 home. Residential neighborhood, close to downtown and campus, full or continental breakfast included.

Florence

Johnson House Bed and Breakfast, 216 Maple Street. (541) 997–8000. Historic home turned top-quality bed-and-breakfast. Six rooms plus a charming little cottage.

Windward Inn, 3757 Highway 101 North. (541) 997–8243. Wood-paneled
restaurant with fireplaces and warm, relaxed atmosphere. Local seafood,
steak, homemade breads, and pastries.

Newport

Sylvia Beach Hotel, 267 Northwest Cliff. (541) 265–5428. Unique hotel on a
cliff above Nye Beach, with rooms dedicated to and furnished in accor-
dance with various authors. Restaurant, library, gift shop, ocean views.

The Whale's Tale, 452 Bay Boulevard SW. (541) 265–8660. On the bayfront.
Known for flavorful omelets and poppyseed pancakes. Light fare and
seafood entrees, all prepared with care.

Seal Rock

Yuzen, 1011 Coast Highway 101 NW. (541) 563–5833. Highly reputed Japanese cuisine. Casual atmosphere, booths and tables, Japanese decor.

Yachats

(There are numerous lodgings in the Yachats area; these are in or very close to
town.)

Adobe Resort, 1555 Highway 101. (541) 547–3141 or (800) 522–3623. Popular resort at the edge of a rocky shore. Restaurant, lounge, great views.

FOR MORE INFORMATION

Convention and Visitors Association of Lane County, Oregon, 115 West
Eighth, Suite 190, Eugene, OR 97401. (541) 484–5307 or (800)
547–5445.

Florence Area Chamber of Commerce, 270 Highway 101, P.O. Box 26000,
Florence, OR 97439. (541) 997–3128.

Greater Newport Chamber of Commerce, 555 Coast Highway SW, Newport, OR 97365. (541) 265–8801 or (800) 262–7844.

Yachats Area Chamber of Commerce, 441 Highway 101, Yachats, OR 97498. (541) 547–3530.

Mount Hood Loop
CIRCLING OREGON'S HIGHEST PEAK

1 NIGHT

Evergreen forests • Waterfalls • Lakes and streams
Highest point in Oregon • Scenic overlooks • Hiking trails
Year-round skiing • Historic lodge • Fruit orchards
Columbia River • Stern-wheeler cruise

From Portland, Mount Hood's peak is a familiar presence, looming 60 miles away on the eastern horizon behind hazy, blue-green foothills. At 11,235 feet, its summit is the highest point in Oregon.

Circling around this massive, broad-shouldered volcano takes you through some of the state's most spectacular scenery, from the lush green fir forests west of the Cascade Range to the ponderosa pines, ranchlands, and acres of orchards on the east. On the mountain's north side, the wide Columbia River flows westward, fed by streams from Hood's snowfields.

A two-day loop tour is a satisfying excursion into this world of natural wonder. This itinerary, designed as a summer trip, combines vigorous recreation with restful sight-seeing. It takes you up on the mountain, into the orchards, and out on the water. With a few changes, you can enjoy many of its features in winter, substituting ski slopes or groomed trails for forest walks.

DAY 1

Morning

From Portland take U.S. Route 26 east toward **Sandy.** If you missed breakfast, stop to eat at **Denney's,** 36641 Highway 26, (503) 668–7323, in the Sandy Marketplace. Hearty breakfasts are served here twenty-four hours daily.

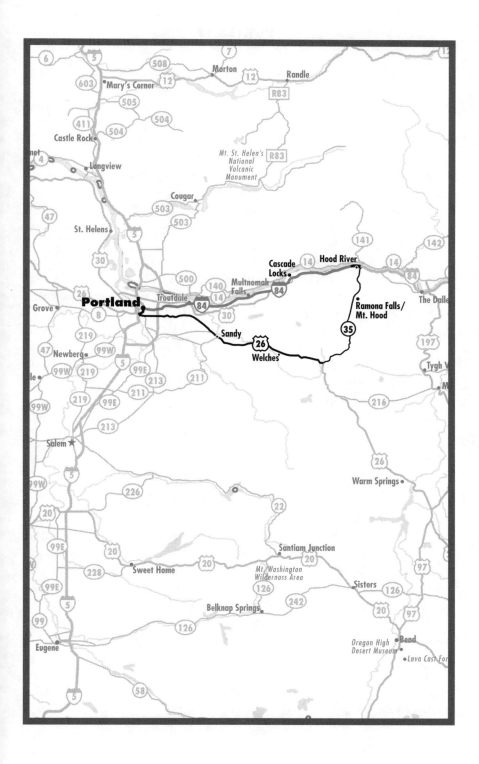

Five and a half miles east of Sandy, stop at the **Oregon Candy Farm** to appease your sweet tooth. For more than fifty years the candy makers, who began their enterprise in Portland, have been selling handmade chocolates and other candies. Watch the candy-making process through glass windows in the factory weekdays from 9:00 A.M. to 5:00 P.M. and weekend afternoons, (503) 668–5066.

Continue on Route 26 to **Welches.** At **Honey Bear Express,** a cafe, bakery, and delicatessen in the Welches shopping center, purchase lunch-to-go. The sandwiches are generously filled; cookies and muffins are home baked. Also in the shopping center are a bookstore, a fly-fishing shop, a ski-rental shop, and a grocery market.

The road rises from here into Mount Hood's foothills, cutting through the forests of fir and hemlock to **Zigzag** (18 miles east of Sandy). Pick up maps and trail information along the way at **Mount Hood Information Center,** 65000 East Highway 26 in Welches.

Take the **Lolo Pass** road north from Zigzag about 4 miles to Road 1825. Turn right and follow the signs to the trailhead for **Ramona Falls,** a 6.8-mile round-trip hike from the lower parking lot. The trail crosses the **Sandy River** and ascends gradually through forestland and open sandy slopes above the river canyon to one of Mount Hood's prettiest waterfalls.

Cascading 100 feet in broad, misty sheets over mossy rocks, Ramona splashes past green ferns into clear, cold **Ramona Creek.**

LUNCH: Picnic at Ramona Falls.

Afternoon

Return to Route 26 past summer homes and ski cabins, and continue east, ascending the mountain toward the 6-mile spur road to **Timberline Lodge.** The grand old lodge, built as a Works Progress Administration (WPA) project in 1937, is a **National Historic Landmark**. Its wood carvings, wrought iron, massive beams, and tribal-motif fabrics make it an extraordinary work of art as well as a significant piece of Northwest history.

Don't miss the fine display of craftsmanship in the **Rachael Griffin Historic Exhibition Center** on the main floor. It's accompanied by a recording of President Franklin D. Roosevelt's speech of dedication at the lodge.

Timberline is the second-oldest developed ski area in the United States and the only one offering summer skiing. In mid-July you can ride the lift up **Palmer Glacier** and ski down.

After (or instead of) glacier skiing, stroll the trails that extend in several directions from the lodge. You are literally at the timberline, so if you head down the mountain you'll be among the trees; walk up its slopes and you're in open, rocky terrain. The trail to **Zigzag Canyon** and **Paradise Park** offers both, as well as rushing streams and wildflower meadows in summer. You may have time to walk part of the trail to a scenic viewpoint above the canyon.

Return to the lodge for a shower and well-deserved evening of relaxation in the **Ram's Head Bar,** a perfect spot for enjoying an aperitif while you watch the sunset's glow on the mountaintop.

DINNER: Cascades Dining Room, Timberline Lodge. American and continental dinners served by candlelight.

LODGING: Timberline Lodge, Timberline, OR 97028. (503) 272–3311. For reservations from Portland, phone 231–5400; (800) 547–1406 nationwide toll-free number. Classic mountain lodge and ski resort on Mount Hood's south flank.

DAY 2

Morning

BREAKFAST: Cascades Dining Room.

Drive back to U.S. Route 26, and head east to State Route 35, which winds northeast around the mountain toward the **Columbia River Gorge.** Near the spot where **Pacific Crest National Scenic Trail** crosses the highway, you'll come to **Barlow Pass.** The pass was named for pioneer Sam Barlow, who developed a toll road around the south side of Mount Hood in 1846. Until then, wagon trains on the Oregon Trail took the precarious Columbia River passage to reach the western side of the Cascades.

Crossing the **White River** (the canyon here is a favorite among cross-country skiers), continue on Route 35 to **Bennett Pass** (elevation 4,670 feet) and the road to **Mount Hood Meadows Ski Area.** This is the largest ski development on the mountain, with numerous lifts and runs. It's also a focus of controversy, as developers seek to expand the facilities.

The East Fork of the Hood River runs by the ski area, beginning in a glacier high on the mountain and coursing down the slopes to create **Umbrella Falls** and, closer to the main road, **Sahalie Falls.** Easy walks take you through the forest to either falls; a longer hike of 1.7 miles connects them.

If you take the detour loop road to Sahalie Falls, you'll come to **Hood River Meadows,** the biggest meadow on Mount Hood, spangled with the colors of wildflowers in late spring.

As the East Fork turns due north, so does the road, crossing brooks that rush down ravines into the river. Shortly after passing Sherwood Campground, you'll come to a parking area for East Fork Trail 650, the **Tamanawas Falls Trail.** The 2-mile trail is a classic for Northwest scenery as it follows bouncy Cold Spring Creek, shaded by tall evergreens, through a narrow canyon to a waterfall that cascades 100 feet.

After your two-hour, round-trip hike, take Route 35 to the turnoff to **Cooper Spur,** a high ridge between Eliot and Newton Clark glaciers. It's about 2¼ miles in from the road.

Drive 6 miles beyond it to **Inspiration Point,** where you'll have a stunning view of the upper **Hood River Valley** and the mountain's north side, with **Wallalute Falls** cascading down from Eliot Glacier.

Still farther—about 11 miles from The Inn at Cooper Spur—is **Cloud Cap Inn,** a starting point for climbers just below Eliot Glacier. The rustic log hotel, constructed in 1889 and now a National Historic Site, is anchored by cables to resist winter storms. The crisp air and incomparable scenery have drawn visitors for a century. Early travelers to the inn rode the train to Hood River, then paid $12.50 for a six-hour ride in an open coach, with two changes of horses on the way. The first automobile to reach Cloud Cap Inn was a 1907 Cadillac. Now maintained by the Crag Rats, a mountain-climbing and rescue organization, Cloud Cap Inn is not open to the public.

The entire Cloud Cap/Tilly Jane area is a National Historic District. Other points of interest include the Tilly Jane Forest Camp, the American Legion Camp, and the massive public shelter built by the Civilian Conservation Corps in 1939. China Fill memorializes the Chinese laborers who toiled with picks to dig and grade the old wagon road in 1889.

LUNCH: The Inn at Cooper Spur, Mount Hood. (541) 352–6692. Homey mountainside restaurant, part of a small resort. Open for lunch Saturday and Sunday. Try the homemade soups and award-winning pie.

A lunch alternative is a picnic on the trail.

Afternoon

Now Route 35, still edging the East Fork, begins its descent into the lush, fertile Hood River Valley, winding through fragrant apple, pear, and cherry orchards. In spring the fields in blossom are as snow-white as the mountain slopes behind them; in autumn the air carries the heady scent of cider.

Stop at **Mount Hood Country Store,** in the small community of Mount Hood, to browse through an old-fashioned country market. Fresh produce, gourmet foods, Northwest wines, and gifts are sold in a nostalgic setting. It's a good place for ice cream on a hot day.

Farther north, drive 1½ miles off the highway to **Panorama Point** for a wide valley vista, with lofty Mount Hood in the background. It's a froth of white in spring but equally beautiful in autumn, when orchard foliage glows yellow-gold and the maples and tamaracks turn rust and orange, with the occasional scarlet-tinged sumac sparking the fall tones. At harvest time, roadside stands are full of produce.

It's a short drive from Panorama Point into **Hood River.**

Turn west on I-84, and you're in the heart of the **Columbia River Gorge.** In this geological wonder, much of it a designated **National Scenic Area,** the wide Columbia flows on your right. On the left, dancing waterfalls spray from steep cliffs and great basaltic masses exposed by ancient floods. On the ridges around them, thick forests shield a network of hiking trails.

For more activities and attractions in Hood River and for more detail on waterfalls and exploring the gorge, see Portland Escape Seven.

Continuing west, you'll pass **Oxbow Salmon Hatchery,** which is open to the public. When you reach **Cascade Locks,** drive to the riverside **Marine Park.** The grassy, tree-shaded park has play equipment, remnants of the old boat locks (used before dam construction made them unnecessary), a museum, and the Oregon Pony, the first steam locomotive built on the Pacific Coast. In the visitors' information center there are a gift shop, historic photographs of early stern-wheeler days, and 50-cent showers—a boon to hikers fresh off the numerous trails in the gorge.

The Pacific Crest Trail passes through Cascade Locks in **Bridge of the Gods Park.** The Bridge of the Gods, spanning the Columbia, was built in 1926 and raised in 1938 to provide clearance when Bonneville Dam was built. Indian legend says that long ago a natural bridge of stone stretched across the gorge near here.

From the wharf at Marine Park, the *Columbia Gorge* stern-wheeler leaves three times a day in summer for two-hour cruises on the river. A hundred years ago stern-wheelers carried passengers and cargo between Portland and The Dalles. Today a 330-ton, three-deck replica of a river paddleboat provides a chance to step into that colorful bygone era. Dinner, dance, and sunset cruises are available.

The Stern-wheeler Columbia Gorge *navigates the majestic Columbia River.*

DINNER: Aboard the *Columbia Gorge* stern-wheeler. Dine on an old-fashioned riverboat as it churns past the gorge's magnificent forests and towering basaltic cliffs. Dinner cruises, available June–October, range from ninety minutes to three hours. For information: 1200 Southwest Front, Suite 110, Portland, OR 97209. (541) 374–8427, for general information; in Portland, 223–3928, for reservations.

From Cascade Locks, it's a thirty-minute drive west on I–84 to Portland.

THERE'S MORE

Fishing. Hood River Marina. Smallmouth bass.

Lost Lake, Mount Hood. Picture–perfect mountain lake with rainbow and German brown trout. One of the most photographed lakes in the nation.

Mouth of Hood River. Steelhead run in spring, October, and January.

Phoenix Farms, 4349 Baldwin Creek Road, Mount Hood, OR 97401. (541) 352–6090. A trout fishing farm, open daily. Fishing rods and bait available. Two miles south of Mount Hood Country Store on Highway 35.

Mount Hood Railroad. Scenic train excursions through the Hood River Valley, mid-April through October. (541) 386–3556.

Mushroom collecting, spring and fall. Mushrooms grow in profusion in Mount Hood's forests. The ranger station has information on the best locations to search. Chanterelles, shaggy manes, boletus, morels, and other exotic species are easy to find; but several poisonous varieties grow here as well. Do not eat mushrooms unless you're certain they are safe. Permits for mushroom picking are required in Mount Hood National Forest and Columbia River Gorge Scenic Area.

SPECIAL EVENTS

Mid-April. Blossom Festival, Hood River Valley. Orchard tours, arts-and-crafts sales, train rides on the Fruit Blossom Special.

Mid-July. Sandy Mountain Festival, Sandy. Celebration of Sandy's pioneer heritage. Folk music, food booths, arts and crafts.

August. Mount Hood Festival of Jazz, Gresham. (503) 232–3000. Nationally acclaimed jazz series with top musicians playing outdoors at Mount Hood Community College.

October. October Harvest Fest, Hood River. Crafts booths, foods, local produce, wines.

OTHER RECOMMENDED RESTAURANTS AND LODGINGS

Government Camp

Falcon's Crest, P.O. Box 185, (503) 272–3403 or (800) 624–7384. E-mail: falconscrest@earthlink.net. Web site address: www.falconscrest.com. Chalet-style mountain home and lodge with five suites. Full breakfast. Walking distance to Ski Bowl, largest nighttime skiing area in the United States.

Rhododendron

Salisbury Restaurant, 69580 East Highway 26. (503) 622–3877. Old-time rustic log restaurant, near Zigzag. Tasty omelets, biscuits and gravy, huge burgers. Popular with local folk.

Sandy

The Elusive Trout Pub, 39333 Proctor Boulevard, (503) 668–7884. Pub selling microbrewed ales, lagers on tap, and foods prepared with care.

Wasson Brothers Winery, 41901 Highway 26. (503) 668–3124. Open for tastings and tours.

Welches

The Resort at the Mountain, 68010 East Fairway Avenue. (503) 622–3101 or (800) 669–7666. Luxury resort with twenty-seven-hole golf course on Salmon River.

FOR MORE INFORMATION

Hood River County Chamber of Commerce, 405 Portway Hood River, OR 97031. (541) 386–2000.

Mount Hood Area Chamber of Commerce, P.O. Box 819, Welches, OR 97067. (503) 622–3017.

Mount Hood Information Center, 65000 East Highway 26, Welches, OR 97067. (503) 622–4822.

Sandy Area Chamber of Commerce, P.O. Box 536, Sandy, OR 97055. (503) 668–4006.

Around Mount St. Helens
EXPLORING THE VOLCANO

1 NIGHT

Mount St. Helens National Volcanic Monument
Volcano museum • Devastation area • Hiking trails
Views of Spirit Lake and crater • Scenic lake • Scenic river
Longest lava tube in the United States

Before May 18, 1980, Mount St. Helens was a pristine, symmetrical white peak, the queen of the Cascade range. But mighty forces were brewing beneath that serene exterior. After two months of minor explosions and earthquakes, the mountain erupted in a blast of rock, ash, gas, and steam.

Within ten minutes an immense plume of pumice and ash leaped 13.6 miles into the atmosphere and continued roaring upward for nine hours. The volume of ash fall could have buried a football field to a depth of 150 miles. Mount St. Helens' height dropped from 9,677 feet to 8,363 feet, with a crater more than 2,000 feet deep.

When the summit and north flank collapsed in a giant landslide, a huge lateral blast blew sideways, obliterating or knocking down trees. Rock and melting ice created mudflows in the stream valleys, uprooting 150 square miles of trees and tearing out bridges and houses. The devastation left a landscape bleak and gray.

Today wisps of gas and ash still rise from the crater, and a lava dome is building. But the mountain remains quiet. Wildlife and plants are returning, along with a million visitors a year. The devastated area is a National Volcanic Monument now, with 200 miles of trails and 50 miles of roads.

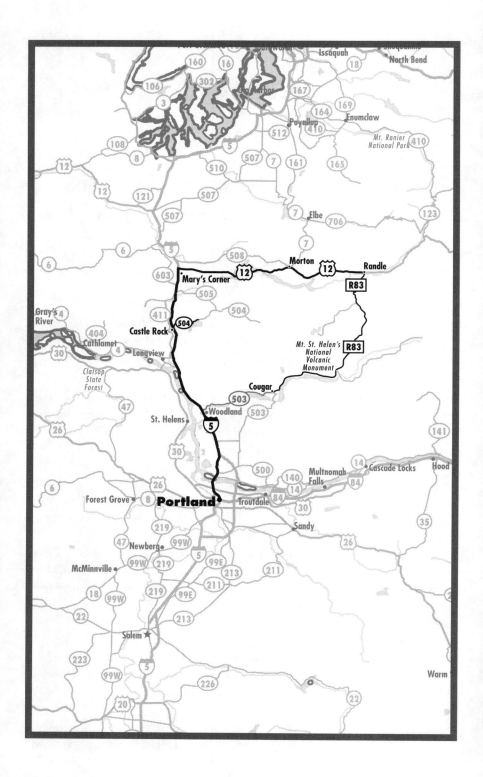

The east side of the mountain is open from Memorial Day until snow closes the roads in October, but you can still do a day trip up the west side of the mountain in winter. On the summer loop trip described here, you spend one day on the west side and one day on the east side of Mount St. Helens. This tour touches the highlights and will give you a sense of the awesome power that changed the structure of a mountain. As you walk, be careful of the fragile vegetation that is beginning to establish new life.

Bring sturdy walking shoes and water; there are few resources. At Mount St. Helens a concession between Meta Lake and Independence Pass sells emergency supplies, film, and food.

DAY 1

Morning

Head north on I–5 to **Castle Rock,** Washington (exit 49). Drive 5 miles east on State Route 504 to **Mount St. Helens Visitors' Center,** a well-designed complex set in a wooded grove near the shore of **Silver Lake.** As national park budgets swing up and down with political fortunes, the center may be open only on certain days of the week, usually from 9:00 A.M. to 5:00 P.M. in the summer. The ongoing rule in the Monument is to check for new times, phone numbers, events, and facilities. Trails (some paved and wheelchair accessible) extend from the center through the forest.

In the center you can obtain maps, information, and sight-seeing suggestions from the helpful staff. Don't miss the theater presentation, shown several times a day, that introduces the Mount St. Helens story.

Exhibits explain the mountain's history of eruptions and graphically illustrate the 1980 devastation. You can even walk into the heart of the volcano— a replica that gives a simulated version of the mountain's interior.

Continue on Route 504 along the **North Fork of the Toutle River.** On the way you'll see an A-frame home that was half-buried in the mudflow; you can walk through the dug-out rooms to see the effects of the disaster.

Stop for magnificent views at milepost 27, where Cowlitz County has opened the **Hoffstadt Bluffs Visitor Center.** You can stand high above the Toutle River and look down the valley to the glistening white flanks of Mount St. Helens. The center offers a few exhibits, but it is primarily an eating and shopping stop. You can take a helicopter ride from here for a closer look at the mountain.

LUNCH: Hoffstadt Bluffs Visitor Center. Eat hot or cold foods indoors, or eat picnic-style on the terrace, where you can keep your eyes on the scenery.

Afternoon

Continue east across the 370-foot-high, ½-mile-long bridge over Hoffstadt Creek. You are now in the blast zone. There are views of Mount St. Helens along the way, but the next big view is from the **Charles W. Bingham Mount St. Helens Forest Learning Center** at milepost 33. This exhibit center, a joint project of the Washington State Department of Transportation and the Weyerhaeuser Company, was designed to show the destruction, recovery, and reforestation of the area. It tells the story from the point of view of the lumber industry. The Rocky Mountain Elk Foundation has joined this project to help provide views of the elk herds in the valley below the center.

At milepost 43, which is almost the end of the road, you will find the 6,000-square-foot **Coldwater Ridge Visitor Center,** facing the volcano crater and with spectacular views of Coldwater Lake. (360) 247–5473. It is open daily year-round, 9:00 A.M. to 6:00 P.M. April through September, until 5:00 P.M. in winter. See the film and learn how many plants and animals have reappeared since the great blast.

Grab an espresso from the adjacent restaurant, and join a ranger for a **Coldwater Ridge Deck Talk.** Follow the ¼-mile **Winds of Change Interpretative Trail** to see how life has emerged from the ashes. Take the barrier-free **Birth of a Lake Trail** to the boardwalk over Coldwater Lake, which was created when debris from the eruption blocked the Coldwater River.

The very end of the road, just beyond the center, has been reserved for the **Johnston Ridge Observatory.**

Ask the park rangers about road conditions on the east side of the mountain. Heavy floods washed out roads and bridges in the mid-1990s, and recovery has been slow. If the east side of the Monument is closed to traffic, you may want to return 43 miles down State Route 504 to Castle Rock and drive an hour home to Portland. This west side of the mountain makes a great day trip.

If you are going on to the east side of the mountain, turn north on I–5 and east again on Highway 12 to **Mary's Corner.** (Shortcut: Turn north off Route 504 before you get to Castle Rock and follow State Route 505 through Toledo to Mary's Corner.) One of the state's first homesteads, **Jackson House,** is in this little community and is occasionally open to the public.

In **Lewis and Clark State Park,** Mary's Corner, you can walk in one of the last stands of **old-growth forest** along the Portland-Seattle corridor. Many of the Douglas fir, hemlock, and cedar trees are 500 years old.

Follow Route 12 east to **Mossyrock,** a small town set in a beguiling valley of farms and rolling green hills. Wild blackberry vines arch over sagging wood fences along this road, and Queen Anne's lace grows tall against red barns. There are acres of Christmas trees, tulip fields, and blueberries. This is logging country, too, and you'll see hills shorn of trees.

East of town there's a view of **Mossyrock Dam;** at 606 feet it's the highest dam in Washington. The dam created **Riffe Lake,** a 23-mile lake stocked with coho and brown trout. Fishing, boating, and sailboarding are popular here.

Morton, a longtime logging town 31 miles east of Mary's Corner, is famous for its annual rough-and-tumble logging show.

DINNER: Roadhouse Inn, Highway 12 and Crumb Road, Morton. (360) 496–5029. Familiar American food in a comfortable setting.

LODGING: St. Helens Manorhouse, 7476 Highway 12, Morton 98356. (360) 498–5243 or (800) 551–3290. Bed-and-breakfast with four rooms in 1910-era home on wooded grounds at the western end of Riffe Lake.

DAY 2

Morning

Enjoy a full breakfast at St. Helens Manorhouse. Then explore a few sites in Morton.

The **Old Settlers Museum,** in **Gus Backstrom Park** on the Tilton River, is filled with pioneer relics and is open occasionally. The park caretaker may open the museum, if you ask.

It's 17 miles from Morton to **Randle.** Along the route you may spot hang gliders riding the wind currents on Dog Mountain. At Randle, turn south on Forest Road 25.

In 9 miles you'll come to Forest Road 26. Pass this road by, remaining on Forest Road 25 for 11 miles until you reach Road 99. Turn west on the two-lane, paved road. Starting in deep green forest, it leads into the blast area that appears to be one of total destruction, but look closely and you'll see evidence of life's beginnings in the small plants.

Your first stop is at **Bear Meadow,** famous as the site where photographs were taken of the 1980 eruption as it occurred. Trails, picnic areas, and rest rooms are in this area.

Nine miles in, at the junction of Forest Roads 99 and 26, you'll see the **Miner's Car.** The 1973 Grand Prix, resting atop downed trees, was hurled 50 feet during the eruption and then placed in its present location.

Meta Lake Trail 210 begins 100 yards west of Miner's Car, off Road 99. This is the only trail offering barrier-free access into the blast zone. A naturalist leads a walk and explains the changing environment, usually at mid-morning and again in mid-afternoon. Check the summer schedules for times and events. On the ⅛-mile, level paved path you'll see small trees that survived the eruption, just 8½ miles away, because they were protected by snow and ice. Birds and insects have returned, and in **Meta Lake,** at the end of the trail, trout, salamanders, and frogs now live.

Three miles from Meta Lake Trail, at **Independence Pass,** Trail 227 leads to striking views of the mountain, the crater with its growing lava dome, and **Spirit Lake.** Ascend to walk the ridge for ¼ mile, and you'll have views in all directions of the blown-down trees and acres of ash-covered slopes.

If you hike 1½ miles to a Spirit Lake overlook, you'll find interpretive signs pointing out the locations of buried campgrounds, Harry Truman's lodge, and cabins on the shores of the lake.

Spirit Lake, once a crystal-clear alpine gem, is regaining its blue clarity. The lateral blast was moving fast when it snapped off thousands of trees. The slower landslide sludge hit the lake and swooshed back uphill to wash the trees back into the basin. Many of those trees still float in the lake; others have sunk and caught on the bottom, perhaps to become a future petrified forest.

Farther on, the trail narrows and passes rock pinnacles, eventually joining **Norway Pass Trail.**

Walk Trail 227 back to Forest Road 99, and drive deeper into the National Monument; in 4 miles you'll reach the end of the road at **Windy Ridge Viewpoint,** which is as close as you can drive to the crater. A parking area is on the edge of the restricted zone, which can be entered only with a permit, but you can hike without a permit if you stay on the trail.

On one side you'll notice a sand-ladder trail against a slope. Climb the stair-step path to the top of the hill, and you'll have a good vantage point into the great, often-steaming crater and devastated area.

Retrace your route back to Forest Road 25, and turn south. Drive 25 miles to join Forest Road 90 at **Swift Reservoir,** a long lake south of Mount St. Helens. The lake has a boat launch, picnic and camping grounds, and some tourist facilities. Take Road 90 to Road 83, turning north to drive 2 miles to the **Trail of Two Forests,** one of the best barrier-free trails for wheelchairs. One forest is an echo of the past; the other is of living, growing lodgepole pines.

An easy, ¼-mile-loop boardwalk (protecting the fragile mosses and plants growing on the lava) passes 2,000-year-old tree molds, formed when a lava flow consumed the forest that once stood here. Interpretive signs tell the tale of the two forests.

Next, take Road 8303 to **Ape Cave,** so called because it was discovered in 1951 by members of a club nicknamed the Mount St. Helens Apes. The cave, formed by an eruption 2,000 years ago, is 12,810 feet long—the longest lava tube in the continental United States. Lanterns and guided trips are usually available. Wear a jacket, carry two-light sources, and wear sturdy shoes. It's 42 degrees Fahrenheit year-round.

Ape Cave has two routes to explore. The lower cave, ¾ mile long and fairly level, is easiest and has unique features such as a "lava ball" wedged in the ceiling. Allow one and one-quarter hours round-trip. The more challenging upper cave has large rock piles to climb and an 8-foot lava fall.

Back on Road 83, turn northeast and travel 9 miles to **Lahar Viewpoint,** which provides a look at the southeast side of the mountain. A short trail leads to an interpretive sign that portrays the path of the lahar (mudflow).

Drive another ¾ mile past the parking lot to the **Muddy River,** and you'll notice the bright colors of stratigraphy bands on the stream bank. With the hill sliced away by debris racing down the channel of Shoestring Glacier, deposits from previous eruptions were revealed. The lower, bright yellow layer was deposited 8,000 to 13,000 years ago.

Return on Road 83 to Road 90 at the western shore of Swift Reservoir. This is one of three reservoirs created by dams on the **Lewis River.**

Drive 8 miles to the town of **Cougar,** on **Yale Reservoir,** a lake known for its outstanding Dolly Varden trout fishing. Stop in at **Cougar Ceramics,** 16834 Lewis River Road, (360) 238–5371, where Lynn and Dave Birch create smooth, marbled works of Mount St. Helens ash. They were among the first to use local volcanic ash in ceramics. Many of their pieces have become collectors' items.

Travel 5 miles south on State Route 503 to **Jack's Sporting Goods and Restaurant,** 13411 Lewis River Road, Ariel. (360) 231–4276. Travelers traditionally purchase supplies here for camping, fishing, and hunting, and it's one of the places where climbers sign in before beginning their trek up Mount St. Helens.

A limited number of free advance and same-day climbing permits have been available, but that may change.

LUNCH: Jack's. This is logger country; omelets and hamburgers are the size of platters. You may also picnic along the way to Cougar or enjoy a snack at the concession at Spirit Lake.

Afternoon

Drive Route 503 west, along **Lake Merwin**'s northern shore, 23 miles to **Woodland.** The visitors' center here sells souvenirs and such gifts as emerald obsidianite, a gemlike stone made from heat-fused volcanic rock; the center also provides maps and helpful information.

From Woodland, it's a 30-mile drive south on I–5 to Portland.

THERE'S MORE

Camping. Beaver Bay Park, east of Cougar on Lewis River Road. Boat launch, fishing, RV sites.

Cougar Park and Campground (tents only). Swimming, boat launch, fishing.

Lewis River RV Park, 3125 Lewis River Road, Woodland, WA 98674. On North Fork Lewis River. Swimming pool, picnic supplies, boat rentals. Near golf course.

Swift Park, east end of Swift Reservoir.

Chief Lelooska Living History Presentation, 5618 Lewis River Road, Ariel, WA 98603. (360) 225–9522. Colorful, evocative, educational programs on Northwest Coastal Indian culture. Ceremonial dances, masks, songs, stories. Afternoon performances for school groups; occasional evening performances. Native American art and artifacts displayed in Exhibit Hall.

Climbing. There is a climbing route on the south side of the mountain. Permits not required in winter; 110 permits a day issued in summer. Self-register at various designated places May 15 to October 31. For information, call Climbing Hotline at (360) 247–5800 or write Mount St. Helens National Volcanic Monument, Route 1, Box 369, Amboy, WA 98601.

Guided walks, with forest interpreters.

Hopkins Hill. Four miles west of Morton, the hill provides a commanding view of the Mount St. Helens crater and, often, a column of steam.

SPECIAL EVENTS

Mid-August. Loggers' Jubilee, Morton. Parades, carnival, arts and crafts, bed races, quilting exhibition, logging skills competition: tree fallers, logrollers, woodchoppers.

OTHER RECOMMENDED RESTAURANTS AND LODGINGS

Cougar

Lone Fir Resort, 16806 Lewis River Road. (360) 238–5210. Nothing fancy, but fifteen motel units, five with kitchens, are clean and well kept. Swimming pool, laundry facilities, RV sites with hookups.

Morton

The Seasons Motel, 200 Westlake. (360) 496–6835. New, modern motel with fifty spacious rooms.

FOR MORE INFORMATION

Mount St. Helens Visitor Center, 3029 Spirit Lake Highway, Castle Rock, WA 98611. (360) 274–2100. Call for road conditions before attempting to drive into the National Monument area.

Astoria and Long Beach
Water Pleasures

EXPLORE BY RIVER AND SEA

3 NIGHTS

*Columbia River views • Sandy beaches • Pioneer museums
Early explorers' fort • Lighthouses • 28-mile beach
Ocean views • Seaside resort town*

When you cross the bridge from Astoria, Oregon, to the recreational pleasures of Long Beach in southwestern Washington, you become part of the great water show of the West. The native canoes and explorers' boats have gone, but the freighters and pleasure boats still ride the broad, 1,000-mile-long Columbia River across that treacherous bar to the Pacific.

Today's travelers cross the Columbia to play on wide beaches and sand dunes around Long Beach, home to gourmet dining, good fishing, raucous kid fun, and a quiet historic village. A three-day loop trip northwest from Portland to Astoria and Long Beach combines the vivid life of the river with the lazier life of the beach.

DAY 1

Morning

Drive U.S. Route 30 west to the 10-block historic district that edges the Columbia in one of Oregon's oldest settlements, **St. Helens.** Visit the handsome Georgian Revival courthouse and pioneer museum. Watch river life

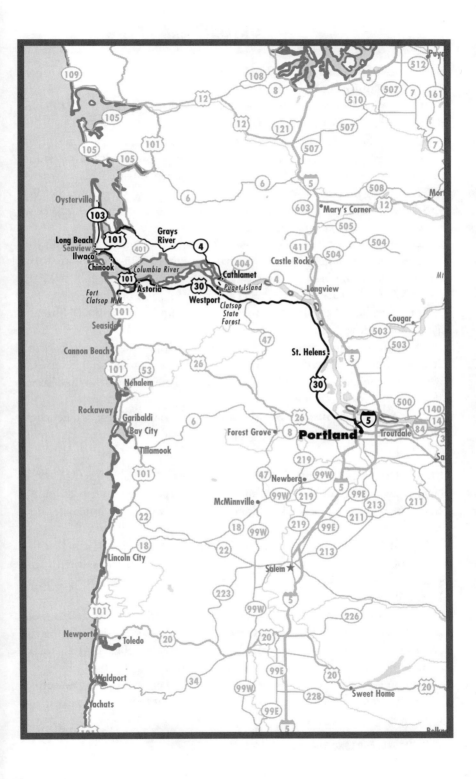

from the old-fashioned gazebo, brick viewing platform, picnic tables, or boat facilities at **Columbia View Park.**

If you missed breakfast, the St. Helens Cafe has served bountiful down-home meals 2 blocks from the plaza since 1915.

Continue heading northwest on Route 30 to **Astoria,** the Northwest's first European-American settlement. In 1811, John Jacob Astor built his fur-trading post and the Fort Astoria stockade in this rain-washed, fish-rich, hilly corner.

Fishing, logging, and canning drew settlers, many from Finland. By 1900 Astoria was the largest city in the state. It's still a sizable fishing port, keenly aware of its historic position and Scandinavian heritage.

Start your exploration on Coxcomb Hill, where a mural depicting historical highlights spirals up **Astoria Column.** Climb the 125-foot column's 166 steps for a sweeping view of the city, the long bridge, and the hills of Washington. Watch the Pacific Ocean meet the river in a roll of thunder.

Tour a replica of the **Fort Astoria log stockade,** a National Historical Landmark, at Fifteenth and Exchange Streets.

Don't miss one of America's finest nautical displays at the ultramodern **Columbia River Maritime Museum.** It exhibits historic sailing vessels, a river steamer wheelhouse, World War II submarine periscopes, and the historic West Coast lightship *Columbia.*

Next stop is **Josephson's Smokehouse,** 106 Marine Drive, where alder-smoked seafood is produced. It is shipped all over the world—there's none better.

LUNCH: Columbian Cafe, 1114 Marine Drive, Astoria. (503) 325–2233. Richly flavored soups, vegetarian and seafood crepes, lovely off-beat atmosphere. Open seven days a week for lunch; Wednesday through Sunday for dinner only.

Park at Flavel House, an ornate 1883 Queen Anne mansion built for a river pilot at 441 Eighth Street. It was saved when a 1922 fire burned much of the town, and the house is now a museum operated by the Clatsop County Historical Society.

Buy a walking-tour map in the museum, and explore seventy gracious old homes bearing historical markers. Check a few shops and galleries along the way. Michael's Antiques and Art Gallery features oriental and Victorian antiques plus the works of Pacific Northwest artists.

Choose your favorite historic clothing style at Personal Vintage Clothing, 100 Tenth Street, which carries hats, beaded bags, jewelry, linens, laces, and period wear.

Ricciardi Gallery, also on Tenth Street, carries paintings, ceramics, fabric art, carved wood, and jewelry by regional artists.

Afternoon

Take U.S. Highway 101 and go 6 miles south of Astoria to **Fort Clatsop National Memorial,** a reproduction of the fort used by the Lewis and Clark expedition during the wet winter of 1805–1806. Enjoy the center, its theaters, and interpretive displays by buckskin-clad rangers who tan hides, cure jerky, make candles, and carry muzzle-loaders just as the explorers used to do.

Follow the coastal road to the northwestern tip of Oregon and **Fort Stevens State Park,** a military reservation built during the Civil War to guard the river mouth from Confederate attack. It is now a 3,800-acre park with campgrounds, bicycle and hiking trails, beaches, and an interpretive center.

The shipwrecked remains of the *Peter Iredale* have poked through the sand here since 1906. Artifacts from the ship are displayed in the **Clatsop County Heritage Museum** at Sixteenth and Exchange Streets.

DINNER: Ship Inn, 1 Second Street, Astoria. (503) 325–0033. Watch the ship traffic as you feast on tender, crisply battered fish and chips.

LODGING: Rosebriar Hotel, 636 Fourteenth Street, Astoria. (503) 325–7427. Large home restored as stylish hotel. Mahogany furniture, fireplaces, televisions, phones. Winner of Astoria's Historic Preservation Award.

DAY 2

Morning

BREAKFAST: A full breakfast is included in the room rate at the Rosebriar Hotel.

Cross the bridge that spans the wide, choppy mouth of the Columbia River. Turn west on U.S. Highway 101 to Chinook, once a fabulously rich fishing town, and Ilwaco, where gill-netters and trappers fought ferociously over fishing grounds at the turn of the century

Learn about the Northwest heritage, from Chinook Indian life to the logging and fishing industries, at **Ilwaco Heritage Museum** on Lake Street (360–642–3446). The museum's loop map will guide your scenic 3-mile trip around the southwestern tip of the peninsula. Outdoor murals grace the walls in Ilwaco and other peninsula towns; they are part of a plan to attract visitors.

Stop at **North Head Lighthouse,** built in 1899 to warn boats approaching from the north. From this bluff above the Pacific you have a panoramic ocean view.

The road then curves toward **Fort Canby State Park** and the **Lewis and Clark Interpretive Center** (open daily in summer, weekends in winter). Inside, you can trace the intrepid explorers' adventures through pictorial displays, which include excerpts from the original journal entries. Ramps take you from the planning of the expedition in 1804 to its final destination here on the Pacific Ocean.

Stormy weather creates surf action at its wildest as monster breakers slam against steep cliffs below the interpretive center. Nearby **Waikiki Beach,** a local picnic favorite, is the only relatively safe swimming beach in the area.

Drive to the Coast Guard station south of the interpretive center and walk the ¼-mile path to the 1856 **Cape Disappointment Lighthouse,** one of the oldest lighthouses on the West Coast. Far below you lie the churning river mouth and the whitecapped sea. Captain John Meares named Cape Disappointment in 1788, when he was unable to cross the rough Columbia bar. More than 200 ships have wrecked or sunk in these treacherous waters.

Take the loop drive back to Ilwaco, one of several Northwest towns claiming the title "Salmon Capital of the World." Drive down to the harbor to see the busy tangle of boats and crab pots, charter fishing companies, canneries, and cafes, all mingling on the waterfront. The harbor has moorage for 1,000 boats.

Dockside Cannery and Gift Shop, on the waterfront, sells fresh seafood and gift packs.

LUNCH: Bubba's Pizza, Ilwaco Harbor. (360) 642–8700. Hamburgers, fish-and-chips, homemade chowder, in a convivial wharfside atmosphere.

Afternoon

Head north 2 miles into **Seaview,** once a fashionable resort town. Turn-of-the-century Portlanders took a Columbia River steamer and a narrow-gauge railway to the village, which still retains a pleasantly drowsy, old-fashioned atmosphere. Take a quiet walk on the sand. Enjoy art galleries like the Sea Chest, which shows work by watercolorist Charles Mulvey.

Long Beach, just north of Seaview, is a lot livelier and more commercial. Youngsters love its go-cart track, moped rentals, and horseback riding and the oddities and kitschy souvenirs of Marsh's Museum. Climb whimsical wooden sculptures in the miniparks.

Buy a kite at Long Beach Kites, and spend an exhilarating hour holding a bright dragon, box kite, or bird against the sky as you fly it on the wide, windy beach, said to be the longest (28 miles) in the world.

Sip an espresso or Italian soda while shopping for clocks, china, and linens at Pastimes, on South Fifth Street and Pacific Highway. Buy sweets made from the local product at Cranberry Pantry. Choose a book for the beach at The Bookvendor, 101 Pacific Highway.

Check in at the Shelburne Inn, and enjoy a Northwest wine or beer at the inn's Heron and Beaver Pub.

DINNER: Shoalwater Restaurant in the Shelburne Inn, Seaview. (360) 642–4142. Gourmet dining emphasizing regional foods and fine wines. Candlelight, linens, stained glass, quiet atmosphere.

LODGING: The Shelburne Inn, P.O. Box 250, Seaview, WA 98644. (360) 642–2442. Antiques-furnished inn, on the National Register of Historic Places. Calico quilts and plenty of charm.

DAY 3

Morning

BREAKFAST: Full country breakfast served family-style in The Shelburne Inn; complimentary to hotel guests.

Drive north up the peninsula, between sand dunes, forests, and cranberry bogs. In this major cranberry-growing center, the roads are bordered with acres of brilliant red berries in the fall. Call ahead to make arrangements for a tour of the bogs. (360) 642–2031.

At **Briscoe Lake** you'll see the rare, majestic trumpeter swans, which migrate to peninsula lakes and Willapa Bay in December and January.

Pass Klipsan Beach and Ocean Park, which have good beach access, and turn east across the peninsula to **Oysterville.**

Great sailing ships loaded with oysters sailed to San Francisco from here during gold rush days, in the mid-1800s, when oysters cost $1.00 apiece. The industry collapsed and the village faded, but the gracious old homes and the pretty church are on the National Register of Historic Places. Pick up a walking-tour map at Oysterville Church, and amble into a previous century.

Drive Stackpole Road north to **Leadbetter Point State Park** at the peninsula's northern tip, a quiet world of sand dunes, beach grasses, and hiking trails. Thousands of shorebirds feed and rest on the tidal flats and salt marshes during their migrations. The dunes are closed to the public to protect the snowy plover during the April-to-August nesting season, but the rest of the park is open year-round.

LUNCH: Picnic in Leadbetter Park.

Enjoy the beach, surf-fish, go clam digging, or bird-watch on **Eliot Hiking Trail.**

Travel Sandridge Road south to **Nahcotta,** once the northern terminus of the railroad that carried vacationers up and down the peninsula. The town is still active in the oyster business, and mountains of shells whiten the docks at the Port of Peninsula.

Buy oysters shucked or in the shell at **Wiegardt Brothers' Jolly Roger Oysters,** Nahcotta Boat Basin, or choose a whole range of seafood from a live tank at **East Point Seafood Company** (closed Sundays).

DINNER: The Ark, at 273rd Street at the Nahcotta docks. (360) 665–4133. Nationally acclaimed restaurant featuring regional seafood specialties, homemade breads, and fabulous desserts. Picturesque setting overlooking Willapa Bay.

LODGING: The Shelburne Inn.

DAY 4

Morning

BREAKFAST: Another Shoalwater breakfast, perhaps with homemade sausage omelet and buttery pastries.

Follow U.S. 101 and State Route 4 north and west to Grays River. A short detour will take you to the Grays River salmon hatchery and a **covered bridge,** the last such bridge remaining on a public road in Washington.

Travel east on State Route 4 to **Skamokawa,** one of the early river settlements, now a National Historic District. **Redmen Hall,** an old-fashioned schoolhouse from 1894, is open to the public on summer weekends. The **River Life Interpretive Center** here tells the history of the area. **Vista Park,** on the Columbia shore, is a worthy stop for its broad river views. The park has picnic facilities, tennis courts, showers, and campsites for recreational vehicles.

You are now on your way to **Cathlamet,** Washington, a peaceful logging and fishing community established in 1846. Visit the **Wahkiakum County Historical Museum** (open 1:00 to 4:00 P.M.) to see how the early pioneers, loggers, fishers, and farmers lived. The museum has a walking-tour map of the town's historical sites: a pioneer church, settlers' homes, and a cemetery.

Descend a slope to the sheltered harbor and **Elochoman Slough Marina** to watch the sturdy gill-netters come and go, reminders of the region's fishing heritage. This is one of the few full-service marinas on the lower Columbia.

Cross the bridge over the Columbia River to **Westport.** Board the twelve-car ferry, which departs every hour from 5:00 A.M. to 11:00 P.M. for **Puget Island.** The ten-minute ride will take you to a bucolic world far from city stress.

LUNCH: Picnic on the little beach near the ferry landing on Puget Island.

Afternoon

Puget Island has miles of quiet country roads that are ideal for bicycling. The roads wind past quaint churches, grazing sheep, tidy dairy farms with rose-covered fences, and whitewashed barns. Fish for salmon and steelhead at the public beach, bird-watch (look for Canada geese and swans), or beachcomb.

When you are ready to go home, follow Route 30 east to Portland.

THERE'S MORE

Boating. Bring your own boat to Long Beach Peninsula.

Boat from Nahcotta to Long Island, in Willapa Bay, and hike up to the last known groves of old-growth cedar in the United States. In this wilderness, home to deer, elk, grouse, bear, and 1,000-year-old trees, you can experience a bit of what the Northwest was like when Lewis and Clark arrived. Note: The bay is subject to tidal action; consult a tide table and use caution.

Fishing. Tiki Charters, Astoria, WA 97103. (503) 325–7818.

Golf. Peninsula Golf, 9604 Pacific Way, North Long Beach, (360) 642–2828. Nine-hole course.

Seaview Antiques and Collectibles Mall, 4705 Pacific Highway South, Seaview. (360) 642–2851. Several dealers sell wares in a colorful old house.

SPECIAL EVENTS

April. Ragtime Rhodie Festival, Long Beach, WA. Weekend performances of Dixieland jazz.

Late April. Great Astoria Crab and Seafood Festival, Astoria, OR. Carnival, wine tastings, arts, crafts, Dungeness crab.

First Saturday in May. Blessing of the Fleet, Ilwaco, WA. Children's parade, salmon barbecue, flowers cast on the waters.

Mid-June. Scandinavian Midsummer Festival, Astoria, OR.

July. Sand Sculpture Contest, Long Beach, WA. Cash prizes for winning sand sculptures.

Mid-August. International Kite Festival, Long Beach, WA. Annual kite-flying competition on the beach; one of the world's largest kite events.

October. The Great Astoria Oktoberfisht, Wallooskee Valley Fairgrounds, 6 miles east of Astoria, OR, on Highway 202. Fun, food, and beer from Oregon microbreweries.

OTHER RECOMMENDED RESTAURANTS AND LODGINGS

Astoria

Columbia River Inn, 1681 Franklin Avenue. (503) 325–5044. Victorian home restored as a charming bed-and-breakfast with pink-and-lace decor. Quiet neighborhood, friendly innkeeper.

Franklin Street Station, 1140 Franklin Avenue. (503) 325–4314 or (800) 448–1098. Walking distance from downtown. Tastefully furnished home with antique reproductions and modern comforts. Full breakfast. Closed during winter months.

Grandview Bed and Breakfast, 1574 Grand Avenue. (503) 325–0000. Web site address: www.bbonline.com/or/grandview/. Airy, attractive rooms in turn-of-the-century home on a hillside above town. Warm hospitality.

Ilwaco

Inn at Ilwaco, 120 Williams Avenue, NE. (360) 642–8686. Former church converted to bed-and-breakfast hotel and performing arts center. Cozily furnished rooms, friendly ambience. Full breakfast.

Seaview

42nd Street Cafe, Forty-second Street and Highway 103. (360) 642–2323. Lunch and dinner in cozy, quiet, nostalgic atmosphere.

Sou'Wester Lodge, Beach Access Road. (360) 642–2542. Historic home of former U.S. senator; very casual, on the beach. Three rooms in lodge plus several cabins and mobile homes.

FOR MORE INFORMATION

Astoria–Warrenton Area Chamber of Commerce, 111 West Marine Drive, P.O. Box 176, Astoria, OR 97103. (503) 325–6311 or (800) 875–6807.

Peninsula Visitors Bureau, P.O. Box 562, Long Beach, WA 98631. (360) 642–2400 or (800) 451–2542.

Columbia River Gorge: Oregon
A NATIONAL SCENIC TREASURE

1 NIGHT

*National Scenic Area • Waterfalls • Wildflowers
Woodland trails • River and mountain views • Bonneville Dam
Orchards • Sailboarding • Wineries*

Nature was more than generous in lavishing scenic beauty on the Pacific Northwest. The Columbia River Gorge, with its thick green forests, rocky bluffs, rushing streams, and misty waterfalls, is a spectacular example. Much of the gorge is a federally designated National Scenic Area.

The broad Columbia divides northern Oregon from southern Washington as it slices through the Cascade Mountains on its way to the sea. Streams rush into the river from the foothills of Mount Hood, on their journey from melting snow to waterfalls to tumbling creeks to the river and the sea.

On either side, sheer basaltic cliffs reveal a geologic history of earthshaking violence: rock that twisted like taffy under the onslaught of ancient floods, lava casts where trees fell before streams of molten lava, gaping holes where hillsides slid into the river.

This getaway immerses you in natural splendor. You'll walk forested trails to overlooks and waterfalls, watch boaters and sailboarders (or join them), taste Northwest cuisine, and tour the largest dam on the river.

DAY 1

Morning

Pack a picnic lunch (or plan to eat at Multnomah Falls Lodge), drive east from

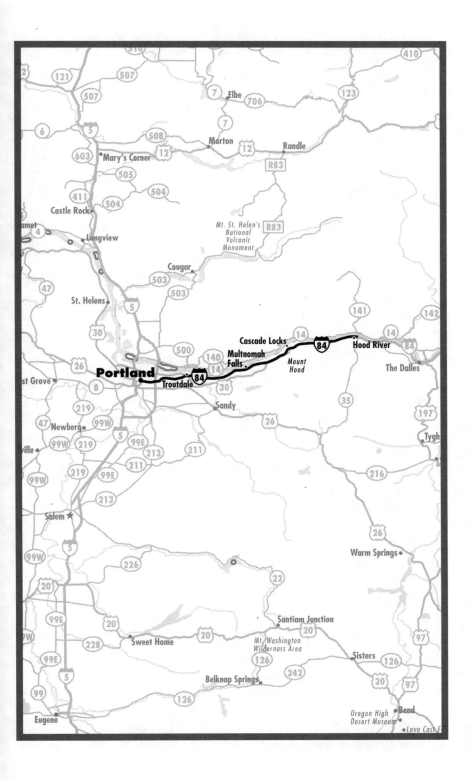

Portland on I–84 to Troutdale (about thirty minutes), and take the **Scenic Highway** exit. The historic road, much of it edged with moss-covered stone walls, cuts into riverside cliffs for 24 miles. Built in 1915, the road rises from river level to **Crown Point,** a basalt ledge jutting 720 feet above the Columbia. Stop here for one of the most romantic views in the world—a panoply of forest, mountains, and sky, with the mighty river glistening far below. **Vista House,** perched atop Crown Point, is a circular stone structure built in 1918 as a monument to pioneers. It contains information about the gorge and has a gift shop selling local handicrafts.

Continue 2.4 miles on the Scenic Highway to **Latourell Falls,** where a 2-mile trail curves up through ferns and mossy undergrowth to the 100-foot cascade. Lichens grow a brilliant yellow-green against rock walls. Hawks, crows, songbirds, and sometimes eagles soar overhead, while scolding squirrels scamper underfoot.

East from Latourell on the Scenic Highway, make a brief stop at **Shepherd's Dell.** Here a ¼-mile paved path, edged with a curving, mossy rock wall, descends to expose the spraying tiers of a stream not visible from the road.

The next stop is **Bridal Veil Falls State Park,** fifteen acres of footpaths and camas meadows on an open bluff above the river. Interpretive signs explain how natives and pioneers dug the bulbs of the sky-blue camas flowers and dried and baked them for winter food.

The park has picnic tables and rest rooms and a fenced, paved trail, accessible to wheelchairs, that loops along the bluff. The views of the river and across it to the immense basalt columns called the **Pillars of Hercules** are stunning.

An easy ⅔-mile walk takes you to an observation platform under a canopy of alder and maple trees, where you can see **Bridal Veil Falls,** a double cascade of dancing white water.

LUNCH: Picnic in Bridal Veil Falls State Park.

Afternoon

Continue east on the Scenic Highway, passing lovely **Wahkeena Falls** as you proceed to **Multnomah Falls,** a shimmering, 620-foot ribbon of spray that is the second-highest waterfall in the United States.

Native American legend says that long ago a chief's daughter plunged over the cliff above the falls as a human sacrifice to save her tribe from a devastat-

Multnomah Falls drops 620 feet from a sheer cliff in the Columbia River Gorge.

ing plague. Sometimes, people say, when the wind blows through the waterfall, you can see the shape of a maiden in the mist.

For an eagle's-eye view of the Columbia, hike up the paved trail to the fenced platform perched at the top of the falls (about 1 mile). The dizzying, over-the-edge view is what the legendary princess saw.

Rather than heading back down on the paved route, take the main trail into the woods along **Multnomah Falls Creek.** Then follow well-marked **Perdition Trail;** it will give you a two-hour walk through the ferny forest, over streams, and across a ridge to the top of Wahkeena Falls.

Along the trail are picturesque staircases, quaint bridges, and breathtaking glimpses of the river. To the north, on the Washington side, you'll see the snowy slopes of **Mount Adams** and **Mount St. Helens.** At Wahkeena, take the path downward toward the road, and connect with the final ¼-mile segment of the walk, which will lead you back to your car at Multnomah Falls.

(If you did not bring a picnic, order lunch in **Multnomah Falls Lodge.** This may be the only place in the world where you can sip a huckleberry daiquiri as you relax in a glass-enclosed lounge and gaze up at a waterfall as high as a sixty-story building.)

Your next stop is **Oneonta Gorge Botanical Area.** In summer, you can walk upstream in a cool, narrow canyon, which ends at a waterfall. Fifty species of wildflowers, shrubs, and trees grow in this fragile habitat; six grow nowhere else.

Just beyond Oneonta is **Horsetail Falls,** then **Ainsworth State Park,** where the Scenic Highway ends.

If this is a day trip, you may decide at this point to head back to Portland on I–84.

To continue exploring the gorge, travel eastward on I–84 and stop at **Bonneville Dam,** the oldest and largest hydroelectric project on the Columbia. Open daily for tours, the dam has a visitors' center with exhibits that explain the structure's operation. Underwater windows view fish ladders, so you can watch migrating salmon on their way back to native spawning grounds.

A mile east of the huge dam is **Eagle Creek Trail,** probably the most scenic in the gorge. As the fir needle–strewn path climbs and twists along steep cliffs, Eagle Creek tumbles beside and then below it, bouncing over boulders on its way to the river. Next to the trail are high cliffs, where thick, spongy moss drips showers of silver.

Two miles in from the trailhead you'll come to **Punchbowl Falls.** There's a viewing point above this lovely deep pool, and a short spur path leads down to its pebbled shore. From a rocky cleft, the falls plummet into the pool, while ferns clinging to the cliffs around it tremble in the mist. The stream plunges northward in a broad cascade at Punchbowl's wider end.

You can either make this your turnaround point, thereby retracing your route back down the Eagle Creek Trail, or continue another 4 miles to **Tunnel Falls.** Such a hike (12 miles round trip) would obviously take much of the day and mean excluding some of the other suggested walks.

At Tunnel Falls, another impressive waterfall, you'll pass through a 25-foot-long tunnel cut into the cliff. Eagle Creek Trail continues to **Wahtum Lake,** 14 miles in from the highway; it's an all-day hike.

When you return to your car and are back on I–84, drive east another 22 miles to the **Hood River Valley.** On the dry side of the Cascade Range, the valley's orchards produce fruit for world markets. In spring, Hood River's apple, pear, and cherry trees provide a glorious display of bloom. Mount Hood, mantled in glaciers, rises steeply behind them on the southwest, while northward across the river Mount Adams and Mount St. Helens are snowy sentinels against the sky.

Dozens of roadside stands sell fresh fruit and cider in the fall, and all year the area's wineries are open for tours and tastings.

Take exit 62 from I–84, and curve around toward the imposing yellow stucco inn that stands on a precipice high above the river. The **Columbia Gorge Hotel,** 4000 Westcliff Drive, is a fine place to relax with a drink in the **Valentino Lounge.** The historic hotel, built in 1921, harks back to the Jazz Age in its furnishings and decor. Adjoining the hotel is **Hood River Vineyards'** tasting room and art gallery, where you can sample local wines.

Continue on I–84 to the next exit, which will take you into downtown Hood River and your hotel.

DINNER: Stonehedge Inn, 3405 Cascade Drive, Hood River. (541) 386–3940. Once a summer home with lovely gardens; now a fine restaurant with a classic continental menu.

LODGING: Hood River Hotel, 102 Oak Street, Hood River, OR 97031. (541) 386–1900 or (800) 386–1859. E-mail: www.HoodRiverHotel.com. Recently restored 1910 hotel in the heart of town. European ambience, warm hospitality, charming period decor in thirty-two rooms and nine spacious suites.

DAY 2

Morning

BREAKFAST: Hood River Hotel restaurant.

After the preceding day's vigorous activity, this is a slower-paced morning for exploring Hood River and its peaceful valley. Start with the visitors' center in **Port Marina Park,** which has information on area attractions.

The **Hood River County Historical Museum** (open Wednesday through Sunday, April through October) is also in Port Marina Park and holds intriguing displays of Native American artifacts and relics from early settlement days.

The park has swimming and boating facilities and is a good place to watch **sailboarders** skim over the waves. On a clear, windy day hundreds of the brilliantly colored sails dot the river. Hood River, widely considered the "sailboarding capital of the world," draws fans of the sport from around the country. The best spot for close-up views of sailboarders is Hood River Event Site, at the north end of Second Street. The site, under development for sailboarding events, has a rigging area and bleachers. Other good viewing sites are the West Jetty and Rushton Park, west of the Columbia Gorge Hotel.

If you want to try sailboarding, several shops in Hood River rent equipment and provide a variety of lesson packages.

Drive up to **Panorama Point** (the turnoff is just south of town on Route 35) for a memorable view of the valley and Mount Hood. The view is most striking in spring, when the orchards are frothy with pink-and-white blossoms. Five miles south of Hood River, at the Odell turnoff on Route 35, is **River Bend Farm and Country Store**, 2363 Tucker Road (800–755–7568). Web site address: www.gorge.net/riverbend. Country gifts and gourmet foods are sold in a quaint setting.

LUNCH: Tugboat Annie's, 1100 East Marina Way. (541) 386–7999. Seafood, hamburgers, tasty fries. At water's edge, with river views.

Afternoon

Check the shops of Hood River, watch the sailboarders, fish, golf, or just relax on the beach.

You might take a self-guided tour of the **Hood River Brewing Company,** 506 Columbia Street. (541) 386–2281. There, you can watch traditional brewing techniques. Taste locally brewed, handcrafted Full Sail Ale in the adjacent **White Cap Pub,** which overlooks the Columbia River.

If you're feeling ambitious and the cool forests and waterfalls of the gorge look inviting, hike one of the dozens of trails that wind from the road up to Mount Hood's lower slopes. Or continue on into Portland.

THERE'S MORE

Cascade Locks. A park and museum are located on the site of the river locks that were used for river navigation before Bonneville Dam inundated the rapids. (See Portland Escape Four for more information.)

Cascade Salmon Hatchery, near Eagle Creek campground.

Hood River Golf Course. Scenic, nine-hole public course 5 miles southwest of Hood River.

Mount Hood Railroad, 110 Railroad Avenue, Hood River, OR 97031. (541) 386–3556. Old-fashioned train excursions (summer only) through Hood River Valley on the Fruit Blossom Special. Dining car, restored historic depot, children's photos with the engineer—and free rides on your birthday.

Swimming and picnicking, at pools of Eagle Creek.

Windsurfing is seen in local and international events near Hood River Expo Center, off I–84, exit 63.

SPECIAL EVENTS

Mid-April. Blossom Festival, Hood River Valley. Arts-and-crafts fairs, dinners, orchard tours, train rides.

Mid-July. Gorge Blowout, Hood River. Open-water, 20-mile sailboard race. International competition.

Late August. Apple Jam, Hood River. Music festival in Port Marina Park by the Columbia River.

Late October. Harvest Fest, Hood River Valley. Two days of entertainment, crafts sales, freshly baked goods, fresh produce.

Day after Thanksgiving. Light Up the Gorge!, Columbia Gorge Hotel. Historic hotel illuminates grounds for the holidays with more than 65,000 lights.

OTHER RECOMMENDED RESTAURANTS AND LODGINGS

Bridal Veil

Bridal Veil Lodge, Historic Columbia River Highway. (503) 695–2333; in Portland, 284–8901. Bed-and-breakfast home, built in the 1920s, across the road from Bridal Veil Falls State Park. Two cozy rooms and a guest cottage in knotty pine, shared bath. Full breakfast.

Hood River

Columbia Gorge Hotel, 4000 Westcliff Drive. (541) 386–5566 or (800) 345–1921. Classic country inn with forty-two rooms, 1920s motif, and river view. Full farm breakfast included. Dining room open to public.

Lakecliff Estate, 3820 Westcliff Drive. (541) 386–7000. Former grand summer home, now on National Register of Historic Places, has four rooms with forest or river views. Full breakfast included.

State Street Inn, 1005 State Street. (541) 386–1899. Classic English home on a hillside in residential Hood River. Clean, bright, stylish, friendly. Room rentals.

Troutdale

Tad's Chicken 'n Dumplings, on Crown Point Highway, a mile east of Troutdale, overlooking the Sandy River. Popular for its country cooking and fried chicken. (503) 666–5337.

FOR MORE INFORMATION

To learn more about the attractions of the Columbia River Gorge, see Portland Escape Four.

Hiking trail maps available ($2.00) from U.S. Forest Service, 319 Southwest Pine Street, Portland, OR 97204.

Hood River County Chamber of Commerce, Port Marina Park, Hood River, OR 97031. (541) 386–2000 or (800) 366–3530.

Oregon Wine Country

WILLAMETTE VALLEY AND

TUALATIN VALLEY

---

1 NIGHT

Vineyards • Pastoral countryside • Wine tastings
Museum • Orchards • Fine dining • Antiques

Oregon's Willamette and Tualatin valleys, with a climate similar to the great European wine-growing regions of Burgundy, Champagne, and the Rhine Valley, continue to produce outstanding, award-winning wines. The numerous wineries are usually open for tours and tastings.

This two-day journey takes you through rolling farmlands, fruit- and nut-laden orchards, and acres of vineyards. You'll stop along the way to glimpse Oregon history, visit art galleries and antiques shops, purchase fresh produce, enjoy a picnic, and check the new wine releases. If your party plans on wine tasting, you'll want to select a designated driver for the tour. Make it a leisurely journey, perhaps passing by some of the wineries suggested in order to fully enjoy the experience.

Tour maps are available at any of the Yamhill wineries, or call the Oregon Winegrowers Association, (503) 228–8403.

DAY 1

Morning

Pack a picnic lunch, and drive west from Portland on U.S. Route 26 to the 185th Street exit. Turn right on 185th, then right again on Springville Road,

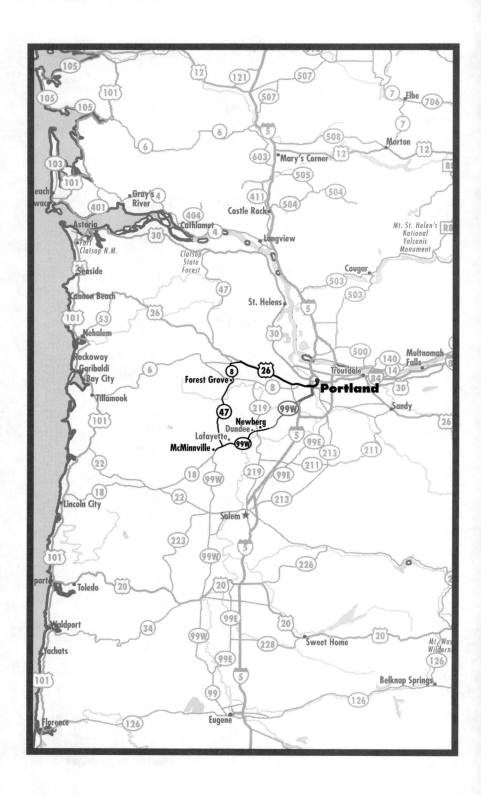

to Portland Community College. On the campus is the **Washington County Museum,** where you can learn about the area's history, from the Atfalati Indians through nineteenth-century settlement to today's high-tech industries.

Back on Route 26, travel west to the Jackson Road exit, turn south on Jackson, and turn right on Old Scotch Church Road. This will take you to a bonny white church that dates from 1878. Set in a grassy pioneer graveyard under tall fir trees, with farmland around it, the **Old Scotch Church** (Tualatin Plains Presbyterian) is a charming example of the appeal of rural Oregon.

Joseph Meek, one of the founders of the first government in the West, is buried in the graveyard. The church is open from 9:00 A.M. to noon Wednesday through Friday, for Sunday morning services, and at other times by arrangement.

After paying obeisance to a pioneer heritage, turn to present-day pleasures: wine tasting at **Tualatin Vineyards,** on Seavy Road (503–357–5005). It's open from noon to 5:00 P.M. on weekends and from 10:00 A.M. to 4:00 P.M. on weekdays. Get there by following Route 26 (also called the Sunset Highway) to State Route 6. There are signs to the winery along the way, and the visitors association can provide you with a map.

The vineyards, spread across eighty-five acres on the slopes above the Tualatin Valley, have at their center a winery with a spacious tasting room and a picnic area overlooking the valley. In the fall, the vines, orchards, and maple groves are brilliant with color.

Follow Route 6 to turn south on Route 8, where signs direct you through the rolling green countryside to **Shafer Vineyard Cellars,** Star Route, Box 269, Forest Grove (503–357–6604). Shafer, open weekend afternoons, serves pinot noir, chardonnay, riesling, gewürztraminer, and sauvignon wines.

Its first wine was produced in 1978. Since then, Shafer has received several awards, including the gold medal for its 1982 chardonnay at the American Wine Competition in New York.

LUNCH: Picnic at Shafer Vineyard.

Afternoon

Continue now on Route 8 to David Hill Road and turn right to **Laurel Ridge Winery** (503–359–5436). It's open daily except major holidays, from noon to 5:00 P.M. Set on one of the oldest vineyard sites in Oregon, Laurel

Ridge overlooks the farms of Tualatin Valley, backed by the green Tualatin Mountains. It produces sparkling wines in the *champenoise* method.

After your wine tasting, head south toward **Forest Grove,** a pleasant college town with tree-shaded sidewalks. **Pacific University,** 2043 College Way, was founded in 1850 by Congregational settlers from New England. The centerpiece of its attractive campus is stately **Old College Hall,** which is listed on the National Register of Historic Places. A museum in part, it can be toured weekday afternoons during the school year and on weekends in summer by appointment (503–357–6151, extension 2455). The hall holds Native American and pioneer artifacts and, in the Oriental Room, items reflecting the missionary spirit that founded Pacific University. Intriguing memorabilia from China, Japan, Turkey, India, and Africa are on display.

Leaving Forest Grove, drive south on Route 47 for 2½ miles to Dilley, where you'll turn right and ascend a hill to **Montinore Vineyards.** Tastings and tours are offered in one of Oregon's newest and largest wineries. Most production is devoted to pinot noir, pinot gris, and chardonnay wines.

Return to Route 47 and the hamlet of Gaston. South of Gaston, take Olson Road, off Route 47, to visit **Elk Cove** and **Kramer,** neighboring vineyards. Elk Cove and Kramer have annual open houses on Memorial and Thanksgiving weekends, along with twenty-two other Yamhill wineries. Most wineries are open for tastings year-round. Visitors are welcome.

Continue south on 47 through Carlton, home to Ken Wright Cellars and Domaine Serene; check out the pinot noir in the tasting room at Highway 47 and Main Street. Go south on Route 47 to join U.S. 99W. Turn right to head south into McMinnville and your lodgings.

DINNER: Nick's Italian Cafe, 521 East Third Street, McMinnville. (503) 434–4471. Outstanding Italian dinners. Brick walls, informal atmosphere. One of the region's best restaurants.

LODGING: Steiger Haus, 360 Wilson Street. (503) 472–0821. Lovely bed-and-breakfast with five rooms in country pine and wicker. Near downtown and college campus. Full breakfast served.

DAY 2

Morning

BREAKFAST: Steiger Haus provides a full breakfast that often includes local fruits and berries.

Return to downtown McMinnville for a tour of the historic district, where the tallest building is four stories high. The chamber of commerce provides maps for self-guided walking tours. Once you've left the commercial highway sprawl, McMinnville has the nostalgic atmosphere of small-town America. There are pleasant parks, tree-shaded sidewalks, shops, and cafes. It's the county seat and the home of **Linfield College,** founded in 1855. See **Pioneer Hall** on the green and leafy campus; it's a local landmark.

In a local shop you may see packages of gourmet candies. They're made locally by the monks in the Brigittine Monastery in Amity. You owe yourself a taste of the chocolate fudge.

Arterberry Winery Cellars, 905 Southeast Tenth Avenue, produces wines from grapes grown in the red hills of Dundee. They include pinot noir, pinot blanc, and sparkling chardonnay and riesling. Phone (503) 472–1587; open Saturday and Sunday, noon to 5:00 P.M., May to Thanksgiving. **Eyrie** and **Panther Creek,** also in McMinnville, are open only by appointment. Ask about Torii Mor Vineyard.

Return to 99W (labeled 99-Wine in these parts) and head north to **Lafayette.** At this village, formerly named Yamhill Falls, fur traders and natives crossed the Willamette River as they traversed the Overland Trail. In a park west of town you can see the remains of the **Yamhill Locks,** where riverboats of a century ago were assisted up the river.

Tour the **Yamhill County Historical Society Museum,** which is housed in an 1893 church, the oldest in the county. The museum contains cases full of items used by early settlers. Similar relics, and many more, are sold in the **Lafayette Schoolhouse Antique Mall** on Highway 99W (503–864–2720).

Near Lafayette, on Mineral Springs Road, is **Chateau Benoit Winery.** This winery began in 1979 and is best known for its sauvignon blancs and sparkling wines and has won awards for its Müller Thurgau. Open daily.

Continue on 99W to 5000 Sokol Blosser Lane and **Sokol Blosser Winery,** open daily. This winery's grapes produce pinot noir, chardonnay, white riesling, and Müller Thurgau wines. The tasting room has a sweeping view of the Willamette Valley and Mount Hood.

Your next stop is Dundee.

LUNCH: Alfie's Wayside Country Inn, 1111 Highway 99W, Dundee. (503) 538–9407. Soups, sandwiches, salads, and pasta served in a Dutch barn–style shingled inn. New features include take-out deli and wine tasting.

Vineyards in the Tualatin Valley, one of Oregon's wine-producing regions.

Afternoon

Several wineries are located in the red hills of Dundee. They include **Lange, Cameron, Erath, Argyle,** and **Duck Pond Cellars.** Map in hand, track down those you have time to visit as you head northeast on Highway 99W.

In Newberg, stop at **Coffee Cottage,** 808 East Hancock (503–538–5126) for rich espresso and cheesecake or a scone. Open daily.

East of Newberg, on the green slopes of the **Tualatin Mountains,** is **Rex Hill Vineyards,** 30835 North Highway 99W. (503) 538–0666. This show-place winery, furnished with antiques, emphasizes vintage-dated, vineyard-designated bottlings of pinot noir and chardonnay and has produced a fine pinot gris. Recently expanded, Rex Hill has a large tasting room and cellar and a sizable picnic area with a view of the valley. Across the highway is **Chehalem Winery,** 31190 Northeast Veritas Lane (503–538–4700), in a pic-turesque setting of vineyards above the northern Willamette Valley.

It's about 20 miles from the wineries back to Portland on Highway 99W. On the way, stop in Sherwood at **Sleighbells,** a fifty-acre Christmas-tree farm and holiday shop where peacocks roam the landscaped grounds. It's open June through December. (503) 625–7966.

THERE'S MORE

Boating. Canoe or kayak in the Yamhill and Willamette rivers. There are boat launches at various points along the riverfront.

Dr. John C. Brougher Museum, George Fox College campus, Newberg. (503) 538–8383. Contains memorabilia of Quakers who founded Newberg and the college. Open by appointment.

Fort Yamhill blockhouse. Used by General Phil Sheridan in Grand Ronde, the structure is now a city park in Dayton, a small town west of Lafayette.

Gallery Players of Oregon, Second and Ford Streets, McMinnville. (503) 472–2227. Community theater with year-round weekend performances.

Golf. Bayou Golf Course, McMinnville. Nine-hole course. (503) 472–4651.

Riverwood Golf Course, Dundee. Nine-hole course. (503) 864–2667.

Historic walking tours, Newberg. Tours pointing out turn-of-the-century homes in several architectural styles.

The **Hoover-Minthorn House,** Newberg. (503) 538–6629. Herbert Hoover's boyhood home from 1885 to 1888, now a museum with original furnishings. Open Wednesday through Sunday, 1:00 to 4:00 P.M.

Valley Art Association, 2022 Main Street, Forest Grove. (503) 357–3703. Regional artists show their works on consignment in this gallery, open Monday through Saturday.

SPECIAL EVENTS

March. Barbershop Ballad Contest and Gay Nineties Contest, Forest Grove. Barbershop quartet competition.

Memorial Day Weekend. Yamhill County wineries host visitors.

June. Portland Rose Festival Air Show, Hillsboro Airport. (503) 227–2681.

July. Concours d'Elegance, Forest Grove. Vintage auto show, entertainment, food.

July. Turkey-rama, McMinnville. Three days of street sales, carnival, music, turkey barbecue, 1950s dance, 8-kilometer run, and biggest-turkey contest. Celebrates local turkey business.

July. Tualatin Valley Fourth of July Barrel Tasting Tour. Open House and tastings at six valley wineries.

Midsummer. International Pinot Noir Celebration, McMinnville. Meet the winemakers and taste pinot noirs from Oregon, France, and California.

Thanksgiving weekend. Holiday Open House, Washington and Yamhill counties. Tours, tastings, food, and entertainment at most wineries.

Weekend after Thanksgiving. Wine Country Thanksgiving, Yamhill County. Music, tastings, foods at most wineries.

OTHER RECOMMENDED RESTAURANTS AND LODGINGS

Aloha

Yankee Tinker Bed-and-Breakfast, 5480 Southwest 183rd. (503) 649–0932. Ranch-style home with three guest rooms, shared bath. Colonial decor, antiques, tinware collection. Full breakfast.

Dayton

Wine Country Farm, 6855 Breyman Orchards Road. (503) 864–3446. Historic home on a hilltop with panoramic views of surrounding vineyards, Willamette Valley. Seven guest rooms with private baths. Wide deck, gardens, Arabian horses. Full farm breakfast. Has its own vineyard.

Dundee

Tina's, 760 Highway 99W. (503) 538–8880. Small, spare restaurant serving exceptional Northwest cuisine with French country zest. Worth a special trip. Lunches Tuesday through Friday; dinners daily. Reservations recommended.

Forest Grove

El Rodeo, 3331 Pacific Avenue. (503) 357–9410. Local favorite for Mexican food.

Ford's, 1923 Pacific Avenue. (503) 357–0317. Well-prepared hamburgers and sandwiches, 1950s decor.

Jan's Food Mill, 1819 Nineteenth Avenue. (503) 357–6623. Steaks and seafood, Sunday brunch in historic granary with homespun family atmosphere.

McMinnville

Orchard View Inn, 16540 Northwest Orchard View Road. (503) 472–0165. Five guest rooms in octagon-shaped home with wraparound deck. Full breakfast included.

Roger's Seafood Restaurant and Lounge, 2121 East Twenty-seventh Street. (503) 472–0917. Dinners overlooking a tranquil stream. Specializes in fresh seafood, charbroiled steaks, and Oregon wines.

Roth's, 1595 South Baker. (503) 472–7406. Grocery store, deli, and bakery. A good place to purchase picnic supplies and Oregon wines. Open daily.

The Sage Restaurant, 406 East Third Street. (503) 472–4445. Lunches on the mezzanine of 1893 Shops. Casual and cozy, with wooden booths and hanging plants. Sandwiches, soups, desserts at low prices.

Umberto's, 828 North Adams Street. (503) 472–1717. Italian dinners, veal specialties. Compares well with better-known Nick's Italian Cafe.

Newberg

Springbook Farm Carriage House, 30295 North Highway 99W. (503) 538–4606. Hideaway cottage in hazelnut orchard near Rex Hill. Kitchen, pond, swimming pool, tennis. Refrigerator stocked with breakfast.

Yamhill

Flying M Ranch, 23029 Northwest Flying M Road. (503) 662–3222. Rustic log lodge and restaurant 10 miles west of Yamhill, on the old stagecoach route. Horseback riding, swimming, tennis, barbecues. Private airstrip. Cabins.

FOR MORE INFORMATION

Forest Grove Chamber of Commerce, 2417 Pacific Avenue, Forest Grove, OR 97116. (503) 357–3006.

McMinnville Chamber of Commerce, 417 North Adams Street, McMinnville, OR 97128. (503) 472–6196.

Newberg Area Chamber of Commerce, 115 North Washington Street, Newberg, OR 97132. (503) 538–2014.

Oregon Wine Center, 1200 Front Avenue NW, Suite 400, Portland, OR 97209. (503) 228–8403.

Washington County Visitors Association, 5075 Griffith Drive SW, Suite 120, Beaverton, OR 97005. (503) 644–5555.

Yamhill County Wineries Association, P.O. Box 871, McMinnville, OR 97128. (503) 434–5814.

John Day Fossil Beds to Shaniko

FOSSILS AND FALLS

1 NIGHT

Waterfalls • Fossils • Ghost town • Antiques shops
Cattle ranches • River rafting • Historic hotel

If you appreciate nature's artistry, history on the grand scale, and a bit of adventure, you'll enjoy this tour. In two days you'll travel through millions of years of geological change, visit a frontier town, raft on a river, and ride through cowboy country. It's all a comparatively short distance from the city but a long way from urban living.

DAY 1

Morning

From Portland, drive east on I–84 to the Bridal Veil exit. Leave the freeway here, and at the top of the hill turn left on the **Scenic Highway.** This was the first federally designated scenic highway in the United States; only a short section remains, but the views are spectacular. In spring, colorful wildflowers bloom beside the winding old road; in all seasons it's surrounded by greenery. Below, on the north, lies the freeway and beyond it the broad **Columbia River** and the hills of Washington.

After passing through the quiet Bridal Veil community, you'll come to **Wahkeenah Falls,** a 242-foot series of falls pouring down the boulder-strewn basaltic cliff. It's a short distance from here along the Scenic Highway to the famous **Multnomah Falls.** Stop for a close look at the long, double cascade and perhaps have coffee and breakfast in the old stone **Multnomah Lodge.**

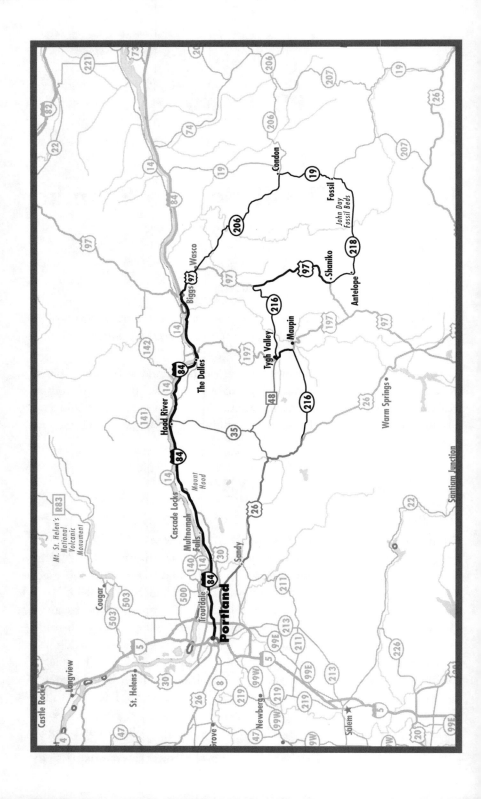

Next is **Oneonta Gorge Botanical Area,** a narrow canyon with rare plants and dense greenery; then comes picturesque **Horsetail Falls,** twisting 176 feet into a pool behind a low stone wall. **Ainsworth State Park** is the last stop on the Scenic Highway, a pleasant place for camping and picnics.

Rejoin I–84 at this point and continue east along the Columbia River toward the town of Hood River, another 28 miles (for more on Hood River, see Portland Escape Seven). You're driving through the great cleft in the Cascade Range, with Mount Hood rising immediately on the south and brawny Mount Adams and chopped-off St. Helens across the river on the north. On a clear day you'll see the peaks of Rainier in the distance. East of the Cascades, the scenery changes. The fir forests, waterfalls, and rugged cliffs are left behind, with rounded hills, sere and brown in summer, lying ahead.

After Hood River, take the Mosier/Rowena exit to travel a scenic byway, where cherry orchards grow on the hillsides and balsamroot and lupine carpet the fields with yellow and blue in April and May. As you climb the hill you'll have sweeping, panoramic views of the river and mountains.

Six miles after you leave I–84, you'll come to **Rowena Dell.** Stop to admire the view from **Rowena Crest View Point** and walk the paths of the **Governor Tom McCall Preserve at Rowena Plateau.** Owned by the Nature Conservancy since 1982, this scenic area offers stunning displays of wildflowers on a plateau above the river. You might also walk the 1½-mile footpath that leads to **McCall Point,** a high overlook.

The cliffs here, composed of dark Columbia basalt, were formed in a series of massive lava flows about fifteen million years ago. Ten million years ago, as the great basalt plain crumbled, erosion carved out Rowena Dell. Later floods and ash from volcanic eruptions created the steep cliffs and landscape visible today.

You can rejoin I–84 after descending from Rowena Dell, or continue on the country byway to Rowena and Mayer State Park, joining I–84 at **The Dalles.** In spring, the countryside around The Dalles is a pastel sea of cherry blossoms, as this is a prime fruit-growing area.

If time allows, take a look around the history-steeped town. For centuries it was a Native American trading center and then the end of the overland Oregon Trail. A walking tour map points out the original **Wasco County Courthouse,** now an interpretive center. Tours are led mid-morning and mid-afternoon from the Chamber of Commerce, 404 West Second Street. The courthouse was built in 1859 when Wasco was the largest county in the United States, extending into present-day Idaho, Montana, and Wyoming.

Old St. Peter's Church dates from 1898. In it, you'll see brilliant stained-glass windows, Italian marble, rich woodwork, and the church's original organ. The former **Surgeon's Quarters** is all that remains of Fort Dalles. In the mid-1800s, it was part of the only military post between Fort Vancouver and Fort Laramie; today the quaint structure is a museum with displays on pioneer life.

Leaving The Dalles, the rocky hills are dotted with fragrant blue-gray sage-brush, while willows and wildflowers grow by the water. From I–84, take exit 97 to State Route 206. **Celilo Park,** between the river and railroad tracks, is a green oasis here, with lawns, trees, and rest rooms.

Traveling on Route 206, you'll cross the Deschutes River and come to **Deschutes River Recreation Area.** This large, attractive riverside park is a popular gathering spot. It has boat launches, grassy slopes under locust trees, and campsites. An **Oregon Trail Historic Marker** tells of pioneers crossing the Deschutes on their way west.

At the Fulton Canyon/Wasco sign, Route 206 heads inland, away from the river. You're driving up a winding road into a steep canyon, where sheep paths crisscross the treeless hills. Then you're up and out of the canyon, surrounded by vast grain fields, with cottonwood trees where there is water. By the road-side, in a grove of locust trees, you'll see Locust Grove Church, with its high steeple and arched windows. Now deserted, gray, and weathered, the quaint little church was built in 1895 and last used for a funeral in 1914.

Crossing U.S. 97, you'll arrive in **Wasco,** a small, intensely quiet town dominated by big grain elevators. There are brick buildings and lilacs, a small city park with play equipment, a city hall, a post office, and the Wasco Mar-ket, where the community goes to learn the latest happenings. Recent signs in the window advertise garage sales, a junior rodeo, the high school sports schedule, a gun show, and an annual rummage and plastic flower show.

Continue through ranch country, where grain and cattle are the mainstays, to the sagebrush of Cottonwood Canyon, and on to the **John Day River.** At J. S. Burres State Park, a simple wayside with a couple of picnic tables and toi-lets, boaters often put in to the river.

From the John Day, ascend out of the canyon to a hilltop with a "Moun-tain Identifier," which names the visible mountains: Jefferson, Hood, St. Helens, Adams, and Rainier.

Forty miles after leaving the Columbia River, arrive in **Condon,** another quiet town where grain elevators loom. The home of the "Blue Devils" and the "gateway to John Day recreation area" has one main street with barber and beauty shops, a few cafes, and numerous empty storefronts. Condon's school neighbors a pretty green park with play equipment and has a pool and tennis courts.

The most interesting place in town for the traveler is **Country Flowers,** which boasts a surprisingly large variety of crafts and gift items—wind chimes, dolls, copper pans, birdhouses, soaps, teddy bears, and many others, all of excellent quality. Fresh flowers and plants are displayed indoors and on the front sidewalk.

LUNCH: Country Flowers Soda Fountain, 201 South Main, Condon. (541) 384–4120. Soups, thick sandwiches, taco salad, Italian sodas, frozen yogurt, ice cream, espresso. There are also a gift shop, florist, and bookstore.

Afternoon

Leave Condon on Route 19 headed south, driving through old lava flows covered with a thin layer of topsoil that supports sagebrush and a few juniper trees. The town of **Fossil** (population 430) is 20 miles south of Condon. Fossil has several points of interest, including a **museum** with well-displayed nineteenth-century artifacts and exhibits on turn-of-the-century fossil hunters, a **car museum** where you can see a collection of vintage autos, and the red brick **Wheeler County Courthouse.** The courthouse has fish-scale shingles, two towers (one with four stories, making this the tallest building around), and a curved brick entrance.

Arthur Glover Park has a playground and picnic tables. Fossil Mercantile sells groceries and sundries.

Turning southwest on Route 218, you'll drive 20 miles to reach **John Day Fossil Beds National Monument,** a journey that reaches far into the past. The National Monument, established in 1975, encompasses 14,000 acres in three separate units: Sheep Rock, Painted Hills, and Clarno. This visit to the northernmost site, the **Clarno Formation,** explores the oldest fossil beds, fifty-four million to thirty-seven million years old. They are some of the best preserved on earth. Beds spanning more than five million years are rare, yet the John Day Fossil Beds show more than forty million years of diverse plant and animal life.

Evidence of ancient subtropical forests abounds, as well as fossils of mammals that roamed the region thirty-four million years ago.

Visitors usually pick up a trail map and hike the short walk to the cliffs, or palisades. The **Clarno Palisades** are high rocks exposed by erosion after volcanic mudflows over millions of years inundated the forests again and again. One trail is fairly steep and leads to a high arch in the rocks; the other is an easier nature trail, with fossils identified. These give you a small sampling; there are many significant sites, deeper in the National Monument, that are not yet open to the public.

Nearby is the **Hancock Field Station,** operated by the Oregon Museum of Science and Industry. It offers field trips and study courses on the geology, paleontology, and ecology of the area.

Leaving the palm trees of the past for the sagebrush of the present, continue on 218 to the John Day River. At the rust-red bridge crossing the John Day, a federally designated Scenic Waterway, you may see rafters and boaters putting in for a ride down the rapids. Then you'll ascend again through mounds where cattle graze near juniper trees and cloud shadows glide over buttes and valleys. In spring, if there has been rain, the landscape is a delicate green sprinkled with yellow flowers.

Tucked into a quiet hollow shaded by poplar trees is **Antelope,** a farm town with a store, a school, and a church. From here, the road turns north for 8 miles to Highway 97, at the crest of a hill, and the ghost town of **Shaniko.** With twenty-five people, it's not quite a ghost town, but that's what it is labeled, as the residents strive to attract tourists to this slice of the Old West.

You can ride a stagecoach, peek into the worn jail, see a collection of well-used buggies and a covered wagon, photograph the picturesque schoolhouse, and shop for antiques. You can even have a western-style wedding at the little **Shaniko Wedding Chapel,** on the boardwalk of the 2-block main street.

Shaniko was once a busy place, the wool shipping capital of the world. Millions of pounds of wool from regional sheep ranches were stored in the big warehouse and shipped out on the rails at the turn of the century. But eventually the train bypassed the town, the economy dropped away, and Shaniko was nearly deserted. In recent years, though, new owners took over the old **Shaniko Hotel** and brought it to life again.

The mood in Shaniko is disturbed only by the rumble of trucks on busy Highway 97, which runs by the edge of town.

DINNER: Shaniko Cafe. Shaniko Hotel's bright and cheerful restaurant features steak, meatloaf, stew, and hamburgers. Try the crispy-tender fried chicken with home fried potatoes—hearty and delicious.

LODGING: Shaniko Hotel, Shaniko, OR. (541) 489–3441. Brick hotel with twenty simple but clean and comfortable second-floor rooms and one ground-floor room. Lace curtains hang at high windows; the atmosphere is updated frontier. On the National Historic Register.

DAY 2

Morning

BREAKFAST: Three breakfast choices are included in the room rate at the Shaniko Hotel—bacon and eggs, French toast, or continental. Or you can order from the menu at additional cost. Portions are generous.

After you've poked around the ghost town, head north on U.S. 97 and take the first right, Bakeoven Road. At this 3,500-foot elevation you can look back toward John Day country, while ahead of you lies the **Deschutes River Canyon.** Mount Hood and Mount Jefferson tower on the horizon, and you can see Mount Adams and Olallie Butte. The near landscape is festooned with power lines, carrying hydroelectric power from The Dalles Dam on the Columbia River.

From the plateau, twist down into the valley where **Maupin** nestles against the Deschutes River. Here you'll meet your **river-rafting guides** and board the van that will take you to a put-in point on the river. (Ewing's, P.O. Box 427, Maupin, OR 97037; phone 541–395–2697.)

The Deschutes is a popular rafting river, with weekends, especially in July and August, very busy. It's carefully regulated, but you'll find that off-season weekdays are considerably less crowded. In the 14-foot raft you'll float the Scenic Waterway back to Maupin, encountering several rapids on the way, and have lunch in the park.

LUNCH: Provided by the **Ewings,** it's set out in the riverside city park at Maupin. Deli sandwiches, chips, fruit, and apple cake are the usual menu. (Executive lunches, at additional cost, include steak or chicken.)

Afternoon

Climb into the raft again and continue down the river to **Sherar Falls,** a series of cascades that pour over rocky ledges. This is a traditional fishing ground, where local tribal members still stand on wooden platforms built out over the falls and dip long-handled nets into the water. Other fishers cast their lines from the shore.

You'll be shuttled back to Maupin when the four-hour ride is over.

From Maupin, travel north on Deschutes River Road, a National Scenic Byway, and parallel your river ride. There are camping and fishing areas all along the road here. Blue Hole Recreation Site has a fishing ramp with handicap access.

On your left, the river rushes by and above it rise steep, rocky cliffs topped by a flat plateau. Past Sherar Falls, where you have a good view of the fishing activity, cross Sherar Bridge. It's often crowded near here, with RV campers parked by the bridge and along the shore. Now you're on Route 216, headed for Tygh Valley.

Three miles from the bridge, watch for the state park sign and turn left at **Tygh Valley Wayside,** where there's an attractive, well-tended day park with lilacs and maple trees, grass and picnic tables. As soon as you arrive you'll hear the roar of the water—**White River Falls,** the most spectacular sight for miles around.

In a series of three cataracts, the falls drops 90 feet through a steep basalt canyon. The White River begins in a glacier on Mount Hood and flows to join the Deschutes. In spring, when there's abundant snowmelt, the falls is at its most powerful, plunging into pools that roil with action. You can see the falls from a fenced viewpoint or walk down a fairly steep dirt trail in order to view all three sections at once. On the site are also the concrete remains of an abandoned hydro plant.

From the wayside, drive on to **Tygh Valley,** home of the All-Indian Rodeo (see "Special Events") and head west on the road to Wamic. This becomes Route 48, the White River Road. The pioneers who chose to travel overland, rather than float their covered wagons down the Columbia from The Dalles, came this way and often traded with the Tygh Indians. Sam Barlow forged a trail around Mount Hood and set up a tollgate to charge travelers coming through on his road.

You can drive part of the Old Barlow Road, which parallels White River Road and goes all the way to Barlow Pass and Highway 35. There are several turnoffs and signs pointing the way from Route 48.

Now you've left the sagebrush and ponderosa pines of central and eastern Oregon and entered the thick fir forests of the western Cascades and **Mount Hood National Forest.** Continue into the foothills of Mount Hood, crossing several creeks, with the great mountain looming directly before you.

When you reach Highway 35, you have two choices: Turn west toward Route 26 and head for Portland around the mountain's south side, or go north on 35 to Hood River and take the freeway, I–84, west to Portland. If you choose the latter course and have time, stop at East Fork 650, just north of Sherwood Campground, for a two-hour walk up to **Tamanawas Falls,** another cascade of breathtaking beauty (see Portland Escape Four for details).

THERE'S MORE

Fishing. The John Day is noted for its smallmouth bass, salmon, and steelhead. The Deschutes is famous for its summer steelhead and trout.

John Day River. The John Day, much less used than the lower Deschutes, offers solitude and quiet within its dramatic canyon walls. It's also good for rafting, especially in spring. The 47-mile run from Service Creek to Clarno is a two-day trip with some rapids.

OTHER RECOMMENDED RESTAURANTS AND LODGINGS

Maupin

The Oasis Resort, 609 Highway 197 South, P.O. Box 365. (541) 395–2611. Eleven small vintage cabins, most with kitchens, on a grassy, tree-shaded slope near the Deschutes River. Campground also available. Reasonable rates. Also has a restaurant known for good food.

SPECIAL EVENTS

Mid-April. Northwest Cherry Festival, The Dalles. Orchard tours, cherry cook-off, street fairs, parade, runs.

Mid-April. Celilo Salmon Feed, The Dalles. Tribal dancing, feast of salmon, venison, root potatoes. Celebrates long Native American fishing tradition in the Columbia.

May. All-Indian Rodeo, Tygh Valley. Bronc riding, wild-horse race, team roping, bulls, Buckaroo breakfast, Native American crafts, fun runs, kids carnival, dances, beer garden.

Early June. Pioneer Days, Shaniko. Three-day event with parade, Old West shoot-outs, dances, pie social, stagecoach rides, mountain man camp.

Early August. Shaniko Festival, Shaniko. Parade, beef barbecue, beer garden, street dance, music, cloggers, flea market, old-time fiddlers.

FOR MORE INFORMATION

The Dallas Chamber of Commerce, 404 West Second Street, The Dalles, OR 97058. (541) 296–2231.

The Dalles Convention and Visitors Bureau, 404 West Second Street, The Dalles, OR 97058. (541) 296–6616 or (800) 255–3385.

Hancock Field Station, Fossil, OR 97830.

Superintendent, John Day Fossil Beds National Monument, HCR 82, Box 126, Kimberley, OR 97848. (541) 987–2333.

PORTLAND

McKenzie River Highway

A CLASSIC NORTHWEST ADVENTURE

1 NIGHT

*Festive markets • Covered bridge • Scenic wild river
Hot springs • Old-growth forest • Stagecoach stop
Waterfalls • Historic village*

Oregon's McKenzie River, which flows from hidden springs in Clear Lake, in the central Cascade Range, through lava fields, forests, and farmlands to join the Willamette, is internationally known for its great fishing and white-water rafting. Dozens of river guides and outfitters are eager to take you out in a raft or McKenzie River drift boat and introduce you to the joys of the river and the gorgeous scenery that surrounds it.

A ribbon of green in a green forest, with high, snow-topped mountains rising against the eastern sky, the McKenzie is one of the state's outstanding scenic attractions, and the road that runs beside it offers a chance to sample its pleasures in a brief getaway. You can always come back for more.

DAY 1

Morning

Drive from Portland on I–5 to **Eugene,** 100 miles to the south. There's a lot to do in this university town, where counterculture meets high culture. You can tour art galleries and attend world-class concerts, or buy beads from street vendors at **Saturday Market.**

Eugene has shaken off the economic doldrums and is full of lively activity. To start your holiday on a vibrant note, head for the **Fifth Street Public**

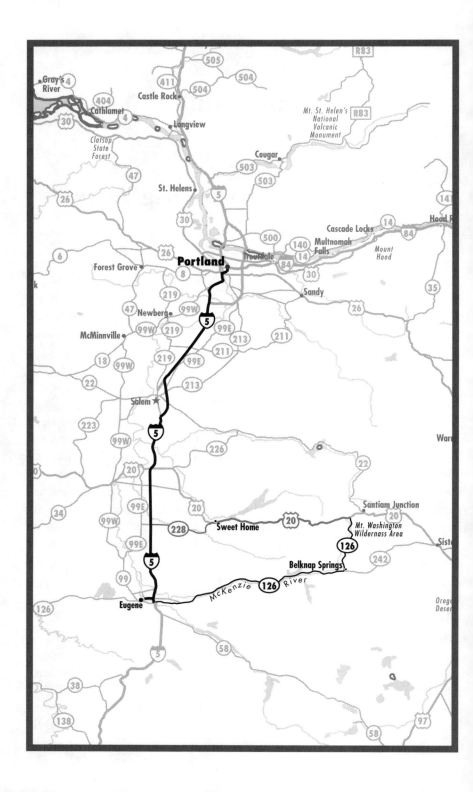

Market, in the historical downtown area. Under one roof, several dozen shops and restaurants on three levels are bursting with wares. Browse through the market, relax in the brick courtyard, listen to the musicians, and watch the fountain play and people go by.

LUNCH: Mekala's, 296 East Fifth Street, Eugene. (541) 342-4872. Extensive menu of perfectly spiced Thai food, to eat indoors or on the terrace. Located in Fifth Street Public Market.

Afternoon

Leave Eugene, driving east on State Route 126; within a few miles you'll be edging the **McKenzie River** shore. (Alternatively, to allow more time by the river, you might skip the Eugene visit and turn directly off I–5 to east Springfield and Route 126.)

Long before white settlers arrived, native tribes from Eastern Oregon were traveling this route. They came to fish during salmon runs, pick berries, hunt game, and gather herbs in the valley. Then came the explorers, pioneers, and loggers. Today, it's sport fishers and tourists.

As you leave the city, homes become more widely spaced and fields and farms predominate. Soon you're passing groves of dark fir trees and the occasional clear-cut area, and you may see a deer standing by the roadside before it leaps into the shrubbery.

When you reach **Leaburg Dam,** 24 miles from I–5, stop to watch the salmon and steelhead as they climb a fish ladder during migration periods. The **trout hatchery** here, open for public observation, annually releases thousands of trout, summer steelhead smolt, and cutthroat trout fingerlings. The ponds also contain albino trout and Columbia River sturgeon.

Twenty-six miles upriver you'll come to **Goodpasture Covered Bridge.** The well-maintained, picturesque bridge, built in 1938 to replace a ferry that crossed the river here, is 165 feet long.

At the 30-mile point is Ben and Kay Dorris State Park. This is the place to watch the tumbling water of **Marten Rapids,** most famous of the McKenzie's white water.

Mom's Pies, Milepost 35.5, McKenzie Highway 126 (541–822–3891), is a small cafe with an old-fashioned soda fountain, outdoor tables on a terrace, and a cook who bakes superb pies. Ten or more varieties are served daily; try the Black-and-Blue, a flavorful combination of black- and blueberries.

White-water rafting draws thousands of thrill-seekers to the McKenzie River.

Continue east to **Blue River.** The river, a tributary of the McKenzie, was named for the blue hues in the riverbed rocks. In the late 1800s, this was active mining country, after the discovery of gold in Blue River and in Lucky Boy mines. Most mining was abandoned in the 1920s, when the richest ore was gone.

Forest Road 15, which curves around the east end of Blue River Reservoir, leads to **Wolf Rock,** a massive hunk of basalt rising 4,500 feet. From gentle slopes covered with Douglas fir, you suddenly reach the base of the towering, solid black stone that erupted as molten lava thousands of years ago. It's an imposing sight, about 15 miles from the highway.

The next point of interest along the McKenzie is **Cougar Dam and Reservoir,** off Forest Road 19, the Aufderheide National Scenic Byway. Here, in Delta Campground, you'll find a trail that loops for ½ mile through an old-growth grove of Douglas fir and western red cedar. Some of the giant conifers are 200 to 500 years old.

A mile past the dam is a large parking area, and beyond it a lovely, ¾-mile trail to **Terwilliger Hot Springs.** Three pools of naturally heated water lie among the rocks and trees. This very popular destination is frequented by counterculture folk; avoid it if you're uncomfortable around nudity.

Tokatee Golf Course, located off Route 126, is an eighteen-hole golfer's paradise. It's considered one of the top courses in the Northwest and is surrounded by magnificent scenery.

Drive 5 miles east of Cougar Reservoir and you'll reach **McKenzie Bridge,** once called Strawberry Flat because of the abundant wild strawberries in the region. The present bridge spanning the river at this point is the fourth since 1869.

DINNER: Log Cabin Restaurant, McKenzie Bridge. (541) 822–3432. Summer hours: Noon to 8:00 P.M., Monday through Saturday; 10:00 A.M. to 8:00 P.M., Sunday. Winter hours: 5:00 to 8:00 P.M., Monday through Friday; 5:00 to 9:00 P.M., Saturday; 10:00 A.M. to 8:00 P.M., Sunday. Varied menu with noted specialties: beer cheese soup, prime rib, buffalo, venison, and marionberry cobbler.

LODGING: Log Cabin Inn, 56483 McKenzie Highway, McKenzie Bridge, OR 97413. (541) 822-3432. Eight log cabins, one with a kitchen, on a meadow by the river. Rustic but modernized. Occupies the site of a former stagecoach stop and hotel, built in 1885 and rebuilt in 1907, when the first structure was destroyed by fire.

DAY 2

Morning

BREAKFAST: Log Cabin Inn. Full breakfast menu with specials.

Route 126 and the river turn north after McKenzie Bridge. Take Scenic Highway 242 north past Proxy Falls to Historic Dee Wright Observatory. You're on Three Sisters Mountain and can see all the way to Mount Hood. From here, take the National Lava Trail or the Pacific Crest Trail. Return to Route 126 and continue north past **Belknap Springs.** The hot mineral springs, discovered in 1859, have long been favored by those seeking the benefits of a hot springs soak. A hotel first opened here in 1972; now there's a resort with an RV park. Nonguests can use the hot mineral pool (102 degrees Fahrenheit) that has been constructed on the riverbank.

To see **Belknap Crater** close up, you have to take the Clear Lake cutoff. From this volcano came the lava flows that over the past 3,000 years formed the ravines and ledges where waterfalls now drop in spectacular cascades. One, at Milepost 70.5 on Route 126, is **Koosah Falls,** which plunges 70 feet into a deep bowl. Another—probably the most impressive of the entire McKenzie water network—is **Sahalie Falls,** just ¼ mile north of Koosah. Sahalie drops 100 feet to a lava ledge, then falls another 40 feet. Easy paths lead from the parking area to the falls.

At **Clear Lake,** ½ mile off the road, rent a rowboat (no motors are allowed on the lake) and row about fifteen minutes to the east shore. There you'll see a submerged forest lying deep within the lake's cold, crystal-clear waters. The trees are nearly 3,000 years old.

Several mountain peaks are visible: Jefferson, Three Fingered Jack, the Sand Mountain cones, Mount Washington, and the Three Sisters.

LUNCH: Sandwiches or hamburgers from the concession at **Clear Lake Resort.**

You've reached the end of Route 126; turn west here on U.S. Route 20, and drive 43 miles to the small town of **Sweet Home.** In **Sankey Park,** a couple of blocks from the main street, stroll **Weddle Bridge,** a 120-foot covered bridge over Ames Creek. The reconstruction of the historic bridge was made possible by local volunteer support. The park also has a playground, picnic area, and log shelters in groves of fir trees. The sturdy shelters were built as a WPA project in the late 1930s.

The **Santiam River** edges the road here, swinging north. Take the short detour to **Brownsville,** a village with a strong sense of history. Established in 1846 on the Calapooia River, it's the third-oldest continuing settlement in Oregon. Those who took land claims in this lush valley said that the grass was so tall you could tie it over your saddle, and the cattle would become lost in the fields.

Brownsville began with a ferry service over the Calapooia, and in the early 1850s the town was laid out. It was a bustling trade center by 1884. In 1919 a fire destroyed much of the town, but some buildings escaped the blaze and are still standing. The **Linn County Museum** provides a free walking-tour map of the historic structures.

The historical museum is outstanding. Its carefully designed exhibits include an old-fashioned Main Street complete with general store, bank, blacksmith shop, and barbershop. Kalapooya Indian artifacts, a miniature wagon collection, and much more are on display. A sign beside the covered wagon lists the costs of crossing the plains (one hundred pounds of coffee, $8.00; a thirty-pound tent, $2.50).

An outstanding example of Brownsville's historic buildings is the **Moyer House,** an elegant Italianate home with fine detailing, built in 1881. It now contains period furnishings and can be seen by appointment or on special occasions.

Afternoon

After enjoying a tour of Brownsville neighborhoods lined with elegant historic buildings, head west on State Route 228.

Watch for **The Living Rock Studios** (541–466–5814), a unique gallery that is a must when exploring the area. The hand-built stone structure and its contents are the results of one man's dream to construct a memorial to the pioneering spirit.

The Howard Taylor family created an exhibition of petrified wood, family heirlooms, mineral specimens, wood carvings, and paintings depicting Oregon's history. The chief exhibit is a series of "Living Rock" biblical pictures made from translucent stone and backlighted to show their vivid colors, along with a petrified wood tree, which stands in the center of the building. Open Tuesday through Saturday.

Rejoin Route 20; at Lebanon, take Route 34 west to join I–5 for the one-and-a-half-hour drive back to Portland.

An alternative would be to continue on Route 20, crossing the freeway into Albany and touring that historic town.

THERE'S MORE

Fishing. Cutthroat and German brown trout, Dolly Varden trout, summer-run steelhead, salmon, and rainbow trout are caught in the McKenzie. There are more than fifty licensed members in the local guides' association. For information, contact Dana Burwell, P.O. Box 1002, Leaburg, OR 97489. (541) 896–3221.

Hiking. Pick up trail maps at the ranger station in Blue River or McKenzie Bridge. Notable hikes include:

McKenzie River National Recreation Trail, a 27-mile path, passes through some of the most historic and dramatic countryside on the McKenzie. It still bears evidence of the Old Santiam Wagon Road. The trail crosses side canyons on log bridges, winds among old-growth Douglas fir, passes by streaming waterfalls, and edges lakes with lava bottoms so porous they dry up and become meadows in summer.

Clear Lake. A gentle, 5-mile trail encircles the lake. On the way you see lava fields, dense forest, and hand-built log bridges.

Hot springs. There are fifty-six hot springs near McKenzie Bridge. For a map and descriptions, contact Oregon Department of Geology and Mineral Industries, 910 State Office Building, 1400 Southwest Fifth Avenue, Portland, OR 97201.

River rafting. The McKenzie is famous for its white-water rafting thrills and float trips. One of the best guides and outfitters is McKenzie River Rafting Company, 7715 Thurston Road, Springfield, OR 97479. (541) 747–9231.

Water Board Park, east of the state trout hatchery at Leaburg Dam. This well-kept, fifty-five-acre park has hiking trails, a softball field, horseshoe pits, a boat landing, a playground, and cooking grills.

SPECIAL EVENTS

Mid-June. Linn County Pioneer Picnic, Brownsville. Oldest continuing celebration in Oregon, begun 1887. Picnic in Pioneer Park, parades, fiddlers' jamboree, arts-and-crafts fair, races, carnival.

June through July. Oregon Bach Festival, Eugene. Top-quality musical performances by internationally renowned artists.

OTHER RECOMMENDED RESTAURANTS AND LODGINGS

Eugene

The House in the Woods, 814 Lorane Highway. (541) 343–3234. Bed-and-breakfast in turn-of-the-century home on wooded country road near the city. Full breakfast.

Leaburg

Marjon Bed-and-Breakfast Inn, 44975 Leaburg Dam Road. (541) 896–3145. Two rooms in a chalet in the woods by the river, 24 miles from Eugene. Wondrous garden of rhododendrons, ferns, and azaleas. Full breakfast.

Vida

The Wayfarer Resort, Star Route. (541) 896–3613. Cozy, well-equipped cabins with fireplaces and decks on the McKenzie and Marten Creek.

FOR MORE INFORMATION

Convention and Visitors Association of Lane County, Oregon, 115 West Eighth, Suite 190, Eugene, OR 97440. (503) 484–5307; within Oregon, (800) 452–3670; outside Oregon, (800) 547–5445.

McKenzie River Chamber of Commerce, Historic Leaburg Hatchery Information Center, 44643 McKenzie Highway, Leaburg, OR 97489. (541) 896–3330.

Central Oregon

HIGH DESERT COUNTRY

2 NIGHTS

*Mountain wilderness • Lava fields • Caves
Panoramic views • Wildlife • Frontier-style town
Native American museum • Boutique shopping • Fine dining
Hiking • Bird-watching • Fishing • Golf*

Sunny central Oregon is a popular weekend getaway for rain-weary Portlanders. On the dry side of the Cascade Range, its weather is predictably pleasant in summer and clear, crisp, and cold in winter. In this land of rugged mountains with powder-snow ski slopes, 235 miles of streams, and more than a hundred lakes, outdoor recreation is a way of life. You can grab a good bite of it in three days and taste a bit of luxury on the way.

This itinerary emphasizes summer activities. In winter, if you're a skier, you know how you'll spend the weekend: on the lifts and runs of Mount Bachelor or Hoodoo, or slicing through the silent forest on cross-country trails. Other winter recreation includes ice skating, sleigh rides, snowshoeing, dog sledding, and relaxing by a cozy fire.

DAY 1

Morning

Drive U.S. Route 26 east from Portland to the 640,000-acre **Warm Springs Indian Reservation.** As you cross the pass at Mount Hood, you'll leave the cool green rain forests behind and enter a dry landscape of sagebrush and

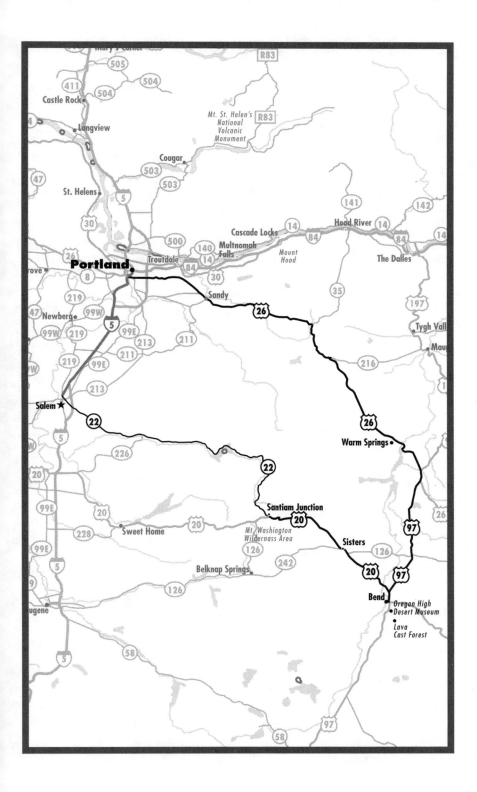

ponderosa pine, steep cliffs and rocky canyons, backdrops to many Western movies.

A must on this route is a tour of the **Museum at Warm Springs,** 2189 State Route 26. The innovative museum, constructed of native stone and timbers and designed to resemble an encampment among the cottonwoods along Shitike Creek, shows the heritage of the Confederated Tribes of the Warm Springs Reservation. Using petroglyph replicas, song, photographs, family heirlooms, and trade items, it tells of native traditions and how they were affected by the settlers. Open daily 10:00 A.M. to 5:00 P.M.

Just past the reservation border, take the **Pelton Dam** exit south for the 25-mile scenic route along the **Deschutes River Canyon.** Overlooks along **Rim Road** present panoramic views across the canyon to cliffs of gray columnar basalt and a wide, sage-covered plain that reaches to the snow-cloaked Cascades. **Mount Jefferson, Three Fingered Jack,** and the **Three Sisters** seem to float on the horizon, white against a deep blue sky.

You'll notice a plaque at one overlook, placed by Fuji Television Network to commemorate the 1984 filming of a popular Japanese TV program, "To Oregon with Love." You are likely to find solitude here, with the only sounds the cries of birds and the occasional roar of a motorboat far below. The air is pungent with the scent of juniper and sage.

South of **Round Butte Dam** and the overlooks, a winding road leads down to a bridge that crosses the Crooked River arm of **Lake Billy Chinook.** The lake, formed by dams holding back the waters of the Deschutes, Squaw Creek, and Crooked River, lies at the heart of 7,000-acre **Cove Palisades State Park.**

Walls of rock, carved by volcanic eruptions ten million years ago, tower above the deep green Billy Chinook and line its 72-mile shore. The lake and its watery arms are favorites with boaters and fishers.

Back on Rim Road, head for Culver and Highway 97, and turn south to Bend.

LUNCH: Deschutes Brewery and Public House, 1044 Northwest Bond Street, Bend. (541) 382-9242. Dark woodwork, light menu, locally brewed beers. A microbrewery with style.

Afternoon

Take Greenwood Avenue east to **Pilot Butte,** and drive—or, if the gate is closed, walk—to the top. A twenty-minute walk to the cinder cone's summit

Skiers flock to Mount Bachelor for its slopes of powder snow and excellent facilities.

will present you with a 360-degree view of Bend, the valley, and the mountains that surround it. Under clear skies you can see virtually all the Oregon Cascades.

Next pay a visit to **Deschutes Historical Center,** housed in a former stone school building on Idaho Street, between Wall and Bond. Displays include pioneer memorabilia, arrowheads, thunder eggs, and a book of biographical sketches of early settlers. (Phone 541–389–1813; open Wednesday through Saturday afternoons.)

Spend the rest of the afternoon browsing through the inviting shops and galleries in downtown **Bend.** Buy note cards from Papers Perfect, select a piece of fine jewelry at Designer's, or look for collectibles in Trivia Antiques.

Step into the new age of global-consciousness and self-awareness in The Curiosity Shoppe.

These shops and dozens more line Wall and its side streets.

DINNER: McKenzie's Restaurant, 1033 Northwest Bond. (541) 388–3891. Steak, seafood, pasta in nice family-style setting downtown.

LODGING: Lara House, 640 Northwest Congress Avenue. (541) 388-4064. Bed-and-breakfast home near Drake Park. Well-furnished, comfortable guest rooms, cozy sunroom.

DAY 2

Morning

BREAKFAST: Lara House serves a full breakfast.

Drive 6 miles south on Route 97 for a tour of the **High Desert Museum,** 59800 South Highway 97 (541–382–4754). This outstanding center of natural and cultural history shows wildlife (beavers, otters, owls) in natural settings, re-creations of historic events, and interpretive programs that help to increase your knowledge of the high desert country. Open daily, 9:00 A.M. to 5:00 P.M.

Continue south on Route 97 for 5 more miles to **Lava Lands Visitor Center.** Watch an introductory slide presentation, then follow interpretive trails through the rough black lava and adjoining pine forest. From here, shuttles carry visitors to the summit of **Lava Butte,** a cinder cone formed 6,160 years ago, for stunning views of the lava flows and Cascade Mountains. You can see Newberry Volcano and the Blue Mountains of eastern Oregon.

Drive a few more miles to **Sunriver,** a self-contained resort community with a lodge, tennis courts, three full golf courses, an airport, and shopping malls. This is one of the Northwest's major planned recreational and retirement developments.

LUNCH: Trout House, Sunriver. (541) 593–8880. Waterside restaurant at the river marina. Hot sandwiches, hamburgers, salads, specials (grilled trout, poached salmon).

Afternoon

Rent a bicycle at the Sunriver shop, and ride the numerous paved, winding paths; or stroll to **Sunriver Nature Center,** where injured birds and animals are sheltered. If you'd prefer a game of golf on a sprawling green course traversed by streams and surrounded by high mountain peaks, club rentals are available at **Sunriver Lodge.**

An alternative to the Sunriver trip is to bring a picnic with you to Lava Lands Visitor Center. After your tour, drive 4 miles west past the center to a picnic area for lunch. Then take the mile-long path that leads downstream, across a footbridge, and on to beautiful **Benham Falls.**

For other short hikes through the spectacular central Cascades, take Highway 97 south 22 miles from Bend and turn east at the signs to Paulina and East Lakes. From here, walk the **Peter Skeen Ogden Trail** to cascading waterfalls, or take the **Newberry Crater Obsidian Trail** (a fifteen-minute walk) to see one of the world's largest obsidian flows.

Drive back to Bend and relax before dinner.

DINNER: Pine Tavern Restaurant, 967 Northwest Brooks Street, Bend. (541) 382–5581. Bend's oldest eatery. Prime rib, lamb, barbecued ribs in a warm, natural wood setting. Windows view tree-shaded lawn and the Deschutes River.

LODGING: Lara House, Bend.

DAY 3

Morning

BREAKFAST: Lara House.

Watch the ducks and Canada geese that claim ownership of **Drake Park,** then head north on U.S. Route 20 toward **Sisters.** You're likely to see llamas behind ranch fences along the way; this is the llama capital of North America. The exotic animals are used for show competition, pack trips, and pets, and their wool is prized by spinners and knitters.

The town of Sisters looks like a scene from the Old West, with its wooden boardwalks and false storefronts. Behind them, boutiques and art galleries sell gifts, trendy clothing, Native American and wildlife art, carved burl furniture, frozen yogurt, and whimsies of all kinds.

Because the frontier town churns with activity in summer, chances are strong that you will find yourself in the midst of one of the many festivals.

Fill your water canteen and buy picnic foods at a deli—there are several— then drive north of Sisters toward **Camp Sherman** and **Black Butte,** a symmetrical cinder cone 6,436 feet high.

The two- to three-hour hike up the butte will present you with splendid views of the pine-covered foothills and jagged white mountains. The trail is an easy grade through the woods and up to open clearings. It culminates in a flat summit with a lookout station. From here, the western views of the Three

Sisters, Mount Jefferson, and Mount Hood are breathtaking. To the east you can see the steep, sheer **Smith Rocks** rising from the desert.

For a longer hike (about four hours) and an even higher perspective, drive 11 miles west of Sisters on Route 242 to **Black Crater Trail.** It's open from July through mid-October. Steep in spots, the hike is challenging but not unreasonable. And the vista is worth the effort.

After climbing wooded slopes and ridges to a 7,251-foot summit of rough lava, you'll see Mount Washington, Three Fingered Jack, the Three Sisters, Mount Jefferson, Olallie Butte, and Mount Hood's snowy cap rising 11,235 feet on the north—all the major peaks of the Oregon Cascades. Clearly evident is the Belknap Crater flow of black lava, spreading below.

LUNCH: Picnic along the trail.

Afternoon

Return to your vehicle, and travel north on Route 20 over **Santiam Pass,** which lies between the Mount Jefferson and Mount Washington wilderness areas. When you reach State Route 22, angle northward to follow the curving, cascading **Santiam River.** On either side of the mountainous road are evergreen and deciduous forests dotted white with dogwood blooms in spring.

The Santiam flows into the deep green, dammed reservoir of **Detroit Lake.** Past the dam, rocky cliffs rise sharply on your right. Waterfalls bounce over them, occasionally splashing the road.

Descending from the mountains, passing small timber towns, you'll eventually reach the lush farmlands of the **Willamette Valley.** Continue on to Salem and the juncture with I–5 for the forty-five-minute drive north on the freeway to Portland.

THERE'S MORE

Cascade Lakes Highway. This 89-mile scenic loop road provides glorious views of lakes, meadows, Mount Bachelor, the Three Sisters, and Broken Top. At Crane Prairie Reservoir, stop to walk a ¼-mile nature trail to see one of the few osprey nesting sites in the United States. (Cascade Lakes Highway is closed to autos in winter.)

Crooked River Railroad Company, 525 South Sixth Street, Redmond. (541) 548–8630. Dinner trains weekend evenings, plus Sunday brunch. Murder mysteries and Western hoedowns on 2½-hour scenic rides.

Horseback riding. Eagle Crest Resort, Redmond. (541) 923–2072; Nova Stables, Inn at the Seventh Mountain, (541) 389–9458; Sunriver Resort, (541) 593–1221 or (541) 504–9799.

Lava Cast Forest, 14 miles south of Bend. From Route 97, turn east on Forest Road 9720, opposite the Sunriver turnoff. This is the world's largest grouping of lava tree molds. A paved, self-guided nature trail leads through the lava flow.

Lava River Cave, 12 miles south of Bend on Route 97. In summer months, lanterns are rented for tours of the mile-long lava cave. Bring walking shoes and a warm jacket.

Operation Santa Claus, 2 miles west of Redmond on State Route 126. World's largest commercial reindeer ranch, with one hundred reindeer. Visitors welcome; open daily.

Petersen Rock Garden, 10 miles north of Bend off Route 97. Four-acre park of miniature bridges, towers, and buildings, all made with various types of rocks. Picnic area, lily ponds, peacocks. Open daily.

Pine Mountain Observatory, 25 miles east of Bend. Observe the skies on Friday and Saturday evenings in spring and summer; reservations required (541–382–8331).

Rock climbing. Smith Rock State Park, north of Redmond in Crooked River Canyon, has massive, colorful rock formations that present a steep challenge to climbers and a fascinating spectator sport for watchers. There's a climbing school and guide service in Terrebonne. (541) 548–5137.

White-water rafting. Cascade River Adventures, P.O. Box 77, Bend, OR 97709. (541) 593–2161 or (800) 770–2161.

SPECIAL EVENTS

January. Sled Dog Race, Chemult. Mushers and spectators gather for "The Old Oregon Championship" dogsled race. (541) 365–7001.

Mid-February. Art-Hopping Tour, downtown Bend. Evening walking tour to get acquainted with the arts. Showings, demonstrations.

May. Pole, Pedal, Paddle Race, Bend. Downhill and cross-country ski, run, bicycle, and canoe on the Deschutes River.

Mid-June. Sisters Rodeo, Sisters. Rodeo extravaganza with top competitors from around the nation.

Late August. Cascade Festival of Music, Bend. Eight-day series of concerts in Drake Park. Jazz, classical, chamber music, Broadway favorites. Concession stands, strolling minstrels, open rehearsals, student workshops.

Fourth of July. Gem and Rock Show, Sisters. Gem dealers gather to buy, sell, and trade. Fireworks, pet parade, crafts in Drake Park, Bend.

Mid-July. Quilt Show, Sisters. Hundreds of handmade quilts on outdoor display.

December. Christmas Festival, Sisters. Santa parade, camels, wise men, llamas, music, and a peppermint bear.

OTHER RECOMMENDED RESTAURANTS AND LODGINGS

Bend

Ernesto's Italian Kitchen, 1203 Northeast Third Street. (541) 389–7274. In a former church.

Goody's, 957 Northwest Wall Street. (541) 389–5185. Old-fashioned soda fountain, candy, toys.

Inn of the Seventh Mountain, 18575 Southwest Century Drive. (541) 382–8711 or (800) 452–6810, for reservations. Family resort on Century Drive, between Bend and Mount Bachelor. Lodge and condo units with kitchens, three swimming pools, ice rink, good restaurants.

Legends Publick House, 125 Northwest Oregon Avenue. (541) 382–5654. America regional cuisine in casual upscale setting.

Pastries by Hans, 915 Northwest Wall Street. (541) 389–9700. Toothsome pastries, sandwiches, coffees in European shop. Closed Sunday and Monday.

Rosette, 150 Northwest Oregon Avenue. (541) 383–2780. Casual restaurant. Dinner Monday through Saturday. Pacific Northwest cuisine with Asian touch.

Westside Cafe and Bakery, 1005½ Northwest Galveston Avenue. (541) 382–3426. Highly popular for breakfast and lunch. Natural foods, great muffins and sandwiches, reasonable prices.

Black Butte

Black Butte Ranch, P.O. Box 8000. (541) 595–6211 or (800) 452–7455. Quiet retreat and top-quality contemporary resort in spectacular setting of wide meadows surrounded by mountains. Golf, tennis, restaurant. Eight miles west of Sisters on Highway 20.

Sisters

Conklin's Guest House, 69013 Camp Polk Road. (541) 549–0123. Homey, friendly bed-and-breakfast on four and a half acres with mountain views. Five guest rooms with private baths. Romantic setting for weddings.

Hotel Sisters, 190 Cascade Street. (541) 549–RIBS. Good food, Sunday specials (chicken and dumplings) in an 1880s-style restaurant. Cowboy boots and spurs hang above the swinging doors to Bronco Billy's Saloon.

Sunriver

Sunriver Lodge and Resort, P.O. Box 3609. (541) 593–1221 or (800) 547–3922. Major resort community, with lodge rooms and rental homes. Many amenities and recreational facilities.

Warm Springs

Kah-Nee-Ta, P.O. Box K. (541) 553–1112 or (800) 831–0100. Resort and convention center on a hilltop in Warm Springs Indian Reservation. Tribal culture and heritage displayed throughout lodge. Swimming, golf, fishing, mineral baths. Comfortable accommodations, good restaurant.

FOR MORE INFORMATION

Bend Chamber of Commerce, 63085 North Highway 97, Bend, OR 97701. (541) 382–3221 or (800) 905–BEND.

Sisters Area Chamber of Commerce, P.O. Box 430, Sisters, OR 97759. (541) 549–0251.

Wilderness maps and trail information available from Deschutes National Forest, 1645 U.S. 20E, Bend, OR 97701. (541) 388–5664 or 388–2715.

SEATTLE
ESCAPES

By Train to Vancouver, Canada
CITY BY THE SEA

2 NIGHTS

*Train of the year • Coastal views • Skytrain
Downtown Vancouver • Granville Island
Westminster Quay • Stanley Park • Science museum*

We will experience Vancouver, the "San Francisco of Canada," on almost every mode of transportation. Train. Skytrain. Seabus. Bus. Foot. Everything but car. No parking, and no driving fatigue, just the rhythm of clean, busy city streets; the aromas that come from small, sophisticated cafes; the outdoor pleasures of Canada's largest city park; and as many world-class museums as you can handle.

We'll take tiny ferries to a "people place" dedicated to work and leisure: Granville Island. We'll take the bus loop to the aquarium, totem poles, picnic sites, and walking trails of Stanley Park. We'll ride the Skytrain to Westminster Quay on the Fraser River, where you can shop the market and watch the tugs struggle upstream.

Pack light so you can carry your luggage yourself.

DAY 1

Morning

Park at the Seattle Kingdome, or at the railway station itself, before boarding the early morning train at the **King Street Station,** 303 South Jackson Street. The *Mount Baker International,* launched in the spring of 1995, was named 1996 Train of the Year for its successful daily runs between Seattle and Vancouver, British Columbia.

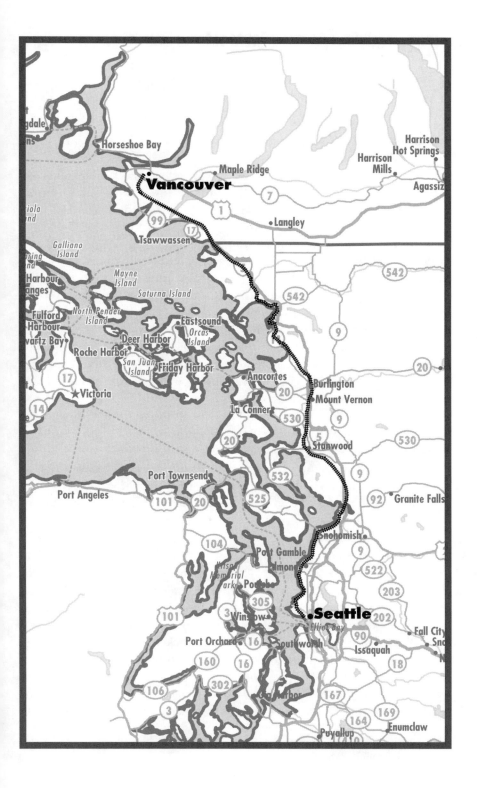

Find a seat, preferably on the scenic left side, in one of the high-tech TALGO Pendular 200 cars, designed and built in Spain. You are ready for a scenic and pleasurable four-hour journey to Vancouver, British Columbia.

BREAKFAST: Order a light continental breakfast in the **Bistro Car,** or just grab a coffee at your seat.

You will enjoy spectacular views as you follow the Washington coast north. The magnificent **Olympic Mountains** rise out of the **Olympic Peninsula** beyond Puget Sound. The **San Juan Islands** make dark-treed shapes in the water to the west.

Travel in April and the tulips may be in full bloom as you cross the **Skagit Valley.** The **Chuckanut Mountains** lead you into **Bellingham.** Look right over your shoulder as you chug-chug another 30 miles north to the Canadian border. That gleaming white snow cone is **Mount Baker,** watching over you as you track on into British Columbia.

This is a very easy border to cross, but you should still carry identification that proves your citizenship and residency. Tip for overseas visitors: If you needed a visa to enter the United States, check before crossing the border that you have a multiple-entry visa that will allow you to reenter the United States when you return from Vancouver.

The skyline of **Vancouver** begins to rise on the horizon as soon as you cross the trestle above **Boundary Bay.** On a clear day you can see the mighty **Coast Range** rising out of the sea into the northern sky.

The *Mount Baker International* pulls into **Pacific Central Station** at 1150 Station Street. This is the home of **ViaRail Canada,** the railway passenger service that is Canada's version of Amtrak. Trains leave here regularly for the Rocky Mountains and eastern Canada.

Carry your minimal luggage across the street to the Main Street **Skytrain** station. Skytrain is the light rail transit system that allows locals and visitors to travel on elevated rails for 17 miles (28 km) from the downtown harbor to the city of New Westminster on the Fraser River. The entire 17 miles takes forty minutes, but we'll only be going four stops on this stage of our journey. All stations except Granville have elevators, and all trains are wheelchair accessible.

Following the directions on the automated ticket machine in the Skytrain station, buy a one-way ticket to **Waterfront Station,** which is at the end of the line downtown.

When you get off at Waterfront Station, you are on the harbor and at the edge of **Gastown.** It may be too early to check into your hotel, so either check your bag in the station or walk through the underground tunnel to the Waterfront Centre Hotel, check your bags with the concierge, and walk back into Gastown.

Gastown is a picturesque area of historic streets lined with restaurants, outdoor cafes, and shops. A bronze statue of **Gassy Jack** watches over the area. John Deighton opened a saloon here in 1867, but he soon earned the name Gassy Jack because he loved to talk.

Walk down the north side of Water Street past **Steamworks Pub and Brewery,** one of many microbreweries in the lower mainland of British Columbia. Check out the Scottish woolens and kilts in **Edinburgh Tartan Shop,** a minimall of English china called **The Landing,** and native Canadian art in **Pacific Rim Art** and **Inuit Gallery.**

LUNCH: **Water Street Cafe,** 300 Water Street, Gastown. (604) 689–2832. Fresh food in a small corner cafe in Gastown.

Afternoon

Gastown runs east for several blocks. Check out **Kites on Clouds, Rock Gems of Canada, Hills Indian Crafts,** and **Images for a Canadian Heritage.** The **House of McLaren** offers ancestor shields, Scottish tartans, and Irish memorabilia.

Retrace your steps on the south side of Water Street to the Skytrain station, and continue on the street or through the Skytrain tunnel to the **Waterfront Centre Hotel,** one of Vancouver's high-end high-rises. It towers above the cruise terminal, with great views of the harbor and Stanley Park.

Check in, and change into your most comfortable walking shoes. On your way out, stop at the concierge desk for a map of the city and bus directions to **Granville Island.** Catch the No. 1 bus in front of the now-familiar Waterfront Skytrain station, and you will get a little tour of the historic **West End** on your way to the **Vancouver Aquatic Centre,** beside the Burrard Bridge.

Walk across a short strip of grass downhill to the **Granville Island Ferries,** tiny aquabuses that leave every few minutes for the five-minute ride across **False Creek,** so named by Captain George Richards of His Majesty's Ship *Plumper* because the inlet turned out to be a dead end.

The twelve-passenger ferry deposits you at the dock of an island that was once used by native hunters and fishers. For most of the twentieth century, the island was a site of heavy industry. Climb the ramp and see what happens when urban planners mix work with leisure in the heart of a great city.

Trucks will be delivering their produce to the **Public Market.** The yellow umbrellas will be up at **Bridges Restaurant.** You'll see boaters and artists crossing paths—and you may see a cement truck arguing with a tour bus.

Stop at the **Information Centre,** and hear how a couple of young Vancouver entrepreneurs started all this by converting an old chemical plant into a people complex. The urban renewal experts followed, with federal grants and a long-range plan.

Pick up a map and turn right down **Foreshore Walk.** Anything that you ever wanted to do on the water, you can do from here: Go fishing, kayaking, or canoeing, or just watch the boaters scraping barnacles.

The **Maritime Market** leads you past **Boatlift Lane, Mast Tower Road,** and **Maritime Mews,** all the hidden sanctuaries of seafood shops and other maritime pleasures.

A few minutes' walk takes you to the mainland end of the island, where you cross the street to the **Kids Only Market.** You can leave the kids at the **Water Park,** explore the **Wall Crawl** or the **Wacky Gator,** take them shopping at the kids' boutiques, or go on to the **Arts Umbrella.**

It's only a few steps from there to the arts-and-craft studios that bring real artists to work here. Check out the crafts in the **Crafthouse,** the **Gallery of B.C. Ceramics,** the offerings of the **Crafts Association of B.C.,** the **Potters' Guild of B.C.,** the **Clay Sculpture Studio,** and all the other creative stops along the way. Don't miss the boat builders at the **Alder Bay Boat Company.**

The **Emily Carr College of Art and Design,** commemorating one of Canada's finest twentieth-century artists, is just around the corner. So is the **Carousel Theatre,** Vancouver's oldest and largest theater school, taught by the city's working actors. You will want to stroll through the Public Market and listen to the street musicians while you watch the sun turn the city to pink and gold.

DINNER: Bridges Restaurant and Pub, which overlooks the ferry dock, the marina, and the skyline of the city. You'll get a very fine menu and a good wine list, whether you sit inside or outside under the yellow umbrellas.

Check out the playbill at either the **Arts Club Main Stage** or the **Arts Club Revue.** Take the ferry and the No. 1 bus back to Waterfront Station, possibly stopping along the way at the popular cafes and shops of **Robson Street.**

LODGING: Waterfront Centre Hotel, 900 Canada Place Way, Vancouver, B.C.V6C 2R9. (604) 691–1991 or toll-free (800) 441–1414. Part of the prestigious Canadian Pacific Hotels and Resorts chain.

DAY 2

Morning

Take the passenger-only **Seabus** from Waterfront Station on its scenic twelve-minute ride across the harbor from Vancouver to the city of **North Vancouver,** the best place to see the saltwater sea, the treed mountains, and the city all in one glance. The Seabus stops at **Lonsdale Quay** in North Vancouver.

BREAKFAST: The food court in Lonsdale Quay.

Spend a little time walking the seawall and shopping, then take the Seabus back to Waterfront Station. Now you will find out just how good this transit system is. Buy a Skytrain ticket from the automated machines to New Westminster Station, which overlooks the north arm of the Fraser River 17 miles (28 km) south. You will have a forty-minute overhead tour of Vancouver's suburbs as you ride.

New Westminster is called the Royal City because Queen Victoria chose it as British Columbia's capital city and named it after her favorite part of London, England: Westminster. New Westminster was the capital for two years before the honor was transferred to the city of Victoria on Vancouver Island.

The Skytrain makes a stop across a footbridge from **Westminster Quay,** a complex of condominiums, restaurants, and market on a river walk that is part of the city's marine history.

LUNCH: Sit upstairs at **Finn's Waterfront Restaurant** and watch the tugs struggling upriver, or buy lunch at the food court, take it outside, and watch the boats go by.

You will be back in Vancouver in time to rest up for the evening. Check the schedule for Vancouver's top-quality theaters. Take the Skytrain to **Stadium Station** for **Queen Elizabeth Theatre,** home to the Vancouver Opera and Ballet British Columbia and stage setting for musicals, dance performances, and Broadway shows. Stadium Station is also the stop for **General Motors Place,** where you can watch the Vancouver Canucks play hockey and the Vancouver Grizzlies play basketball.

DINNER: Raintree Restaurant at the Landing, 375 Water Street, at the Landing in Gastown. (604) 688–5570. Try the regional food and wine and watch the view.

LODGING: Waterfront Centre Hotel.

DAY 3

Morning

BREAKFAST: Waterfront Centre Hotel or food court in bustling deli in Waterfront Centre.

You'll be checking out, so leave your luggage with the concierge or at Waterfront Station. Walk 2 blocks down Howe Street to the north side of Pender Street, and catch the No. 19 bus to **Stanley Park.** On weekends, you can transfer to the **Stanley Park Loop** bus, No. 52, which circles past park attractions. Or consider a $17 day pass from Vancouver Trolley Company. The pass will let you get off and on at fifteen stops citywide, including Stanley Park. The trolley returns every fifteen minutes. (604) 801–5515.

In the park, stop at the **Vancouver Public Aquarium,** which is small enough to enjoy but large enough to hold whales, otters, and sea lions. You will see locals jogging along the seawall, playing cricket or lawn bowling, or just lolling on the grass. Be sure to see the **totem poles.** You can ride a horse-drawn carriage, rent a bicycle for the 50 miles (80 km) of roads, ride the miniature steam train, photograph the totem poles, or just sit on the grass and enjoy it all. Don't miss Stanley Park. After lunch in the park, continue around the loop and take the No. 19 bus back to your starting point at Pender and Howe, 2 blocks from your hotel.

LUNCH: Teahouse Restaurant, 7501 Stanley Park, on Ferguson Point. (604) 669–3281. Charming old house in the park, with spectacular views.

Afternoon

Walk across the street from the hotel to the five huge "sails" that identify the roofline of **Canada Place.** Follow the marked walkway around the building for stunning views of the harbor. You'll see the fireboat, the Seabus, the floatplanes, the floating gasoline stations for boats, and the freighters coming in against a magnificent backdrop of mountains. Check out the five-story screen of the **Imax Theatre** in Canada Place.

Pick up your luggage and take the Skytrain back to the Main Street/Science Centre station. Drop off your bags at the railway station, and go on to the giant silver ball, built for Expo '86 and now **Science World.** Enjoy the hands-on exhibits for children, the **Omnimax Theatre,** and the **3-D Laser Theatre.**

Go back to the railway station, and board the *Mount Baker International* for its return journey to Seattle.

DINNER: The dining car of the *Mount Baker International.* You will arrive back in Seattle late in the evening, in time to pick up your car and go home.

THERE'S MORE

Queen Elizabeth Park and Bloedel Conservatory. Off Cambie Street and West Thirty-third. Beautiful gardens built on and around 492-foot-high (150-meter) Little Mountain. Rose, sunken, and quarry gardens, plus arboretum and great hilltop views. Take No. 15 bus on Burrard Street. (604) 257–8584.

University of British Columbia. 6,103 acres (2,470 hectares) high above the harbor. Take the No. 4 or No. 10 bus from Granville Mall to campus, the Botanical Gardens on Marine Drive, or the Museum of Anthropology on Point Grey Cliffs.

Vancouver Art Gallery. 750 Hornby. (604) 662–4719. You will never see a better collection of the work of Canadian artist Emily Carr, who defined this coast with her paintbrush.

SPECIAL EVENTS

May. Children's Festival, foremost such event in North America.

June. DuMaurier International Jazz Festival.

International Dragon Boat Festival. A worldwide competion of dragon-boat teams.

July. Vancouver Folk Festival. Features performers from around the world.

Sea Festival. Includes bathtub races, fireworks, wooden and heritage boats, and chocolate mermaids.

August. Pacific National Exhibition. Showcases livestock, equestrian events, arts, crafts, entertainment, and Canada's largest wooden roller coaster.

December. Caroling ships on the harbor.

OTHER RECOMMENDED RESTAURANTS AND LODGINGS

New Westminster

Inn at Westminster Quay, 900 Quayside Drive. (604) 520–1776. Stay here at the south end of Skytrain, a forty-minute ride from downtown Vancouver.

Vancouver

Bosman's Motor Hotel, 1060 Howe Street. (604) 682–3171. Moderate, as downtown Vancouver hotels go.

Coast Plaza Suites at Stanley Park, 1763 Comox Street. (604) 688–7711 or (800) 663–1144. Converted from apartments, so rooms are large. Set near shops and restaurants of the West End.

Georgian Court Hotel, 773 Beatty Street. (604) 682–5555. Opposite British Columbia Place Stadium.

Granville Island Hotel, 1253 Johnston Street (604) 683–7373. Small restored hotel on Granville Island.

Sylvia Hotel, 1154 Gilford Street. (604) 681–9321. Reserve early for this popular, inexpensive little hotel on English Bay. You'll feel at home.

Umberto Al Porto Restaurant, 321 Water Street, Gastown. (604) 683–8376. Northern Italian food in an old warehouse. Two dining levels face the harbor.

William Tell Restaurant in the Georgian Court Hotel, 773 Beatty Street. (604) 688–3504. French and Swiss cuisine plus healthy menu.

FOR MORE INFORMATION

Amtrak. (800) USA-RAIL.

British Columbia Information and accommodations reservations (800) 663–6000.

Vancouver TouristInfo Centre, Waterfront Centre, Plaza Level, 200 Burrard Street, Vancouver, B.C. V6C 3L6. (604) 683–2000.

SEATTLE

San Juan and Orcas Islands
ISLANDS IN THE SUN

2 NIGHTS

*Ferry rides • Scenic view • Waterfront resort • Whale watching
Historic sites • Mount Constitution • Sea life*

You will see all kinds of sea life when you ferry to the San Juan Islands: sea gulls, whales, seals, eagles, boaters, fishers, islanders, and tourists in funny hats. With luck, you'll see some of the three pods of black-and-white orca whales that live year-round in these waters.

Not all of the 172 islands of the San Juan Archipelago are accessible by ferry. We'll see the four biggest islands. Our Washington State ferry leaves from Anacortes, on Fidalgo Island, and stops at Lopez and Orcas islands on its way to San Juan Island. Friday Harbor, on San Juan Island, is the only real town in the archipelago and has all the necessary facilities.

This escape is by car but can be adjusted for other transportation, including bicycle, taxi, and van shuttle. Go off-season or as a foot passenger to avoid long car-ferry waits in summer, when 50,000 island travelers swell to 250,000. Call (800) 84–FERRY for schedules.

DAY 1

Morning

From **Anacortes,** 85 miles north of Seattle, catch a ferry west for a one-and-a-quarter-hour ride through island-dotted waters to **Orcas Island.** Orcas was named not for whales but for the Mexican viceroy who charted the island along with Spanish explorer Francisco Eliza in 1791. He saw what you'll see,

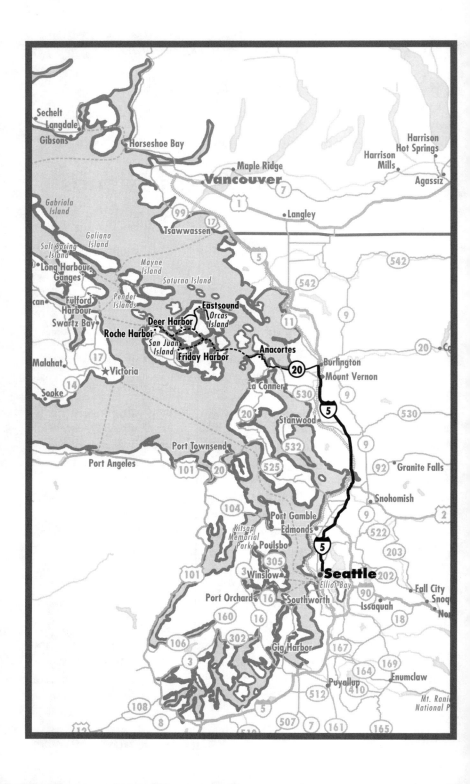

a 57-square-mile U-shaped island of thickly forested hills, with fjordlike inlets and 125 miles of pebbled shoreline.

Drive Horseshoe Highway 13 miles north from the ferry dock to **Eastsound,** a snug community at the head of the island's largest bay and the only commercial settlement.

Much of the valuable tribal collection housed in the **Orcas Island Historical Museum** was saved by Ethan Allen, the San Juan Islands' superintendent of schools around the turn of the century. His hand-built boat, used to row among the islands when he visited the schools, is in the exhibition, which is set in six homestead cabins.

LUNCH: Comet Cafe and Rose's Bakery, Eastsound Square, Eastsound. You'll love the aroma of fresh-baked French bread at Rose's (360–376–5805) and the soups, salads, sandwiches, and vegetarian entrees at the adjoining Comet Cafe (360–376–4220). The bakery is open from 8:00 A.M. to 6:00 P.M., Monday through Saturday; the cafe, from 8:00 A.M. to 5:00 P.M., Monday through Saturday.

Afternoon

Browse through Eastsound shops, especially **Darvill's,** a combination bookstore–rare print shop. It's the oldest art gallery in the San Juan Islands and has an extensive collection of antique and contemporary prints.

Drive Horseshoe Highway 5 miles southeast to 5,175-acre **Moran State Park,** where a narrow, steep road leads another 5 miles to the top of **Mount Constitution,** highest point in the San Juans at 2,409 feet. From the 50-foot stone lookout tower, built in 1936 by the Civilian Conservation Corps, there's a see-forever view.

At your feet the forested mountain, lakes sparkling on its slopes, drops to a blue ocean and an archipelago of green islands that stretch to the horizon. To the east, on the mainland, you can see the snowy peaks of **Mount Baker** and **Mount Rainier.**

An afternoon in or near the park can include biking, fishing, sailing, or kayaking. (See "There's More.") **Cascade Lake,** the biggest lake on the island, offers three campgrounds, a playground, picnic tables, rest rooms, and rental boats. Swimming is good, but the area is crowded in summer.

Rent a rowboat and fish for trout in the stocked lake. Or hike the 2½-mile loop trail that starts west of the picnic area. It winds along a bluff above the lake, crosses a log bridge, and curves through forests of Douglas fir before circling back to the starting place. You may spy ducks, muskrat, otters, and great blue herons.

Continue east down Horseshoe Highway 2 miles beyond the state park to **Olga.** The tiny community is centered by a post office and a combined art gallery and cafe: **Cafe Olga** (360–376–5098) and the **Orcas Island Artworks** (360–376–4408) where more than fifty artists display their wares. (Open daily March through December.)

Or you can drive south past the Olga turnoff to Doe Bay Road and begin a kayaking adventure at **Doe Bay Village Resort. Shearwater Sea Kayak Tours** (360–376–4699) offers several kayak trips, encompassing all skill levels. No experience is necessary. On one ride that's suitable for all ages, you'll paddle to **Doe Island Marine Park** and **Gorilla Rock,** returning via Rosario Strait. You're likely to spot dolphins, whales, and bald and golden eagles.

Follow the signs on Horseshoe Highway to **Rosario Resort,** which faces Cascade Bay on the edge of the sound. The centerpiece of the resort is the mansion built by Robert Moran, a shipbuilder and one-time mayor of Seattle. Consider attending the regular organ concert and a lively talk on the history of the estate. Moran came here in 1905 thinking he had only a short time to live. In his fifty-four-room home he installed a swimming pool, a bowling alley, and a music room containing an enormous pipe organ. Moran then lived on to a ripe old age. In 1920 he donated much of what is now **Moran State Park** to the state of Washington.

DINNER: Rosario Resort, Eastsound. (360) 376–2222 or (800) 562–8820. Multilevel restaurant overlooking the sheltered waters of Cascade Bay. Serves a variety of American and continental dishes.

LODGING: Turtleback Farm Inn, 1981 Crow Valley Road, Eastsound, WA 98245. (360) 376–4914. Take Horseshoe Highway back through Eastsound to this classic farmhouse-turned-country-inn. Seven comfortable rooms with private baths, common room with fireplace, and expansive deck overlooking eighty acres of pasture and woodland. Susan and Bill Fletcher operate the best bed-and-breakfast on the island; book a room early.

DAY 2

Morning

BREAKFAST: A full and fortifying breakfast at Turtleback Farm Inn.

Take a scenic drive down **Deer Harbor Road** to the lighthouse, then circle back around West Sound and down Horseshoe Highway to the ferry terminal. Park your car and choose between two great morning adventures: biking and whale watching.

Orcas Island Eclipse Charters, (360) 376–4663 or (800) 376–6566, tracks whales for its 4½-hour whale watching trips that leave the ferry dock area at about 9:00 A.M. and 2:00 P.M., Friday through Monday in summer, noon daily the rest of the year.

Dolphin Bay Bicycles, (360) 376–3093, rents bicycles near the ferry terminal. Bill Fletcher of Turtleback Inn suggests a two-hour route. Circle east on White Beach Road, go northwest on Dolphin Bay Road, take a brief detour to West Sound, then go south down Horseshoe Highway back to the ferry. You can do this circle either clockwise or counterclockwise, but time it to avoid heavy traffic going on or off the ferry.

LUNCH: Try the seafood chowder at either the **Westsound Store and Deli** (360–376–4440) at the corner of Crow Valley Road and Deer Harbor Road or at the historic **Orcas Hotel** across the road from the ferry landing.

Afternoon

Ferry schedules change but the forty-five-minute direct ferry to San Juan Island typically leaves at 10:45 A.M. and 4:40 P.M. A midday ferry via Shaw and Lopez islands might take an hour and a half.

You will land in **Friday Harbor,** a bustling wharfside village on San Juan Island. Pick up maps and brochures at the visitors' center in the nearby Cannery Landing Building, behind the open-air market.

The **San Juan Island National Historic Park** office, 125 Spring Street (open daily in summer), and the **San Juan Island Historical Museum,** 413 Price Street (open 2:00 to 4:00 P.M. Wednesday and Saturday in summer), offer historic exhibits that explain the island's contentious past.

During the mid-1800s, Britain and the United States shared the island in an uneasy truce. When an American farmer shot a British pig that was disturbing his potato patch, the British authorities threatened to arrest the U.S. citizen. The farmer appealed for help, and soon both sides were lined up for war (not solely because of the pig; San Juan Island has a most strategic location).

The dispute was settled peaceably, however, with the two camps establishing headquarters at opposite ends of the island. Arbitration finally agreed in favor of American rule. Now the incident is remembered as the **Pig War.**

San Juan Transit (360–378–8887 or 800–887–8387) will take you on an island tour in season. **Susie's Moped,** 2 Spring Street, Friday Harbor (360–378–5244), rents mopeds by the hour or day. If you're driving yourself, head northwest for 10 miles on Roche Harbor Road to a historic complex that combines resort, marina, church, and cottages in **Roche Harbor.**

Walk the docks and photograph the old church, then turn south again to **British Camp,** at Garrison Bay. This portion of San Juan Island National Historical Park is where British troops were stationed during the infamous Pig War. Four restored buildings house interpretive exhibits. From the small formal garden, a trail rises to an overlook where officers were quartered.

Walk the **Bell Point Trail,** a level 1-mile hike above Garrison Bay, to reach a beach and a view of neighboring Westcott Bay. Or walk from the barracks exhibit to a cemetery for servicemen who died during the British occupation. Another ½-mile trail leads up 650-foot Mount Young for a far-reaching view of the sea, scattered islands, and the Olympic and Cascade mountains.

From British Camp, drive south to **Lime Kiln Point State Park,** where a trail leads to picturesque **Lime Kiln Lighthouse,** built in 1919 and now on the National Register of Historic Places.

Head south again to **Whalewatch Park,** the best location on the island to observe the three pods of black-and-white orcas that live in the waters around the San Juans. Signs and pictures tell you how to identify porpoises and orca and minke whales.

If you sight whales, call the toll-free Whale Hotline, (800) 562–8832 in Washington and (800) 334–8832 in British Columbia. Reports of sightings help the Moclips Cetological Society to further its research.

Continue south to the southern tip of the island and **American Camp.** This section of the National Historical Park may seem bleak, with its windswept shores and open fields, but it, too, played an important part in island history. From the Exhibit Center an interpretive loop trail leads to the **Officers' Quarters** and the **Hudson's Bay Company** farm site. Farther down the road you'll find a parking area and several more walking paths. The hike to **Jakle's Lagoon,** along the old roadbed, passes through a grove of Douglas firs, and a walk up **Mount Finlayson** (290 feet high) presents another broad seascape and mountain vista.

On **South Beach,** the longest public beach on San Juan Island, birdwatchers will spot terns, plovers, greater and lesser yellowlegs, and bald eagles. Tide pools hold an abundance of marine life. You can salmon-fish from the beach if you have a license. Return to Friday Harbor.

DINNER: Duck Soup Inn, 3090 Roche Harbor Road, Friday Harbor. (360) 378–4878. Fresh seafood and a varied wine list. Entree choices change regularly. Located north of town, closed in winter.

LODGING: Hillside House Bed and Breakfast, 365 Carter Avenue, Friday Harbor, WA 98250. (360) 378–4730 or (800) 232–4730. E-mail: info@hillsidehouse.com. Web site address: www.hillsidehouse.com. Contemporary home on an acre of woodland, ½ mile from downtown district. Seven rooms, some with water views.

DAY 3

Morning

BREAKFAST: Enjoy a full country breakfast with fresh eggs from the henhouse at Hillside House.

Visit the **Whale Museum,** 162 First Street North, (360) 378-4710, one of the great attractions on the island. Life-size models of orca whales and numerous exhibits provide a quick education on whale life and habits.

Wander through the art galleries and gift shops. In Churchill Square's Atelier Gallerie, monoprints and finely detailed scrimshaw work are displayed. Calohan Studio exhibits marine art and sculpture. Waterworks Gallery has changing shows, usually themed (flowers, landscapes, and mythology are examples), with works by regional artists.

The Emerald Seas Diving and Marine Centers, at the ferry landing, offers snorkeling and scuba diving classes as well as charter diving boats and guides. You can also go whale watching, fishing, or sailing with various skippers who operate out of these docks. (See "There's More.")

LUNCH: Front Street Cafe, 7 Front Street, Friday Harbor. (360) 378–2245. Simple, cafeteria-style eatery serving sandwiches, chili, soups, and ice cream.

Afternoon

Watch for your ferry while you have lunch. It is a one-and-a-half-hour ferry ride back to Anacortes. Expect to pass through U.S. Customs when you disembark; since you haven't been across the border into Canada, it's a momentary procedure.

From Anacortes, drive east on Highway 20 to I–5 or return to Seattle via **Whidbey Island.**

THERE'S MORE

Lopez Island

The ferry stops between Orcas and San Juan islands at Lopez Island, popular with bicyclists because of its level roads.

Orcas Island

Biking. Wildlife Cycles, (360) 376–4708.

By air. Magic Air Tours Inc., (360) 376–2733 or (800) 376–1929. E-mail: biplaneguy@aol.com. Web site address: www.magicair.com. Scenic guided tour flights with music in a yellow and red vintage biplane. Leather helmet, goggles, and scarf provided. Hangar with aeronautic memorabilia and hands-on activities for children.

West Isle Air, 4000 Airport Road, Anacortes. (800) 874–4434. Flies to the island.

Cruises. Sharon L. Charters, Box 10, Orcas, WA 98280. (360) 376–4305. Picnic and three-hour sunset/moonlight sail in classic wooden boat.

Shopping. Right Place Pottery Shop and The Naked Lamb Wool Shop on Crow Valley Road. Orcas Island Pottery in the log cabin setting of Orcas's original pottery studio in West Beach.

Whale watching. Deer Harbor Charters, (360) 376–5989 or (800) 544–5758. You can sail bareboat or with a skipper, rent small boats by the hour or day, take a water taxi to any island destination, go whale watching, charter a guided fishing trip, or take a sunset cruise.

San Juan Island

By air. Kenmore Air flies to San Juan Island from the Seattle suburb of Bellevue. (800) 543-9595.

Cruises. San Juan Boat Tours, Box 2281, Friday Harbor, WA 98250. (360) 378–3499 or (800) 232-6722. Wildlife and whale-watching tours.

Western Prince Cruises, P.O. Box 418, Friday Harbor, WA 98250. (360) 378–5315. In summer, four-hour wildlife cruises, daily except Tuesday. Narrated by Whale Museum naturalist.

Way to Go, P.O. Box 4341, Roche Harbor, WA 98250. This 30-foot hydro-foil offers whale-watching and bird-watching charter cruises. Call Fair Weather Water Taxi Tours, (360) 378–8029.

Fishing. Trophy Charters, P.O. Box 2444, Friday Harbor, WA 98250. (360) 378–2110. Fishing, sailing, powerboat charters.

Buffalo Works, P.O. Box 1314, Friday Harbor, WA 98250. (360) 378–4612. Saltwater fishing on a sportfisher called *Net Profit.*

Island Bicycles, 180 West Street, Friday Harbor. (360) 378–4941. Bike rentals, sales, repairs.

San Juan Kayak Expeditions, 3090B Roche Harbor Road, Friday Harbor, WA 98250. (360) 378–4436. Two- to five-day sea-kayak expeditions around the San Juans and Canadian Gulf Islands.

SPECIAL EVENTS

May. Memorial Day weekend. "A" Street Festival, Eastsound, Orcas Island. Crafts shows, dance and music performances for Waldorf Dolphin Bay School, an alternative school.

July. Saturday after the Fourth of July. Historical Day, Eastsound, Orcas Island. Parade, pie-eating contest, games, music, fireworks.

Late July. San Juan Goodtime Jazz Festival, fairgrounds outside Friday Harbor, San Juan Island. Top jazz bands perform all weekend. Free bus service between downtown Friday Harbor and fairgrounds.

OTHER RECOMMENDED RESTAURANTS AND LODGINGS

Orcas Island

Christina's, North Beach Road and Horseshoe Highway. (360) 376–4904. Famous (and expensive) restaurant serving imaginative, well-prepared Northwest cuisine. Ask for a table on the porch for the best views of East Sound.

Rosario Resort, One Rosario Way. (360) 376–2222 or (800) 562–8820. Former private estate on gorgeous Cascade Bay. Rooms in outlying buildings have basic motel amenities; the mansion has a restaurant and lounge, indoor and outdoor pools, and spa facilities.

Orcas Hotel, P.O. Box 155. (360) 376–4300. Remodeled historic hotel with Victorian flavor. Overlooks ferry landing.

Friday Harbor

Lonesome Cove, 5810 Lonesome Cove Road. (360) 378–4477. Secluded retreat on Speiden Channel. Six log cabins, all with kitchens and fireplaces.

Olympic Lights, 4531A Cattle Point Road. (360) 378–3186. Bed-and-breakfast in 1895 farmhouse on five acres at south end of the island. Five rooms with contemporary furnishings, white carpets. Full breakfast included.

San Juan Coffee Roasting Company, P.O. Box 2998, Cannery Landing. (360) 378–4443. Small cafe conveniently located next to ferry landing. Snacks, desserts, tea, coffee.

San Juan Inn, 50 Spring Street. (360) 378–2070. Victorian inn half a block from the ferry landing. View of the harbor. Continental breakfast.

Trumpeter Inn Bed and Breakfast, 420 Trumpeter Way. (360) 378–3884. Quiet country inn of charm and grace.

Wharfside Bed and Breakfast, P.O. Box 1212. (360) 378–5661. Two cozy rooms aboard the *Jacquelyn,* a sloop docked in the harbor. Bountiful breakfast included.

FOR MORE INFORMATION

Orcas Island Chamber of Commerce, P.O. Box 252, Eastsound, WA 98245. (360) 376–3766.

San Juan Island Chamber of Commerce, P.O. Box 98, Friday Harbor, WA 98250. (360) 378–5240.

San Juan Islands Visitors' Information Service, P.O. Box 65, Lopez Island, WA 98261. (360) 468–3663.

Washington State Ferries, 801 Alaskan Way, Pier 52, Colman Dock, Seattle, WA 98104. (206) 464–6400; within Washington, (800) 84–FERRY.

Strait of Juan de Fuca

TOURING THE NORTHERN
OLYMPIC PENINSULA

2 NIGHTS

*Ferry rides • Views of Puget Sound and Strait of Juan de Fuca
Historical museums • National Wildlife Refuge • Herb farm
Native American museum • Northwest corner of United States
Makah Indian reservation • Hiking trails • Rugged coastline*

Between the Olympic Peninsula's verdant wilderness and the southern rim of
Vancouver Island lies the Strait of Juan de Fuca, dividing the United States
from Canada. The sometimes-treacherous, always-fascinating waterway separates Puget Sound and the San Juan and Gulf islands from the wild Pacific.

The 110-mile road edging the strait takes you through a microcosm of the
variety found on the peninsula. From its eastern tip, where a quaint town clings
to its Victorian heyday, to the native fishing village and fog-shrouded coast on
the far western corner, the peninsula provides glimpses of great diversity.

DAY 1

Morning

Take the Winslow ferry from Elliott Bay, Seattle, to Bainbridge Island, and
head for the Hood Canal Bridge. Cross the bridge to the **Olympic Peninsula,** and turn north on Paradise Bay Road, which follows the coastline (passing Port Ludlow Golf Resort and housing development) and curves inland

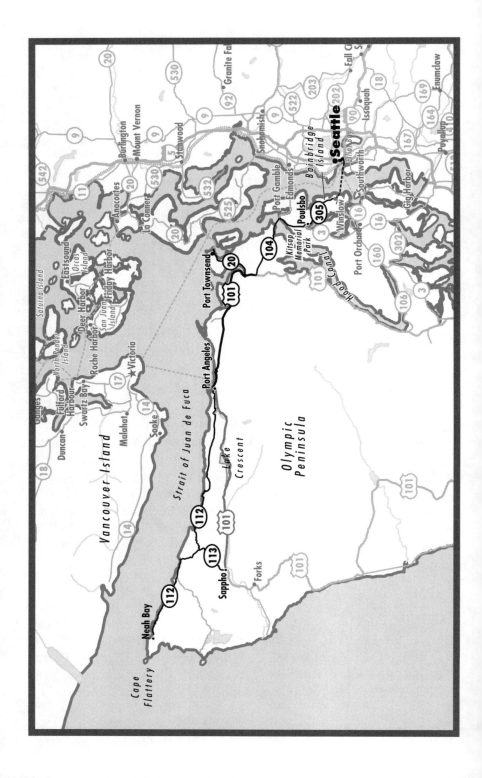

toward U.S. Route 20. Through the trees you'll catch glimpses of pleasure boats on **Admiralty Inlet** as you continue north to **Port Townsend.**

Much of this attractive town, which is divided between a downtown waterfront district and a residential area on a bluff above it, is a designated **National Historic District.** Victorian homes and commercial buildings, built in the late nineteenth century when Port Townsend was expected to become a great seaport, have been restored with pride.

The town was named in 1792 by Captain George Vancouver in honor of an English marquis, but it wasn't officially established until 1851, when the first settlers built a log cabin at the corner of Water and Tyler Streets. The community grew, and its prospects as a center of commerce seemed limitless until the transcontinental railroad was laid—and stopped at Seattle.

Out on the peninsula, Port Townsend was left to languish until its charm as a little-changed Victorian seaport was recognized in the 1970s. Now it booms with tourism and as an arts center.

At the chamber of commerce office, pick up brochures and a tour map that points out seventy-two historic homes and sites. Then continue into town to the end of Water Street and the city hall and museum. Park your car in this area; most of the tour is easy walking from here.

Start at City Hall, which houses the **Jefferson County Historical Museum.** Built in 1891, this was once the county courthouse. Now it houses an eclectic assortment of memorabilia: early photos, Victorian and native artifacts, a rifle and sword collection, Chinese fans and tea canisters. In one corner there stands a chair made of buffalo horn and bearskin; in another lies a mastodon tusk.

Those who advocate no frills for prisoners will approve of the dungeon-like jail cells in the basement. Rumor says that author Jack London once spent a night here.

LUNCH: The Landfall, 412 Water Street. (360) 385–5814. Casual, friendly spot serving hamburgers, alder-barbecued seafood, Mexican dishes. Overlooks marina at Point Hudson.

Afternoon

Highlights you'll see as you explore this history-steeped town include the following:

The Haller Fountain, Taylor and Washington Streets. The bronze figure, variously named Galatea, Venus, and Innocence, was shown at the Chicago

Exhibition of 1893. It was donated to Port Townsend by Theodore Haller in honor of the early pioneers.

Chinese Tree of Heaven, a spreading, one-hundred-year-old tree said to be a gift from the emperor of China. It was intended for San Francisco, but the ship carrying it was blown off course near Port Townsend. In thanks for his happy stay here, the ship's captain left the tree.

Jefferson County Courthouse, Jefferson Street. Built in 1892, the castlelike building is one of the two oldest courthouses still in use in the state. Its 100-foot clock tower is a beacon to sailors.

Old Bell Tower, on a bluff at Tyler and Jefferson Streets, overlooking the downtown district, dates from 1890. It's the only one of its kind in the United States.

Rothschild House, Taylor and Washington Streets. This 1868 home of an early Port Townsend merchant is open for tours daily in summer, weekends in winter.

Ann Starrett Mansion, Clay and Adams Streets. The most elaborate Victorian mansion in Port Townsend was built in 1899 in classic stick style. Its circular staircase, ceiling frescoes, and elaborate furnishings make afternoon tours popular with visitors. The house is now in use as a bed-and-breakfast inn.

After your walking tour of this waterfront town, check the myriad **shops of Water Street and "Uptown,"** a business district on Lawrence Street that was originally begun so that respectable ladies would not have to venture to the rougher waterfront area to shop.

Sooner or later everyone stops for ice cream or a delectable espresso-chip brownie at **Elevated Ice Cream,** 627 Water Street. The bright little shop is reputed to have the best ice cream in the state.

A drive out to **Fort Worden State Park** will take you to the location where *An Officer and a Gentleman* was filmed. Built at the turn of the century as a base to defend Puget Sound, Fort Worden is a 330-acre estate with an army cemetery, officers' quarters, theater, parade grounds, gun emplacements, bronze foundry, and Point Wilson Light Station.

The Centrum Foundation, a nonprofit arts organization, is based here. Numerous workshops, classes, and programs are presented regularly.

At the **Port Townsend Marine Science Center,** in a historic building on the public fishing pier at Fort Worden, visitors can touch and handle sea creatures at open "wet tables." Starfish, sea cucumbers, tube worms, and other marine life live in the touch tanks. The center holds classes in marine ecology, shows informative slide shows, and runs workshops. It's open afternoons in summer, Tuesday through Sunday, and weekends in fall and spring (other times by request; call 360–385–5582 or 385–4730).

On the return trip into town, stop at **Chetzemoka Park** to stroll the grassy grounds and enjoy the fragrant rose garden. The park is named for a Clallam Indian chief who assisted the community in its earliest days. Chetzemoka Park has a bandstand, picnic tables, playground equipment, and access to the beach.

DINNER: Fountain Cafe, 920 Washington Street. (360) 385–1364. Small, unpretentious restaurant on a hillside above the downtown area. Sublime chowder, pastas, dinners, and desserts.

LODGING: James House, 1238 Washington Street, Port Townsend, WA 98368. (360) 385–1238. Grand Victorian home built in 1891. Three floors of antiques-furnished rooms, most with private baths.

DAY 2

Morning

BREAKFAST: Fruit, yogurt, and granola, plus a basket of hot scones and muffins, served in the kitchen at James House.

Drive 13 miles south on Route 20 to U.S. Highway 101; turn right to curve around Discovery Bay and Sequim Bay. Continue 17 miles west to **Port Angeles.** On your right is the **Strait of Juan de Fuca,** a wide channel that defines the border between Washington and Vancouver Island, Canada. On the left the Olympic Range rises 7,000 feet, snow clad and craggy, in Olympic National Park.

Drive to **Port Angeles Fine Art Center,** 1203 East Eighth Street. This gallery is in an award-winning home on five parklike acres overlooking the city, with views of the mountains and water. Visual arts exhibitions are shown year-round. The center is open from 11:00 A.M. to 5:00 P.M. Thursday through Sunday.

If it's a weekday, tour the **Clallam County Historical Museum,** Fourth and Lincoln Streets (360–452–7831; open 10:00 A.M. to 4:00 P.M. Monday through Friday). On the second floor of the brick, Georgian-style courthouse are photographs of early Port Angeles, maritime exhibits, and a replica of an old-fashioned country store complete with a checkers game set up on a barrel.

The courthouse itself is interesting. Built in 1914 and now on the state and national historic registers, it has a stained-glass skylight, a clock tower, and a view of **Port Angeles harbor** 4 blocks down the hill. On a clear day you can see across the strait to downtown Victoria. Hike or bike the 6-mile waterfront trail past the port district.

LUNCH: Chestnut Cottage, 929 East Front Street. (360) 452–8344. Big salads, fresh pasta in a light, airy, smoke-free atmosphere. Owner Diane Nagler also owns First Street Haven, a delightful little place at 107 East Front Street.

Afternoon

Drive west on 101 for 5 miles, and branch onto Route 112, which skirts the rim of the peninsula. Far less traveled than the main highway, the route has a greater sense of wilderness. On your right is the rolling surf of Juan de Fuca and beyond it Vancouver Island, its hills looming hazily green and peaked with frost. Eagles perch in the trees and soar above the water; smoke from wood stoves drifts through the air.

At **Salt Creek Recreation Area,** stop to explore the tide pools among the rocks. Now a county park, Salt Creek was once a World War II defense site. You can still see bunkers and gun emplacements. The park has hiking trails, a kitchen shelter and picnic area, showers, a playground, a softball field, and horseshoe pits.

Farther west, **Clallam Bay** and **Sekiu,** neighboring communities divided by a harbor, host thousands of visitors yearly who come in search of salmon and immense halibut. Resorts and charter companies offer boat rentals and ocean trips. Scuba divers seek abalone and octopus off the coast.

The tide pools at **Slip Point** are particularly interesting for their teeming sea life. You may encounter scuba divers in search of abalone and octopus. Around the point are ancient fossil beds exposed by natural erosion.

Continue to the **Makah Indian Reservation** and the village of **Neah Bay** (67 miles west of Port Angeles). This is the home of the **Makah Cultural and Research Center,** a highlight of the trip.

The $2-million museum, built in 1979, contains a superb collection of Northwest Indian artifacts—more than 55,000. Most were found in the Makah archeological dig at **Lake Ozette.** There are canoes, intricate weavings of cedar and bird feathers, whale and seal harpoons, baskets, and a replica of a native longhouse. One striking exhibit is a cedar carving of a whale's fin inlaid with more than 700 otter teeth.

The museum, which has a gift shop selling the works of Makah artists, is open daily in summer from 10:00 A.M. to 5:00 P.M. Mid-September through

May it's closed Monday and Tuesday. (360) 645–2711.

From Neah Bay, it's an 8½-mile drive to **Cape Flattery.** Walk the wooded (often muddy) trail to the tip of the cape (a 30-minute trip) and you are standing at the northwesternmost point in the contiguous United States. The tree-clad cliff, 150 feet high, faces **Tatoosh Island.** Far below, ocean waves crash against jagged rocks, sending plumes of spray skyward. Whales and sea lions swim these waters, and seabirds nest in rock hollows.

Retrace your drive on Route 112 east to Route 113 and onto the Sappho turnoff and turn south. At Sappho head east on Highway 101, along the **Sol Duc River** toward Olympic National Park and **Lake Crescent.** The deep blue, glacier-formed lake has some 4,700 surface acres and varies in width from ½ mile to 2 miles. The lake is completely surrounded by national parklands.

DINNER: Log Cabin Resort restaurant, on the north shore of the lake. Rustic and casual, serving family fare with a great view. (360) 928–3325.

After dinner, enjoy a stroll by the lake or relax before the big stone fireplace in the antiques-furnished lobby.

LODGING: Lake Crescent Lodge, 416 Lake Crescent Road, Port Angeles, WA 98363. (360) 928–3211. Historic, peaceful hotel facing the lake and forested mountains. Old-fashioned lodge rooms, modern motel units, and separate cottages available. Some fireplaces, no kitchens. Open May through October.

DAY 3

Morning

BREAKFAST: Substantial, tasty breakfasts are served in Lake Crescent Lodge restaurant, which overlooks the lake.

The restaurant kitchen will prepare a box lunch if you request.

There are many ways to enjoy a morning at Lake Crescent. You can rent a rowboat, fish for Beardslee trout, sit in a lawn chair and read, or go hiking. Don't miss a walk up to lovely **Marymere Falls.** The ¾-mile trail can be reached from the lodge or from the nearby Storm King Ranger Station. The path winds through ancient fir and hemlock trees, over a stream on rustic wooden bridges, past mushrooms and flowering plants, and finally ascends sharply to an observation point with a full view of the 90-foot cascade of water. The first ½ mile of the trail is wheelchair accessible.

Lake Crescent Lodge is a classic hotel on the Olympic Peninsula.

From the Marymere Falls Trail, you can continue on **Mount Storm King Trail** for a 2¾-mile climb that offers high views of Lake Crescent.

LUNCH: Picnic by the lake or in the forest, or return to Lake Crescent and eat in the restaurant.

Afternoon

For a different perspective on the lake, drive to the northeast shore and take East Beach Road. Park at the end of the road; from here you can hike all or part of **Spruce Railroad Trail,** which travels for 4 miles through the only roadless wilderness area around Lake Crescent.

Then retrace your route back to Seattle, 144 miles from Lake Crescent.

THERE'S MORE

Arthur D. Feiro Marine Laboratory, City Pier, Port Angeles. Displays of local marine specimens, including a large octopus. Starfish and other creatures in the touch tank. Open daily.

Bicycling. The city of Port Townsend lends bicycles; find them at various downtown locations such as the corner of Quincy and Water Streets.

Boating. Boat rentals at Lake Crescent, Port Angeles, and Sequim.

Kayak Port Townsend, P.O. Box 1387, Port Townsend, WA 98362. (360) 385–6240.

City Pier, Port Angeles. This shoreline park has an observation tower, lawns, picnic area, boat moorage, and promenade decks.

Dungeness Spit, near Sequim. Longest sand jetty in the United States, 7 miles of sand, agates, and driftwood. National Wildlife Refuge with waterfowl, shorebirds, seals.

First Friday Gallery Walk, Port Townsend. On the first Friday evening of the month, galleries and studios are open late.

Fishing. Salmon season starts in late spring, closes September. Bottom fishing from February to November. Fish for the famous Beardslee trout in Lake Crescent.

Port Angeles Charters represents three charter fishing companies in the area. (360) 457–7629.

Golf. Dungeness Golf Course, Sequim. (360) 683–6344. Eighteen-hole course, driving range, clubhouse, restaurant.

Port Ludlow Golf Course, Port Ludlow. (360) 437–0272. Twenty-seven holes on hillside above Admiralty Inlet, east Olympic Peninsula.

Hiking. Olympic National Park has 600 miles of hiking trails. Before hiking on beaches, consult a tide table. Headland crossings can be dangerous. The *Strip of Wilderness* pamphlet, available at visitors' centers, is helpful.

Hurricane Ridge, 17 miles inland from Port Angeles. Mountain ridge with forest and meadow trails, breathtaking views.

SPECIAL EVENTS

Early May. Irrigation Festival, Sequim. Oldest festival in Washington; features parade, fireworks, logging show.

Mid-May. Rhododendron Festival, Port Townsend. Parade, bed race, flower show, arts-and-crafts fair, dancing, fireworks.

Mid-July. Clallam–Sekiu Fun Days, Clallam Bay. Parade, fun run, logging show, arts-and-crafts booths, salmon bake, fireworks, salmon derby.

Late July. Port Townsend Jazz Festival. Musicians from around the country perform on the Fort Worden main stage in daytime and in the evenings in downtown pubs.

Last weekend in August. Makah Days, Neah Bay. Traditional Makah Indian salmon bakes, costumes, dances, canoe races, parades.

Early September. Wooden Boat Festival, Port Townsend. Handcrafted wooden boats on display. Films, demonstrations.

Late September. Historic Homes Tours, Port Townsend. Self-guided tours of the city's Victorian architecture: mansions, cottages, country inns, public buildings.

OTHER RECOMMENDED RESTAURANTS AND LODGINGS

Port Angeles

The Bavarian Inn, 1126 East Seventh Street. (360) 457–4098. European-style home with flower boxes and Bavarian decor. Three guest rooms, two with private bath. Full breakfast served.

Port Ludlow

The Resort at Port Ludlow, 200 Olympic Place, Port Ludow, WA 98365. (360) 437–2222 or (800) 732–1239. Resort on Admiralty Inlet with 188 condominium rentals. Tennis, golf, pools, bicycles, croquet, kayak rentals, restaurant, lounge.

Port Townsend

Ann Starrett Mansion, 744 Clay Street. (360) 385–3205 or (800) 321–0644. Web site address: www.olympus.net\starrett. The most opulent bed-and-breakfast in town. Historic home with Victorian gingerbread, eleven guest rooms. Full breakfast.

Bread and Roses Bakery, 230 Quincy Street. (360) 385–1044. Home-baked pastries, soups, sandwiches, espresso.

Lizzie's, 731 Pierce Street. (360) 385–4168. Victorian bed-and-breakfast home with eight guest rooms. Full breakfast.

Ravenscroft Inn, 533 Quincy Street. (360) 385–2784. E-mail: ravenscroft@ olympus.net. Web site address: www.ravenscroftinn.com. Eight spacious rooms in a hillside inn with a colonial-style look. Peaceful atmosphere, full breakfast.

Salal Cafe, 634 Water Street. (360) 385–6532. Healthy, home-style foods; vegetarian entrees available. Plant-filled solarium.

FOR MORE INFORMATION

North Olympic Peninsula Visitor & Convention Bureau, 338 West First Street, No. 104, P.O. Box 670, Port Angeles, WA 98362. (800) 942–4042.

Olympic National Park, 600 East Park Avenue, Port Angeles, WA 98362. (360) 452–4501.

Port Angeles Visitors' Information Center, 121 East Railroad Avenue, Port Angeles, WA 98362. (360) 452–2363.

Port Townsend Visitors' Information Center, 2437 Sims Way, Port Townsend, WA 98368. (360) 385–2722.

Washington State Ferries, 801 Alaskan Way, Pier 52 Colman Dock, Seattle, WA 98104. (206) 464–6400; within Washington, (800) 84–FERRY.

The Hoh River Valley, Olympic Peninsula

EXPLORING THE RAIN FOREST

1 NIGHT

Rain forest • Wilderness trails • Isolated beaches
Scenic ocean and mountain views • Hot springs • Trout fishing

A temperate rain forest is so intensely green it's almost eerie. Even the sunlight has a green cast as it filters through the treetops, ferns, and hanging moss. The air, hushed and humid, smells of decay and fresh new growth.

There are only three such forests on earth. One is in southern Chile, another in New Zealand, and a third on the western side of the Olympic Peninsula in Washington. Here the crumpled, snow-topped Olympic Range intercepts air masses that flow in from the Pacific and wrings from them 140 inches of rain a year, creating a lush, verdant jungle.

This two-day venture into that jungle will give you a satisfying glimpse of a primeval world, inspiring you to return and further explore its wild depths.

DAY 1

Morning

BREAKFAST: In Edmonds (north of Seattle), at **brusseau's,** 117 Fifth Avenue South. (425) 774–4166. The cafe, which has an outdoor patio, is known for its freshly baked muffins and pastries.

Take the ferry west from Edmonds to Kingston, on the Kitsap Peninsula, a thirty-minute ride across Puget Sound. From the ferry, you can see, on a

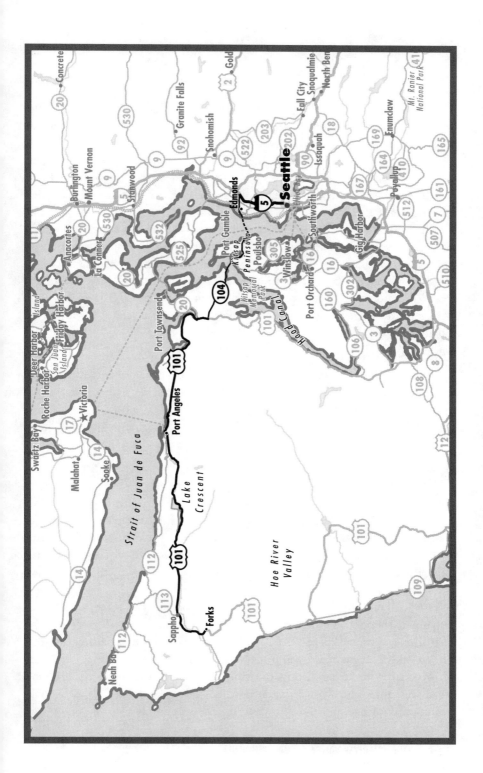

clear day, the majestic, snow-clad Olympic Mountains rising above forested slopes.

Follow State Route 104 to cross the bridge over **Hood Canal.** This is the longest bridge over an inland waterway in the United States; it stretches to the eastern coast of the Olympic Peninsula.

When you arrive on the peninsula, continue 15 miles on 104 to join Highway 101. Turn north on 101, which skirts the **Strait of Juan de Fuca** on the northern shore of the peninsula (see Seattle Escape One for a detailed itinerary of this region).

Five miles beyond Port Angeles, Highway 101 branches south and curves around the south rim of **Lake Crescent.** The lake's cobalt blue waters, 600 feet deep, are surrounded by deep green forests of fir, hemlock, spruce, and cedar.

Stop at **Storm King Information Station** on the lake's eastern edge for maps, brochures, and hiking suggestions; then continue on 101 to Sol Duc River Road. Turn left and drive 12 miles beside the river to Sol Duc Hot Springs Resort.

LUNCH: Sol Duc Hot Springs Resort. At the informal resort's poolside deli window, purchase a sandwich or hamburger and beverage (beer is available) to eat at an outside table. (360) 327–3583. The main restaurant here is open only for breakfast and dinner.

Alternatively, you can bring a picnic lunch from home or one purchased in Port Angeles.

Afternoon

Drive to the end of Sol Duc River Road for a 1-mile hike through the dense, mossy rain forest, ending at lovely **Sol Duc Falls. Lover's Lane** continues past the falls to make a 5-mile loop that takes you back to the resort. **Mink Lake Trail,** which begins at the hot springs, is another 5-mile round-trip hike. It climbs 1,100 feet through thickly forested country to the lake, where you can fish for trout.

At Sol Duc Hot Springs Resort you can, for a nominal fee, swim in an Olympic-size pool and soak in three pools of hot (102 to 109 degrees Fahrenheit) mineral water. There are few more satisfying ways to ease tired muscles after a hike. The resort is open from May to October.

Retrace your route along the Sol Duc River to Highway 101, and head west through the river-webbed woodland to **Forks.** Forks is the only community of size on the northwestern peninsula and is arguably one of the rainiest in the United States. It has been a farming and timber settlement since the late 1880s.

DINNER: South North Garden. (360) 374–9779. Good Chinese food, mostly spicy Szechuan.

LODGING: Miller Tree Inn, 654 East Division Street, P.O. Box 1565, Forks, WA 98331. (360) 374–6806. Bed-and-breakfast in a 1917 homestead on three parklike acres. Seven rooms with private or shared baths.

DAY 2

Morning

BREAKFAST: Prue and Ted Miller serve an ample breakfast at Miller Tree Inn— pancakes, fruit, cereal, eggs cooked to order, and plenty of hot coffee will prepare you for an active day.

Purchase picnic foods at the **Shop-Rite** supermarket deli in the middle of Forks on Highway 101 and travel 12 miles to Hoh Valley Road. The **Hoh Rain Forest Visitor Center** is another 19 miles into the park, along the Hoh River. Tour the attractive, well-designed center to learn about the botany, wildlife, and natural history of the rain forest. The staff is knowledgeable and helpful.

There are three trails in the **Hoh River Valley,** plus a paved minitrail accessible to wheelchairs. Each begins at the visitors' center.

The **Hall of Mosses,** a ¾-mile loop, is a striking sample of life in this damp, iridescent world. The path is silent and spongy beneath immense big-leaf maples, Sitka spruce, western hemlock, and Douglas fir. The ground is carpeted with lettuce lichens, ferns, and sorrel. Tree branches are shaggy with club moss and licorice fern, and a green canopy curtains the sky. When a breeze ripples leaves and fronds, you feel that you've stepped into an aquarium, with undersea plants swaying above you.

The **Hoh River Trail** extends deeper into the wilderness, following the river path for 12 miles, then angling up the shoulder of Mount Olympus to the edge of Blue Glacier. The long, broad finger of oozing ice marks the starting place for climbers ascending the 8,000-foot peak.

The **Spruce Nature Trail,** a 1¼-mile loop walk, leads to a sandy bank of the Hoh River, a good resting and picnicking stop. You may see elk and deer.

LUNCH: Picnic along the trail.

Afternoon

Continue your exploration of the Hoh River Valley, or turn back to Highway 101 and drive northward. One mile north of Forks, turn west and drive 13 miles to **Rialto Beach.** A ⅛-mile paved trail takes you to a beach overlook with a view of James Island and Cake Rock.

Rialto is a favorite among those who know the peninsula's beaches. The scenery is spectacular, with offshore sea stacks and thundering surf. At low tide you can stroll the sand, and when the tide's in, search among the pebbles for agates and pick your way through piles of drift logs, "the bones of the forest." One mile north of Rialto is the sea-carved rock arch called Hole-in-the-Wall.

Return to Highway 101, and drive north and east toward Port Angeles, rejoining Route 104 for the return to Seattle. You can either take the ferry from Kingston to Edmonds or head south to Route 305 and Bainbridge Island. Have dinner in **Winslow,** then ferry across Puget Sound to the Seattle waterfront.

DINNER: Winslow Way Cafe, 122 Winslow Way East, Winslow. (206) 842–1517. Serves Northwest cuisine, gourmet pizza, and pastas. This tiny cafe also has a full bar and schedules live jazz every night.

THERE'S MORE

Camping. Several campgrounds along the Hoh River. Reserve space early. Obtain information through Olympic National Park Headquarters (address below).

Forks Timber Museum, on Highway 101 across from the city park. Displays show local logging industry history. (206) 374–9663. (Open daily April to October.)

Olympic West Arttrek, a 70-mile driving tour of unique shops and art studios. Forks. (800) 44–FORKS.

SPECIAL EVENTS

Mid-April. Rainfest, Forks. Three-day arts celebration.

June 30–July 4. Old-fashioned Fourth of July, Forks. Grand parade, kiddies' parade, frog-jumping contest, talent show, logging show, dog show, Moonlight Madness sales, teen dance, Firecracker Fun Run.

OTHER RECOMMENDED RESTAURANTS AND LODGINGS

Beaver

Eagle Point Inn, Milepost 202, 384 Stormin' Norman Lane. (360) 327–3236. A log lodge on the Sol Duc River 10 miles north of Forks.

Forks

Manitou Lodge, P.O. Box 600. (360) 374–6295. Secluded log lodge on the Sol Duc River, 3½ miles from Rialto Beach. Six rooms, one with fireplace. Full breakfast included.

FOR MORE INFORMATION

Forks Chamber of Commerce, P.O. Box 1249, Forks, WA 98331. (360) 374–2531 or (800) 44–FORKS. Web site address: www.forkswa.com.

North Olympic Peninsula Visitor & Convention Bureau, P.O. Box 670, Port Angeles, WA 98362. (800) 942–4042.

Olympic National Park, 600 East Park Avenue, Port Angeles, WA 98362. (360) 452–4501.

Washington State Ferries, 801 Alaskan Way, Pier 52 Colman Dock, Seattle, WA 98104. (206) 464–6400; within Washington, (800) 84–FERRY.

SEATTLE

Snoqualmie Falls and Fall City
WATERFALL OF THE MOON PEOPLE

1 NIGHT

*Dramatic waterfall • Steam train ride • Luxury resort
Golf courses • Herb farm • Winery • Bicycling
Hiking • Antiques shopping*

Long before the explorers and hop growers reached Snoqualmie Valley, Native American tribes met for trade and council beside the thundering torrent now called Snoqualmie Falls. Early settlers referred to the natives who lived along the riverbanks as the "moon people," for their name was said to be derived from *Snoqualm,* meaning "moon."

The first white settlers arrived in 1855. By the early twentieth century, hops, timber, and electrical power that harnessed the falls' tremendous energy were important segments of the local economy. Today it's tourism.

The scenic valley, just 30 miles east of Seattle, is webbed with quiet backroads that pass farmlands, forests, mountains, and gurgling streams on their way to the Snoqualmie River. This getaway offers both a chance to refresh the spirit and a variety of recreation.

DAY 1

Morning

Travel on I–90 east from Seattle to exit 27, a thirty–minute drive. Follow the signs to **Snoqualmie.** Plan to arrive about 10:00 A.M. so that you'll have an hour to explore the little town and its quaint, restored **train depot** before

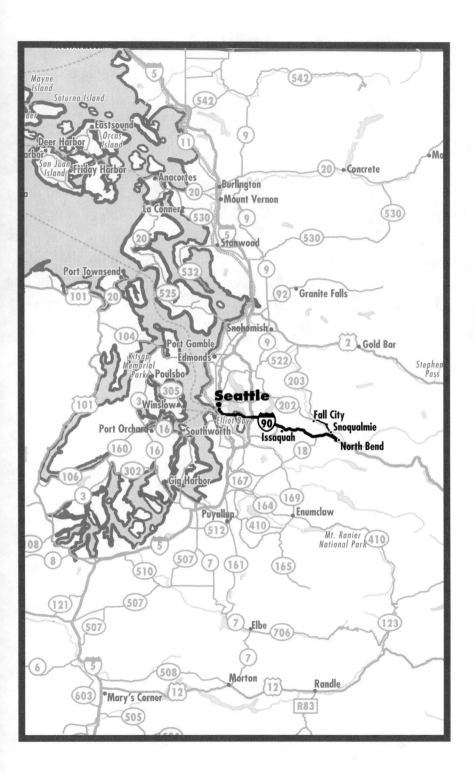

Salish Lodge, a luxury inn, perches on the cliff above thundering Snoqualmie Falls.

your train ride. The depot, built in 1890, is on the National Register of Historic Places. Its displays include a sizable collection of rolling stock from steam, electric, and logging railroads.

At 11:00 A.M., board the old-fashioned steam- or diesel-powered train for a 10-mile trip through the scenic valley. The vintage coaches pass by the base of rugged **Mount Si,** the top of **Snoqualmie Falls,** and through dense forests. They clickety clack over bridges and through lush green fields to a scenic viewing point before making the return trip to the Snoqualmie depot.

Trains, which begin in April, run on summer weekends and on Memorial Day, Independence Day, and Labor Day. Fares are $6.00 for adults, $5.00 for seniors over sixty-two, and $4.00 for children three to twelve. The ride takes seventy minutes. For information, phone (360) 746–4025.

LUNCH: Isadora's, 132 Railroad Avenue. (425) 888–1345. Cafe serving homemade soups, quiche, sandwiches, tea, espresso, scones. Also a gift, antiques, and book shop.

Afternoon

After lunch, or carrying your picnic, continue on 384th Avenue to the freeway on-ramp and Winery Road (watch for the sign to Snoqualmie Winery; the road goes under the freeway). At the winery you can sample local wines while enjoying your picnic and a panoramic view of the Cascades and Snoqualmie Valley.

Turn back toward Snoqualmie and follow the signs to Snoqualmie Falls, which are 1 mile from town. Fenced, paved paths along the cliff offer viewing points for watching the great cascade—100 feet higher than Niagara—as it roars to a misty pool at the bottom.

To get closer to the falls, walk the ½-mile trail that descends to a rocky beach at the falls' base. Behind the powerhouse that stands above the beach you'll find a plank walk leading to an elevated platform, which provides a satisfying overlook.

The trails and landscaped park on the cliff near the lodge were developed by Puget Power, which has received awards of recognition for park design and environmental contributions.

Check in at the **Salish Lodge,** a resort hotel perched at the brink of the falls. Borrow a bicycle—Salish lends mountain bikes—and wheel along the area's country roads. The lodge also lends fishing gear, if you'd rather try your luck at casting for steelhead in the river.

Golfers can head for one of the four nearby courses (for details, see "There's More" at the end of the chapter). If your top priority is simply relaxation, you'll enjoy lounging on the hotel terrace while the Snoqualmie torrent thunders below, or you could take a health treatment at the largest resort spa in the Northwest.

DINNER: Salish Lodge. Northwest cuisine emphasizing regional produce, game, and fish. Special touches include potlatch salmon and farm-raised game meats smoked with apple and cherry woods. Superb service, a fine view, and a large wine cellar.

LODGING: Salish Lodge, P.O. Box 1109, Snoqualmie, WA 98065. (425) 888–2556 or (800) 826–6124. Outstanding, luxury accommodations in an informal country atmosphere. Down comforters, stone fireplaces, two-person whirlpool tubs, balconies viewing the river and falls (some views much better than others).

DAY 2

Morning

BREAKFAST: Salish Lodge. The highly popular breakfast is a five-course extravaganza that includes fresh fruit, hot oatmeal, sourdough biscuits with honey, pancakes, and a main course such as trout with game sausage, eggs Florentine, or smoked salmon in scrambled eggs.

Drive south to **North Bend,** turn left at the traffic signal (the only one in the valley), continue to Mount Si Road, and turn north. Follow this road across the **Snoqualmie River** to 432nd Avenue SE, and park at a gravel area near the bridge. Walk a few yards on 432nd Avenue to the trailhead for **Little Mount Si.**

The 2-mile trail, forested to the top of the mountain, leads to a 1,000-foot summit with sweeping views of the valley, Mount Si, and the Cascade Range in the distance. The hike up Mount Si itself is more time consuming and a greater challenge. The trail zigzags to the top of the great monolith, 4,190 feet high. A panoramic summit view makes the 4-mile trip worthwhile and popular; Mount Si is the second-most-hiked mountain in the state.

If you (or someone in your party) are not interested in hiking, you might visit the **Snoqualmie Valley Historical Museum** at 320 North Bend Boulevard. In this former private home, volunteers maintain exhibits of pioneer memorabilia.

A few blocks from the museum is a large, village-style complex of factory discount outlets. The recently opened stores represent numerous brand name manufacturers.

After your hike and/or museum and shopping tour, drive north on State Route 202 to **Fall City** and the **Herbfarm,** 32804 Issaquah–Fall City Road (800–866–HERB). Here you'll find a peaceful world where caged doves coo and the air carries the fragrance of more than 450 herbs.

The Herbfarm holds classes in herb uses and basketry, sells gifts and books, and has a small deli that offers snacks and picnic fixings.

LUNCH: Construction of the Herbfarm's six-suite country-inn bed-and-breakfast began in 1999. While the inn is under construction, the owners will serve their famous nine-course meals at **Hedges** (425–391–4060) in Issaquah. As always, the Herbfarm's goal is to "give you one of the best meals of your life."

Afternoon

Take I–90 west to exit 17 and leave the freeway for **Issaquah,** a pretty village with a tree-shaded creek running through it. Signs direct you to the **state fish hatchery,** where you can see thousands of salmon fingerlings being reared with loving care.

Also treated with great care are the hand-dipped chocolates at **Boehm's Candies.** The Edelweiss Chalet on Gilman Boulevard is the headquarters for the renowned candy company.

Drive north on Gilman and you'll find **Gilman Village,** a complex of fifty-odd shops, restaurants, and tearooms, many of them in old homes that were moved to the site. They're connected by boardwalks.

A short distance past Gilman Village is **Gilman Antique Gallery,** a must for antiques lovers. Here 170 exhibitors display thousands of antiques of all kinds.

If you'd like a stroll on a sandy beach to finish the journey, stop at **Lake Sammamish,** northwest of Issaquah off I–90. By then you'll probably be ready to head the last few miles into Seattle.

THERE'S MORE

Golfing. There are four eighteen-hole courses in the valley:

> Carnation Golf Course, 1810 West Snoqualmie River Road NE, Carnation. (425) 333–4151.
>
> Mount Si Golf Course, 9010 Boalch Road, Snoqualmie. (425) 888–1541.
>
> Snoqualmie Falls Golf Course, 35109 SE Fish Hatchery Road, P.O. Box 790, Fall City. (425) 222–5244.
>
> Tall Chief Golf Course, 1313 West Snoqualmie River Road SE, Carnation. (425) 222–5911.

Snoqualmie Falls Forest Theatre and Family Park, Fall City. Outdoor dinner theater; summer weekends only. (425) 222–7044.

SPECIAL EVENTS

Early August. Snoqualmie Days, Snoqualmie. Arts-and-crafts booths, parade, music, food concessions, children's games, helicopter rides.

OTHER RECOMMENDED RESTAURANTS AND LODGINGS

Carnation

River Inn, 4548 Tolt River Road. (425) 333–4262. Luxurious solar villa on seven riverside acres. Sauna, banquet facilities, some balconies. Complete breakfast, with vegetarian option.

North Bend

George's Bakery, 127 West North Bend Way. (425) 888–0632. Noted for delicious pastries, baked fresh daily.

Snoqualmie

The Old Honey Farm Country Inn, 8910 384th Avenue SE. (425) 888–9399. Bed-and-breakfast hotel offering country comfort in ten rooms, five with views of Mount Si and the Cascades.

FOR MORE INFORMATION

Issaquah Chamber of Commerce, 155 Northwest Gilman Boulevard, Issaquah, WA 98027. (425) 392–7024.

North Bend Chamber of Commerce, P.O. Box 357, North Bend, WA 98045. (425) 888–4440.

Puget Sound Railway Historical Association, P.O. Box 459, Snoqualmie, WA 98065. (425) 746–4025.

Snoqualmie Falls Chamber of Commerce, 108 Railroad Avenue, P.O. Box 356, Snoqualmie, WA 98065. (425) 888–4440.

Leavenworth to Ellensburg

APPLE ORCHARDS AND

RANCH COUNTRY

2 NIGHTS

Mountain scenery • Waterfalls • Pioneer village • Wild rivers
Apple orchards • Bavarian town • Historical museums
Hiking • Boating • Horseback riding • Columbia River

One of Seattle's great attractions is its proximity to magnificent mountainous wilderness. You can breakfast in a cosmopolitan restaurant and be deep in a silent forest by lunchtime. This three-day getaway will take you east through the rugged North Cascades, into the softer valleys where 60 percent of the nation's apples are grown, and on to dry ranching country. On the way you'll encounter breathtaking scenery, rivers that invite white-water adventure, beckoning trails, and a few surprises.

DAY 1

Morning

Drive north from Seattle to State Route 202, headed toward Woodinville, and stop for a tour of the famed **Chateau Ste. Michelle Winery.** The state's leading winery is in a turreted chateau.

Tours and tastings are available every day. Stroll eighty-seven acres of landscaped grounds. There are trout ponds, manicured lawns, formal gardens, experimental vineyards, and picnic tables.

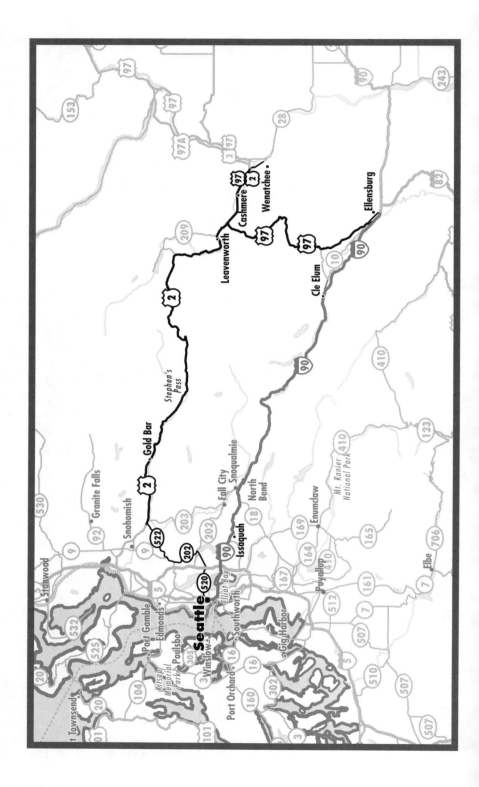

North of the winery, join State Route 522 headed northeast toward U.S. Route 2. Traveling east on the scenic highway, you'll follow the **Skykomish River,** a ribbon of clear blue water that flows west from the high lakes of the Alpine Wilderness. Popular with rafters for both its rapids and its serene stretches, the Skykomish offers steelhead fishing, riverside trails, and gold panning, as well as float trips. Eagles soar above all the activity, indifferent and majestic.

Amid the new-growth forests found on either side of the river are the stumps of virgin old growth, long since logged. The stumps indicate the size of these giants; some are 6 feet in diameter.

Two miles east of Gold Bar, at **Wallace Falls State Park,** stop to hike the trail, which climbs to 1,200 feet and affords grand views of **Wallace Falls,** a 365-foot cascade. South of the Skykomish you'll see imposing **Mount Index,** nearly 6,000 feet high.

The next stop on the highway is the village of **Index.** It is a funky assortment of dark-red clapboard buildings that include historic tavern, museum, general store, city hall, and pioneer park, all clustered around the first corner as you cross the bridge into town. Go to the second corner, and you're ready for lunch.

LUNCH: Bush House Country Inn, 300 Fifth Street, Index. (360) 793–2312 or (800) 428–BUSH. Rustic dining room with river-rock fireplace. Soups, sandwiches, salads, light entrees, homemade desserts. Open daily.

Afternoon

Near **Skykomish,** a timber town that fills with hikers and backpackers in summer and with skiers in winter, you can take a short walk to **Deception Falls,** a tumbling waterfall that splashes down the mountainside and under the highway bridge. The **Iron Goat Trail,** signed on Route 2, follows the route that the Great Northern Railway cut through Stevens Pass in 1893. Walk past old collapsed snow sheds, tunnels, and work campsites.

Continuing on Route 2, you'll leave the Skykomish River and drive through coniferous forest, passing Alpine Falls and rising into the Cascade Mountains to **Stevens Pass,** at an elevation of 4,061 feet. One thousand feet below runs a 7-mile tunnel, the longest railroad tunnel in North America. If you walk from the summit to **Stevens Pass Ski Area,** you'll have a peerless view of the snowy peaks of the Cascade Range.

Descending now on the east side of the Cascades, drive 20 more miles to **Coles Corner.** From here, State Route 207 leads 4 miles to **Lake Wenatchee State Park.** This busy recreation area on the edge of **Lake Wenatchee** offers skiing, fishing, boating, and beaches.

Take Route 2 through the **Tumwater Canyon,** along the bouncing, cascading **Wenatchee River** as it rushes toward the Columbia. In any season the landscape is lovely, but in autumn, when the woodlands blaze with color, it's particularly glorious.

Sixteen miles south of Coles Corner, in **Icicle Valley,** you'll enter **Leavenworth.** Almost the entire town is designed to resemble a quaint Bavarian village, with chalets, carved railings, peaked gables, and hundreds of hanging flower baskets.

In the 1960s, when the local economy was rapidly fading, the townsfolk began the Bavarian village project as a way to stimulate tourism. It has succeeded beyond imagining, drawing visitors by the thousands every year to shop, gawk, eat, and participate in the lively festivals (see "Special Events").

The alpine setting is an even-greater draw. Leavenworth is a gateway to wilderness adventure, white-water rivers, mountain lakes, fishing, rock climbing, and skiing.

For the rest of the afternoon you might choose to hike or bird-watch, play golf, or linger in the dozens of quaint shops. Browse through the hand-painted country pine items in **Pie in the Sky,** the many cuckoo clocks at the **Cuckoo Clock Shop,** and see artisans at work in the **Woodcarver Gallery.** There are many fascinating shops, but be sure to see the Northwest artifacts at **Cabin Fever Rustics,** the quilts next door at **Dee's Country Accents,** the 3,500 distinctive music boxes in **Die Musik Box,** and the Christmas crafts at **Kris Kringl.** Check out the **Nussknacker Haus** and the **Leavenworth Nutcracker Museum** upstairs from it. The U.S. Forest Service Information Center in downtown Leavenworth has maps that direct you to mountain trails and wildflower displays.

Don't miss a walk along the Wenatchee River in tranquil **Waterfront Park,** off Commercial Street. Just a block and a half from the busy shopping area, the park is a quiet spot with benches, trees, and views of the river and the steep peaks around Icicle Canyon. The Wenatchee River is one of the state's most popular rafting rivers.

DINNER: Lorraine's Edel Haus, 320 Ninth Street. (509) 548–4412. Casual elegance. Innovative Northwest and New German cuisine served in a white house near the river.

LODGING: Run of the River, 9308 East Leavenworth Road, P.O. Box 285, Leavenworth, WA 98826. (509) 548–7171. Bed-and-breakfast in a log lodge on the river a mile from downtown. Six comfortable rooms, warm hospitality, deck with hot tub.

DAY 2

Morning

BREAKFAST: A bountiful country breakfast is served in the open dining room at Run of the River.

Continue on Route 2 to **Cashmere,** passing miles of apple orchards that bloom white and pink in spring and are laden with fruit in fall. Apples are big business in Washington; seven billion are grown annually, 60 percent of the nation's apple production.

In Cashmere, at Liberty Acres, the home of the **Aplets and Cotlets** manufacturing plant, 117 Mission Street (509–782–2191), take the brief tour and watch the making of the famous fruit-and-nut confections.

Bob's Apple Barrel, on Route 2, sells cider, apple butter and jam, and has a large selection of Washington wines.

Not to be missed is **Chelan County Historical Museum,** 600 Cotlets Way (509–782–3230), where you step from the highway into the past. On the museum grounds, a typical pioneer village, complete with blacksmith shop, mission, assay office, saloon, dentist's office, hotel, millinery shop, and jail house, is open to the public.

From Cashmere, drive on to **Wenatchee,** the apple capital, where the Wenatchee and Columbia Rivers meet. The **North Central Washington Museum,** in downtown Wenatchee, features out-of-the-ordinary displays. A coin-operated 1892 railroad diorama, aviation exhibits showing the historic 1931 trans-Pacific crossing, a nine-rank Wurlitzer theater organ, and Native American artifacts are part of the disparate collection.

A side trip north on U.S. Route 97 Alt., on the west bank of the river, leads you to the **Washington Apple Commission Visitor Center,** 2900 Euclid Avenue (509–663–9600). It's open daily from May through December 23 and on weekdays the rest of the year. The gift shop is open Monday through Friday year round. You'll get an in-depth look at the apple industry at the center, which offers souvenirs, an eighteen-minute video, pies, and free samples of Washington's famous apples. Continue north on U.S. 97 Alt. to nationally known **Ohme Gardens,** where you can look down on the junction of the Wenatchee and Columbia Rivers. Drive on another few miles to **Rocky Reach Dam,** a 5,000-foot-long structure with a 1,700-foot-long fish ladder and 10,000 years of history in the Gallery of the Columbia.

Afternoon

Drive south on U.S. 97, leaving the orchards to head into the forests of the Wenatchee Mountains and descend from there into cowboy country. The climate here is hot and dry in summer, while winters are harsh, with far more snowfall than occurs west of the Cascade Range.

The scenic route, over the old Blewett Pass Road, is narrow and winding and closed in winter. It is a shortcut that leaves, then rejoins Route 97, which is open all year.

When you reach **Ellensburg,** stop at the Chamber of Commerce on Sprague Street for a walking-tour map of the historic downtown. It's full of interesting architecture, with red-brick buildings dating from the late 1800s, an Art Deco theater, and modern structures on the Central Washington University campus. Antiques shops abound, along with stores selling the famous Ellensburg Blue agate (found only in this region).

In the **Clymer Gallery** view the paintings of John Clymer, a noted western artist; in the **Kittitas County Historic Museum** see what frontier life was like. Tour the **Thorp Grist Mill,** built back in 1883 when Ellensburg (having changed its name from Robbers' Roost) was booming.

Southeast of town, off I–90, is **Olmstead Place State Park,** where you can step into one of the first farms in Kittitas Valley. There's a log cabin, built in 1875, and several buildings, including a barn and schoolhouse, open for tours in summer.

DINNER: In summer, **Circle H Holiday Ranch.** Meals are included in the room rate, with western-style dinners cooked on the grill— T-bone steak or spareribs, salad, and strawberry shortcake are examples. In other seasons **Valley Cafe,** 105 West Third, Ellensburg. (509) 925–3050. Art Deco surroundings, good European dishes.

LODGING: Circle H Holiday Ranch, 810 Watt Canyon Road, Thorp, WA 98946. (509) 964–2000. Louie and Nancy Jo Tutino run a thirty-acre ranch with five cabins in a western theme. Riding trails, horses and other animals, pond, play equipment.

DAY 3

Morning

BREAKFAST: The Circle H serves a full breakfast.

Take a **horseback ride** through the hills behind the ranch, in the **L. T. Murray Wildlife Recreation Area.** It offers 100,000 acres of wilderness, honeycombed with walking and riding trails. If you're not enthused about horses, go hiking, relax at the ranch, or go to Ellensburg to see what you missed the day before.

You might choose a **rafting trip** on the Yakima River instead (Betsy Ogden will make the arrangements for you), or travel 25 miles east to Vantage, on the Columbia River. This section of the river is a dam-created lake, **Wanapum Lake.** The views are spectacular, overlooking the river and surrounding dry, brushy hills. Nearby is **Ginkgo Petrified Forest State Park,** where you can see prehistoric petrified woods of many species. In the park there are petroglyphs, an interpretive center, walking trails, wildlife, and picnic areas.

LUNCH: The Circle H provides a saddlebag lunch; eat at the ranch or take it with you for a picnic in Ginkgo Petrified Forest State Park.

Afternoon

Leaving your peaceful ranch retreat, take I–90 northwest (or a byway, State Route 10) to Cle Elum. Once a coal-mining and railroad town, it's now a gateway to mountain and lake outdoor recreation. Stop at the **Cle Elum Bakery** for caramel-nut rolls and coffee. (509) 674–2233. Closed Sunday. Also check out **Glondo's Sausage Company** for Yugoslav sausage and Polish kielbasa. Almost every town has its special museum; Cle Elum preserves phone history in the **Cle Elum Historical Telephone Museum.** Another interesting spot is the **Carpenter House,** a stately mansion that now houses exhibits from life in an earlier day in the region.

Continue west to **Roslyn,** a quiet, pleasant little community with a couple of good cafes and what is said to be the oldest operating saloon in Washington state, **The Brick.** Roslyn is famous for its dozens of ethnic cemeteries, where miners are buried among their own cultural groups, banded together on a hillside west of town.

Proceeding northwest on I–90, you'll come to **Kachess Lake,** a recreation area with beautiful old trees, walking paths, and a pretty lake where you can swim, boat, and fish.

Continue on I–90 through thick forests and mountain terrain over Sno-qualmie Pass and on to **Snoqualmie Falls** (for more information on the Snoqualmie Falls area, see Seattle Escape Five).

On your way back to Seattle, if there's time, stop in **Issaquah** for coffee or tea and a look around the shops of Gilman Village. While you're so close, you might as well pick up a sample from **Boehm's Candies**—a sweet touch to end your trip.

THERE'S MORE

Animal Lovers, reserve for a Saturday or Sunday **Chimposium** at the Chimpanzee and Human Communication Institute, Central Washington University, Ellensburg. (509) 963–2244. Watch chimps "talk" in sign language.

Bicycling. Bicycle routes for all abilities surround the Leavenworth area. Rent bicycles at Der Sportsman (509–548–5623) or Leavenworth Sports Center (509–548–7864). Run of the River Bed and Breakfast (509–548–7171) offers the "Tour de Pomme," a bicycling route from inn to inn.

Golf. Leavenworth Golf Course. Eighteen holes. (509) 548–7267.

Rock Island Golf Course, east of Wenatchee. Eighteen holes. (509) 884–2806.

Rafting. Raft the white water of the Wenatchee River with Leavenworth Outfitters. (509) 763–3733 or (800) 347–7934. Web site address: www.thrillmakers.com. Scenic float trips also available.

Skiing. Leavenworth: Cross-country ski trails are numerous in the Leavenworth/Wenatchee area. Icicle River Trail and Lake Wenatchee are popular, and so are the golf course and city park in Leavenworth.

Stevens Pass: Open November to mid-April. Downhill: Six double chair lifts, two triples, longest run 6,047 feet. (206) 634–1645.

Wenatchee: Mission Ridge has four chair lifts and runs up to 5 miles long. (509) 663–7631.

SPECIAL EVENTS

Late April/early May. Apple Blossom Festival, Wenatchee. Parades, carnival, arts-and-crafts fair.

Mid–May. Maifest, Leavenworth. Maypole dance, bandstand entertainment, hand-bell ringers, outdoor breakfast, flea market, antiques bazaar, street dancing, flowers.

Early June. Founders Day, Cashmere. Celebrate the historic figures who first settled the Northwest's apple country.

June. Leavenworth International Accordian Celebration, Leavenworth. Old World architecture, flowering gardens, and artisans provide the backdrop for this musical celebration.

Early September (Labor Day weekend). Ellensburg Rodeo. One of the major U.S. rodeos. Four-day event, with cowhands competing for cash prizes. Also carnival rides, produce and craft displays, homemade pies, and music.

Early September. Chelan County Fair, Cashmere.

Late September/early October. Autumn Leaf Festival, Leavenworth. Grand parade, accordion and oompah music in bandstand, art displays, street dance, food booths, pancake breakfast.

Mid–October. Cashmere Apple Days, Cashmere. Pie-baking contest, races, music, dancing, pioneer entertainment. Fund-raiser for Chelan County Museum.

Late November. Christkindlmarkt, Leavenworth. A German-style Christmas village with booths filled with holiday foods and gift items. Christmas music and an Olde World Puppet Theatre for children.

Early December. Christmas Lighting, Leavenworth. Snowman contest, sledding, food booths, concerts, lighting of village.

OTHER RECOMMENDED RESTAURANTS AND LODGINGS

Cle Elum

Hidden Valley Guest Ranch, 3942 Hidden Valley Road. (509) 857–2322. Wilderness ranch with cabins, horses, swimming pool, hiking trails, cross-country skiing, hot tub. Gold panning also available. All meals included.

The Moore House, 526 Marie Street, P.O. Box 629, South Cle Elum. (509) 674–5939 or (800) 22–TWAIN. A former bunkhouse for railroad workers, restored as an attractive bed-and-breakfast with a railroad theme. Full breakfast.

Ellensburg

Best Western Ellensburg Inn, 1700 Canyon Road. (509) 925–9801. Clean and comfortable rooms, restaurant, lounge, pool, putting green.

Murphy's Country Bed and Breakfast, 2830 South Thorp Highway. (509) 925–7986. Turn-of-the-century frontier bungalow on a country road.

Pub at Inglewood, 402 North Pearl. (509) 962–2260. Lamb and seafood, pasta, light meals at tables with linens and candlelight.

Leavenworth

All Seasons River Inn, 8751 Icicle Road. (509) 548–1425. Adults only. Bed-and-breakfast with six spacious rooms. All but one room have whirlpool tubs. Private decks, river views, antiques, hearty breakfast.

Enzian Motor Inn, 590 Highway 2. (509) 548–5269 or (800) 223–8511. Hotel combining Old World atmosphere with contemporary comfort. Heated pool, hot tub, 104 rooms, some fireplaces. Full European buffet breakfast included.

Homefires Bakery, 13013 Bayne Road. (509) 548–7362. Freshly made whole grain breads, European and specialty breads, pies, cinnamon rolls, and cookies, baked in a wood-fired masonry oven.

Mountain Home Lodge, P.O. Box 687. (509) 548–7077. Intimate getaway in roomy stone-and-wood lodge with pool. In the hills, 3 miles from town. Full breakfast included. All meals served during winter months.

Pension Anna, 926 Commercial. (509) 548–6273. Fifteen units in a Bavarian-style inn. Traditional European breakfast included.

Sleeping Lady Resort, 2½ miles from town at 7375 Icicle Road. (509) 548–6344. A sixty-seven-acre conference retreat center with guest rooms, gourmet meals, and music concerts in a natural setting dedicated to pre-serving the environment. Ideal for larger groups. Individuals must stay two nights and reserve within sixty days of arrival.

Tumwater Restaurant and Lounge, Ninth and Commercial. (509) 548–4232. Cozy atmosphere, good food and service.

Monroe

Ixtapa, 19303 Highway 2. (360) 794–8484. Moved, expanded, better-than-ever cafe serving spicy, well-prepared Mexican food. Lunch and dinner.

FOR MORE INFORMATION

Cashmere Chamber of Commerce, P.O. Box 384, Cashmere, WA 98815. (509) 782–7404. E-mail: page@crewnet.com; Web site address: www.cashmereweb.org.

Cle Elum/Uppper Kittitas County Chamber of Commerce, 221 East First Street, Cle Elum, WA 98922. (509) 674–5958.

Ellensburg Chamber of Commerce, 436 North Sprague, Ellensburg, WA 98925. (509) 925–3137.

Monroe/Sultan Chamber of Commerce, P.O. Box 38, 211 East Main Street, Monroe, WA 98272. (360) 794–5488.

Leavenworth Chamber of Commerce, P.O. Box 327, Leavenworth, WA 98826. (509) 548–5807.

Wenatchee Area Visitor and Convention Bureau, 2 South Chelam Avenue, P.O. Box 850, Wenatchee, WA 98807. (509) 662–4774.

North Cascades
UNTAMED WILDERNESS

2 NIGHTS

*Alpine peaks • Wildflowers • Forests • Waterfalls
Glaciers • Hiking trails • Bald eagle refuge • Old West town*

Because of their jagged peaks, immense glaciers, and high meadows splashed with summer wildflowers, the North Cascades are often called the American Alps. The wilderness around them, a 505,000-acre national park bisected by only one road, provides a remarkable retreat from crowded streets into natural beauty.

Along the route through North Cascades National Park, and on the occasional side roads that extend from it, you'll encounter numerous opportunities for outdoor adventure. This three-day trip suggests a few. It's a summer excursion, as much of the road is closed in winter. To reach the skiing areas mentioned during the ski season, you have to take a different route, approaching from the south.

DAY 1

Morning

Travel north from Seattle on State Route 9 to **Snohomish,** about 30 miles. The river town, founded in 1859 on the banks of the Snohomish and Pilchuck Rivers, is one of Washington's oldest communities. It's thus fitting that Snohomish not only has examples of Victorian architecture but is known

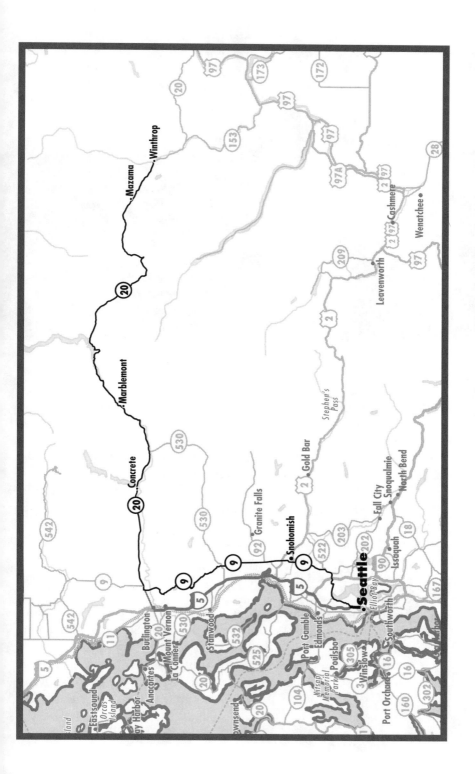

Glaciers and snowfields abound on the slopes of the rugged North Cascades.

as the antiques capital of the Northwest. Dozens of shops, many within a 4-block radius, sell antiques of all kinds.

The three-level **Star Center Mall,** 829 Second Street, houses 150 dealers who sell everything from native artifacts to art nouveau. It's open every day (360–568–2131). **First Bank Antiques,** 1019 First Street (360–588–7609), carries oak and mahogany furniture and country primitives; **The Antique Market Place Mall** represents twenty dealers offering Hummel figures, glassware, furniture, china, and collectibles.

At the **Pioneer Village Museum,** on Second and Pine Streets, and at **Blackman House Museum,** 118 Avenue B, you can see how many of these antiques were once used in daily life. Both museums are open daily for tours in summer.

At **Townsend's Deli and Espresso,** 102 Avenue D, buy sandwiches-to-go. Then head north toward **Lake Stevens,** curving to State Route 92 toward Granite Falls.

On this scenic route, known as the **Mount Loop Highway** (part of it is closed in winter), you'll follow the **South Fork of the Stillaguamish River** and pass through the evergreen forests of **Boulder River Wilderness,** eventually turning north toward Darrington and the North Cascades Highway.

From **Granite Falls,** follow Route 92 east 11 miles to Verlot. The ranger station, across the road from 5,324-foot Mount Pilchuck, will provide maps and suggestions. The 7-mile road leading to the trail up the mountain is east of Verlot. From the trailhead, the hike up Mount Pilchuck is 2½ miles, leading to **Mount Pilchuck Lookout.** From here you gain one of the finest viewing points in the state for scenic splendor.

The forest fire observation tower was built in 1918 on the western edge of the Cascade Range, near Boulder River Wilderness. From the lookout you can see for miles, a view encompassing White Horse and Three Fingers mountains.

As you enter the **Mount Baker–Snoqualmie National Forest,** edging the Stillaguamish shore, you'll drive for 14 miles, through Silverton to the turnoff for the **Big Four Mountain.** At the base of the immense escarpment, which soars 6,120 feet, a popular inn once stood. It was destroyed by fire long ago, but the site is a good picnic spot.

LUNCH: Picnic at **Mount Pilchuck** or Big Four Mountain.

Afternoon

Follow the trail to the **Big Four Ice Caves,** which some say is the lowest-lying glacier in the contiguous United States. The ¼-mile-long ice field is fed from a snow cone on Big Four.

Continue now over **Barlow Pass** (elevation 2,600 feet), turning north to travel beside the tumultuous **South Fork of the Sauk River** for 19 miles to Darrington. The road is unpaved, but it's well graded.

The slate-blue Sauk is a favorite with white-water rafters and kayakers because of its swift rapids. Through the trees on this narrow, winding road you'll glimpse mountain peaks—Sloan, Pugh, and White Chuck—and the Monte Cristo Range in **Henry M. Jackson Wilderness.** The Monte Cristo area was once the site of gold, copper, and silver mines.

When you reach **Rockport,** you'll see **Rockport State Park** on the bank of the **Skagit River.** The attractive park has campsites and a network of trails, partially accessible to wheelchairs.

On the western border of the park, a 7-mile road winds up Sauk Mountain, leading to **Sauk Mountain Trail.** This trail, a one-and-a-half-hour walk, is considered by many hikers to be one of the most beautiful walks in the North Cascades, with wildflowers and panoramic views from the mountain. You may see hang gliders here.

After your hike, drive west 12 miles on State Route 20 to your night's lodging.

DINNER: North Cascades Inn, 4286 Highway 20, Concrete. (360) 853–8771. Standard, dependable American fare.

LODGING: Cascade Mountain Inn, 40418 Pioneer Lane, Concrete, WA 98237. (360) 826–4333. European-style inn with five rooms on ten acres of grounds. Down comforters, friendly hosts. View of Sauk Mountain.

DAY 2

Morning

BREAKFAST: Enjoy expansive views and a full breakfast in the dining room or on the patio of Cascade Mountain Inn.

Take the picnic lunch the innkeepers have packed for you (request this in advance), and drive east on Route 20, the North Cascades Highway. Considered the most scenic mountain drive in Washington, this route is closed in winter.

Again keep an eye out for eagles, especially between **Rockport State Park** and **Marblemount.** In Marblemount you can pick up maps and back-country permits (and gasoline—this is the last gas stop for 75 miles).

If you didn't bring a picnic, check out the buffalo menu at **Buffalo Run Restaurant** on Route 20. (360) 873–2461. Sandwiches, soups, and salads are available in a casual atmosphere.

Route 20 and the Skagit River flowing beside it divide the northern portion of North Cascades National Park from its southern part. There are almost no other roads in the national park, a wonderland of high mountains, jagged ridges, countless waterfalls, and glacially sculpted valleys. There are 318 glaciers, more than half of all the glaciers in the contiguous United States. On off-road trails, you'll hear crashing icefalls and see broad snowfields and flower-dotted slopes.

Two short walks are located near the manicured village of **Newhalem. Trail of the Cedars** is a nature walk, handicapped accessible, with interpretive signs that explain the forest's growth. The **Ladder Creek Rock Garden** walk winds up a hillside, passing fountains and landscaped plantings to reach Ladder Creek Falls.

LUNCH: Picnic in Newhalem or along the trail, or eat at Buffalo Run Restaurant in Marblemount.

Afternoon

Continue in leisurely fashion on Route 20, stopping at the numerous turnouts to admire particularly striking views of ridges and green valleys. At **Diablo Lake Overlook,** enjoy a panoramic vista of the smooth blue lake, Sourdough Mountain, Davis Peak, Colonial Peak, Pyramid Peak, and the Skagit River.

Beyond Diablo is **Ross Lake,** its blue-green glacial waters extending far north into the wilderness, across the Canadian border. The only access to the lake is by boat or trail.

Ross Lake is named after James Ross, the engineer who designed dams on the Skagit River. Another Ross, Alexander, explored the southern section of the present park in 1814. After him came more explorers, then miners (mining efforts were abandoned because of the arduous terrain) and a few homesteaders.

The dams were built by Seattle City Light to generate electricity; today, the power company runs railway and boat tours to Diablo and Ross dams (see "There's More" for additional information).

Fall is especially beautiful in the North Cascades. An example of the leaf color you can see, flaming red and orange against the hillsides, is at **Ruby Creek,** 20 miles past Newhalem.

Rainy Pass has an elevation of 4,860 feet. It's crossed by the Pacific Crest National Scenic Trail. Near the Rainy Lake rest stop is the **Rainy Lake National Recreation Trail,** a 1-mile paved path, wheelchair accessible, that leads to **Rainy Lake.** There's a memorable view here of the subalpine lake and waterfall streaming in from snowfields.

Whistler Basin Viewpoint provides an opportunity for a close look at the wildflowers that grow in alpine meadows. In July and August, these fragile, open spaces are full of color.

For the most splendid close-up view of the Cascades, don't miss the **Washington Pass Overlook** (elevation 5,400 feet). **Liberty Bell Mountain** soars 7,808 feet above the valley. Next to it, almost as high, are the **Early Winter Spires; Silver Star Mountain** rises a steep 8,875 feet on the east. Against the dark ridges and snow-filled ravines, the leaves of Lyall larch glow a brilliant yellow.

Now, as the road descends east of the Cascades into Washington's dry side, the scenery changes. There are no dense rain forests, thick with ferns and mosses; the vegetation thins, and firs give way to widely spaced pines. To the north lie the mountains and forests of the rugged, roadless **Pasayten**

Wilderness. In recent years, wolves have been found living deep in the wild—a welcome comeback, since they were thought to have disappeared.

Twelve miles from Washington Pass you'll come to **Mazama,** a popular ski center.

DINNER: Mazama Country Inn. Pasta, chicken, and barbecued ribs are favorites here. Light suppers of soup, salad, and bread available.

LODGING: Mazama Country Inn, P.O. Box 275, Mazama, WA 98833. (509) 996–2681; within Washington, (800) 843–7951. Spacious cedar lodge, simple but immaculate rooms. Stone fireplace in living/dining area, windows on three sides offering views of forest. Two separate cabins and ranch house available. Bicycle rentals and horseback rides.

DAY 3

Morning

BREAKFAST: Mazama Country Inn. The lodge serves three meals a day (included in the American Plan rates in winter only).

Drive eastward on Route 20 into the lovely **Methow Valley,** carved by glaciers 11,000 years ago. Farmers' fields, punctuated with rocky outcroppings, extend from the meandering **Methow River,** while its banks are outlined by poplar and ponderosa pines.

Drive 13 miles from Mazama, and you'll arrive in **Winthrop,** a town nestled in the upper Methow Valley, almost surrounded by national forestland. Here migrant Native American tribes once camped along the river, digging for camas root and fishing for salmon. White settlers and miners arrived after 1883.

When you visit Winthrop, you might think the townsfolk never left the late 1800s. The entire town has a frontier motif, with boardwalks, Old West storefronts, and saloon replicas.

Guy Waring and his wife and two children were among the early settlers. They came from Massachusetts and named the town after the governor of that state, John Winthrop. The Warings' home, built in 1897 after most of the town was destroyed by fire, is now the **Shafer Museum.** It contains historical artifacts, wagons, and a stagecoach.

With 300 days of sunshine a year and an abundance of lakes, forests, mountainous terrain, and clean country air, the Methow Valley offers virtually limitless outdoor recreation. Fishing, photography, boating, river rafting, and skiing are among the most popular activities.

LUNCH: Duck Brand Cantina, 248 Riverside Avenue, Winthrop. (509) 996–2192. Tasty Mexican dishes, as well as sandwiches, steaks, pies, and chocolate cake.

Afternoon

Turn west on Route 20 for the return trip, stopping at the overlooks and trails you missed on the way out, continuing this abundant feast for the senses.

In Marblemount, stop at Buffalo Run Restaurant for a coffee break; then continue westward toward Sedro Woolley. At Burlington, join I–5 for the forty-five-minute drive south to Seattle.

THERE'S MORE

Boating. Ross Lake provides superb high-country canoeing in the wilderness. From Ross Dam parking lot, portage your canoe down a ¾-mile trail. You can choose to paddle to Ross Dam from Diablo Lake; for a fee, Ross Lake Resort will haul you up to the lake. Call Ross Lake Resort, Radiotelephone Newhalem 7735.

Dam and river tours. Seattle City Light offers a four-hour tour (summers only) that includes a ride on the historic Incline Railway, which rises 560 feet up Sourdough Mountain, and a cruise on Diablo Lake to Ross Dam Powerhouse. The tour ends with an all-you-can-eat, bunkhouse-style dinner. A ninety-minute tour gives you the railway ride, slide show, and tour of the Art Deco Diablo Powerhouse. Phone (206) 684–3030. After May 1, call (206) 233–2709 for individual tours and (206) 233–1955 for group tours.

Fishing. In streams and lakes, fish for brook, Dolly Varden, golden, and rainbow trout.

Horseback riding. Horse Country, 8507 Highway 92, P.O. Box 2, Granite Falls, WA 98252. (360) 691–7509. Trail rides in the Cascade foothills, along the Pilchuck River. Just forty-five minutes from downtown Seattle. Ponies, lessons, family trail rides, and spring and summer camps are also available.

Skiing. Methow Valley Ski Touring Association, Box 147, Winthrop, WA 98862. Provides information and maps on Nordic ski trails in Sun Mountain, Rendezvous, and Mazama areas. Methow Valley Sport Trails Association gives recorded updates on trail conditions. (800) 682–5787. The Methow Valley, with 100-odd miles of cross-country ski trails, is known as one of the best Nordic skiing centers in the world.

SPECIAL EVENTS

July. Bluegrass Festival, Darrington.

Late September. Norba Mountain Bike Races, Glacier.

Late September. Historic Home Tour, Snohomish.

Early October. Granite Falls Railroad Days, Granite Falls.

OTHER RECOMMENDED RESTAURANTS AND LODGINGS

Winthrop

Sun Mountain Lodge, P.O. Box 1000. (509) 996–2211; within Washington, (800) 572–0493. Rustic, log-beamed lodge in the Methow Valley. Rock fireplace, swimming pool, tennis, beautiful mountain setting.

FOR MORE INFORMATION

Concrete Chamber of Commerce, P.O. Box 739, Concrete, WA 98237. (360) 853–7042.

National Park Service, 800 State Street, Sedro Woolley, WA 98284. (360) 873–4500.

North Cascades National Park and Ross Lake National Recreation Area, Skagit District Office, Marblemount, WA 98267. (360) 873–4590.

Snohomish Chamber of Commerce, 116 Avenue B, Snohomish, WA 98290. (360) 568–2526.

Winthrop Visitors' Center, P.O. Box 39, Winthrop, WA 98862. (509) 996–2125; within Washington, (800) 551–0111 or (888) 463–8469.

SEATTLE

Mount Rainier Loop

CASCADES GRANDEUR

1 NIGHT

Mount Rainier National Park • Historic lodge • Wildlife park
Backcountry hiking • Steam-train ride • Daffodil fields

The highest mountain in the Cascade Range can be seen for 200 miles when the weather is clear. Mount Rainier's snowy bulk rises 14,411 feet, enticing climbers, hikers, and other lovers of the wilderness. Twenty-six massive glaciers hold an icy grip on the tallest volcanic mountain in the contiguous United States.

Old-growth forests encircle the mountain. Douglas fir, red cedar, and western hemlock soar 200 feet above the moss-covered valley floors. Through those trees, more than 300 miles of trails meander, leading to wildflower-spangled meadows and clear ponds. Glacier-fed streams rush through every valley, tumbling in rapids and waterfalls.

Rainier is moody, and its weather unpredictable. Rain and snow may suddenly appear on a mild day and retreat as quickly. Glimpsed through the clouds, the mountain is beautiful. Under sunny skies, when Rainier appears in all its dazzling glory, it is magnificent.

Much of the route outlined here is open only in summer; check with the visitors' information centers for road conditions.

DAY 1

Morning

From Seattle, take I–90 east to I–405 south to Route 167 south to Highway 410. At Greenwater, the road turns south and within a few miles enters

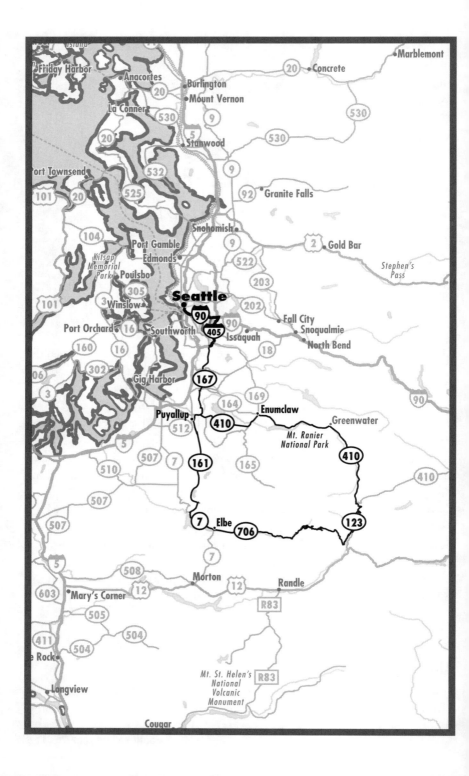

Mount Rainier National Park. You're on the Mather Memorial Parkway, paralleling the White River in the shadow of Sunrise Ridge. At the Sunrise/White River road, turn right and drive 17 miles to the 6,400-foot ridge top. Trails lead from the visitors' center through the fragile, subalpine vegetation to ever-higher and more breathtaking views of glaciers and rocky crags.

From **Sunrise Point,** the summit's crater rim and **Emmons Glacier,** 4½ miles long, are clearly visible. Mount Adams lies to the south, and Mount Baker rests on the northern horizon.

LUNCH: Picnic at Sunrise.

Afternoon

Return to Highway 410, continue south to **Cayuse Pass** (4,694 feet), and veer left toward **Chinook Pass** (5,430 feet). Drive 3 miles for a striking view of Mount Rainier's east side.

Return to Cayuse Pass and take Route 123 south. Near the **Stevens Canyon** entrance, at the southeastern end of the national park, watch for signs to the **Grove of the Patriarchs.** Walk the 1-mile trail, crossing the Ohanapecosh River on a footbridge, to an island where you'll be in the midst of an ancient forest. The princely trees that grow on the island—Douglas fir, western red cedar, and western hemlock—are 1,000 years old.

Drive the Stevens Canyon road west to **Paradise.** The road angles through thick forest, across rivers and creeks, rounding the bend at **Backbone Ridge** and heading north to **Box Canyon.** Through this narrow canyon, scoured by glaciers and carved by water, runs the Muddy Fork of the Cowlitz River.

Traveling west from Box Canyon, you'll see Stevens Ridge looming high on the right, with Stevens Creek below. In the fall, the vine maples on the slopes of the ridge in this U-shaped valley blaze with color.

As the road twists toward the southern shores of Louise and Reflection Lakes, at the base of the **Tatoosh Peaks** you'll see the three most prominent peaks, Stevens, Unicorn, and Pinnacle, thrusting sharply skyward, dramatically punctuating the rugged landscape.

When you reach the Paradise Valley Road, turn right and climb upward until you arrive at last in Paradise. **Nisqually Glacier** and **Wilson Glacier** hang above, with Rainier's peak capping the view. At **Henry M. Jackson Visitors' Center,** pick up maps and trail information. The center offers slide and film programs on Rainier and the park's history, as well as 360-degree views of the awe-inspiring surroundings.

During July and August, the slopes of **Paradise Park** become tapestries of color and beauty, as delicate subalpine flowers bloom by the thousands. Trails wind through the meadows and over trickling brooks, luring you to explore.

Head out on your own, or join one of the **naturalist-led walks** that begin at the visitors' center. An easy one-hour walk exploring the flower fields starts at 2:00 P.M. Another undemanding hike leaves the center at 2:30 P.M. and concentrates on the geology, glaciers, and fine views of the dirty snout and pristine, almost-blue interior of Nisqually Glacier.

Take **Skyline Trail** to **Panorama Point** for a comfortable, half-day hike replete with grand vistas. Marmots whistle and streams sing in the crisp, clear mountain air. A side trail crosses snowfields to end at Ice Caves, remnants of the once-immense caves carved by water flowing under glaciers.

DINNER: Paradise Inn. Grilled salmon, steak, and chicken, served in the dining room of a grand old lodge.

At 7:30 P.M., meet a park naturalist in the lobby for a one-hour **evening stroll** in the valley. It's an excellent opportunity for taking photographs and for observing wildlife.

At 9:00 P.M., interpreters give **slide-illustrated talks** in the lodge lobby. Topics vary: Meadow ecology, volcanic geology, human effects on the mountain, and Native American views are a few.

LODGING: Paradise Inn. Imposing, 126-room lodge of Alaskan cedar. Simple rooms; some share baths. The views are incomparable. For reservations (a must), contact Mount Rainier Guest Services, P.O. Box 108, Ashford, WA 98304. (360) 569-2275; (360) 569-2411 for reservations only.

DAY 2

Morning

Rise at dawn for an early hike, if the weather is clear. There are few sights more exhilarating than Rainier's rosy-hued glaciers under the first rays of the morning sun.

BREAKFAST: Paradise Inn. Standard breakfast menu, lavish Sunday brunch.

Head south from Paradise Park to the small community of **Longmire,** and stop for a tour of the second-oldest national park museum in the country. Open daily, the small museum offers exhibits that cover Rainier's geology, wildlife, and history.

As you drive west toward the Nisqually entrance, 6 ⁹⁄₁₀ miles from Long-mire, you're surrounded by trees 600 to 800 years old. Their high branches create a green canopy above the road.

From the park's entrance, continue west on Route 706, along the banks of the **Nisqually River.** At Elbe, follow the signs to **Mount Rainier Scenic Railroad,** Box 921, Elbe, WA 98330. (360) 569–2588. The old-fashioned train operates daily mid-June through September, weekends in winter, on a 14-mile ride. Behind a vintage steam engine, open cars chug, steam, and whistle across high bridges and through deep forest to Mineral Lake. The train ride takes ninety minutes. The dinner train ride on Sundays lasts four hours.

From Elbe, take Route 7 and Route 161 to Eatonville and **Northwest Trek,** a 600-acre wildlife park. (360) 832–6116 or (800) 433–TREK. Here the visitors are enclosed in a bus for a forty-five-minute tour, and the animals roam freely in their natural habitat. Bison, moose, bighorn sheep, and caribou move undisturbed through the woodlands and open meadows. Cougar, wolves, eagles, and owls are kept in spacious, enclosed areas. Spring is a good time to see the newborns.

Northwest Trek has 5 miles of nature trails; one is accessible to wheelchairs.

LUNCH: Northwest Trek snack bar. Sandwiches, soups, and hamburgers. Eat indoors or take your lunch to the picnic meadow, where tame deer may wish to share your meal.

Afternoon

Continue on Route 161 north to **Puyallup,** home of the daffodil and once the bulb basket of the world. Valley farmers shipped worldwide a generation ago, and tourists flocked in to admire the acres of fragrant flowers and watch the street parade held in spring in their honor.

That was before urban development covered many fields and before fresh-cut flowers became a lucrative business; now most of the daffodils are cut and shipped while they're unopened buds. But you can still see a few fields in bloom—glorious yellow carpets, with Mount Rainier an immense white backdrop. The April festival and parade remain a major annual event in both Puyallup and Tacoma.

In Puyallup, tour **Meeker Mansion,** a seventeen-room home of the 1890s. Among its ornate splendors are six fireplaces with carved ceramic tiles, Victorian furnishings, and floral painted ceilings. Well worth a visit, the mansion is open afternoons, Wednesday through Sunday, March through December.

Another restored home, this one in neighboring Sumner, is **Ryan House,** built in 1875 by the town's first mayor. He was a hops farmer and lumberman.

To return to Seattle, drive north on State Route 167 or take Route 161 to I–5 for the final 15 miles.

THERE'S MORE

Hiking. Naches Loop Trail, near Chinook Pass and Tipsoo Lake (off Route 410, on the eastern border of the national park), is enchanting, with its subalpine firs and mountain hemlock trees, wooden bridge, and summer wildflowers. The trail connects with the Pacific Crest Trail, which extends from Mexico to Canada.

Silver Falls Trail, above Laughingwater Creek on the Ohanapecosh River, is a 3-mile loop trip from Ohanapecosh Campground, 2 miles south of the Stevens Canyon junction on Route 123. The trail leads to an 80-foot cascade of water so clear it has a silver cast. The vibrant green of the ferns and mosses in the Silver Falls gorge is stunning on a cloudy day.

Trail of the Shadows is a ½-mile trail through a meadow with bubbling mineral springs; you may see a beaver family. The trail begins across the road from Longmire Museum.

Farmers' Market at Pioneer Park, Puyallup. Fresh fruit and produce from local farms on summer Saturdays.

Mountain Climbing. Climbing Rainier demands skill and experience. One-day seminars and equipment rentals are available from Rainier Mountaineering Inc., Paradise, WA 98398. (360) 569–2227. They have exclusive rights to conduct guided climbs of the mountains. Winter address: 201 St. Helens Avenue, Tacoma, WA 98402. (253) 627–6242.

Skiing. Crystal Mountain, one of the state's major ski areas; at 7,000 feet, it's Washington's highest. Commercial resort with ski lifts.

Camp Muir snowfield. Gentle slope, snow covered all year, on Rainier's south side. No lifts. Hike up and ski down.

Reflection Lakes. Safe cross-country trail skiing, easy access, and scenic grandeur. Camping allowed when snowpack is 3 feet deep. Park at Narada Falls, near Paradise.

Van Lierop Bulb Farm, 13407 Eightieth Street East, Puyallup, WA 98372. (253) 848–7272. Stroll brick walkways in a small garden with flowering trees and a gazebo. Buy bulbs and plants in the gift shop. Put your name on the mailing list for a lovely catalog.

SPECIAL EVENTS

Mid-April. Daffodil Festival, Puyallup and Tacoma. Elaborate parade, flower show, bake sale, dog show, barbecues, auction, dances.

Late June and early July. Meeker Days, Puyallup. Honors an early Puyallup pioneer. Arts-and-crafts fair, fun run, pancake breakfast, family track meet, chicken barbecue, and ice cream social.

September. Western Washington Fair, Puyallup. One of the state's major fairs and the sixth-largest state fair in the U.S., with livestock exhibitions, races, carnival rides, food booths, handicrafts, and big-name entertainers.

OTHER RECOMMENDED RESTAURANTS AND LODGINGS

Ashford

Alexander's Country Inn, Route 706. (360) 569–2300; within Washington, (800) 654–7615. Landmark country restaurant and inn with twelve rooms. Fresh fish entrees and memorable blackberry pie.

Wild Berry Restaurant and Cabin at the Berry, Route 706 East. (360) 569–2628. Good sandwiches, great pie. Rustic but comfortable log cabin across the road sleeps eight.

Crystal Mountain

Crystal Mountain Resort, P.O. Box 1. (360) 663–2265. Some of Washington's best ski slopes and cross-country trails. Condominium rentals, a sports shop, restaurants. Summit House Restaurant, highest in state at 6,872 feet, has a great view. Open mid-November to mid-April.

Longmire

National Park Inn. Historic cedar lodge, remodeled 1989–1990. Rustic and woodsy, with twenty-six rooms (two handicapped accessible) and a view across Longmire Meadow to mountain's peak. The only lodge in the park open all year. Reservations: Mount Rainier Guest Services, P.O. Box 108, Ashford, WA 98304. (360) 569–2275.

Packwood

Hotel Packwood, 103 Main Street. (360) 494–5431. Renovated Victorian inn 10 miles from Mount Rainier National Park. Nine comfortable, antiques-furnished rooms, two with private baths. Theodore Roosevelt stayed here.

Puyallup

Earthquake Burgers, 11526 Meridien South. (253) 848–9850. Small cafe serving platter-sized hamburgers. For those with large appetites.

Manna Teriyaki, 127 Fifteenth Street SE. (253) 845–4222. Specializes in teriyaki dishes and sushi. All entrees available for take-out.

Sumner

Manfred Vierthaler Winery and Restaurant, 17136 Highway 410 East. (206) 863–1633. Unusual dining room on a hill, offering view of valley and vineyards. German-style wines in the tasting room, steak and Bavarian dishes on the menu.

FOR MORE INFORMATION

Enumclaw Chamber of Commerce, 1421 Cole Street, Enumclaw, WA 98022. (360) 825–7666.

Mount Rainier National Park, Tahoma Woods, Star Route, Ashford, WA 98304. (360) 569–2211.

Puyallup Chamber of Commerce, 322 Second Street SW, Puyallup, WA 98372. (253) 845–6755.

North Kitsap Peninsula
A NORTHWEST HERITAGE

---

1 NIGHT

Ferry rides • Chief Seattle's grave • Native American museum
"Little Norway" Secluded country resort
Oldest operating sawmill in America • Historic Victorian village

There's a lot of diversity within a comparatively small area on the northern Kitsap Peninsula. You can drive from a Scandinavian-style village to a New England mill town in less than a half hour, with time out for sight-seeing, or you can watch Suquamish Indians carve a dugout canoe a few miles from fine dining opportunities on a country estate.

DAY 1

Morning

Kitsap Peninsula lies west of Seattle, across Puget Sound. Board the Winslow ferry at Elliott Bay for the thirty-five-minute crossing to **Winslow,** on **Bainbridge Island.** Have breakfast here at the **Streamliner Diner,** 397 Winslow Way (360–842–8595), or drive Route 305 north toward Agate Passage and the bridge to the peninsula.

Take an immediate right on Suquamish Way, and follow the signs to the grave of **Chief Seattle** (or Sealth). The grave of the famous Salish Indian leader, who died in 1866 and for whom Seattle is named, lies in a hilltop cemetery beside a small church. Marked by a cross and framed with traditional dugout canoes, the great chief's resting place overlooks the waters of the sound. On the horizon rise the tall buildings of Seattle's skyline.

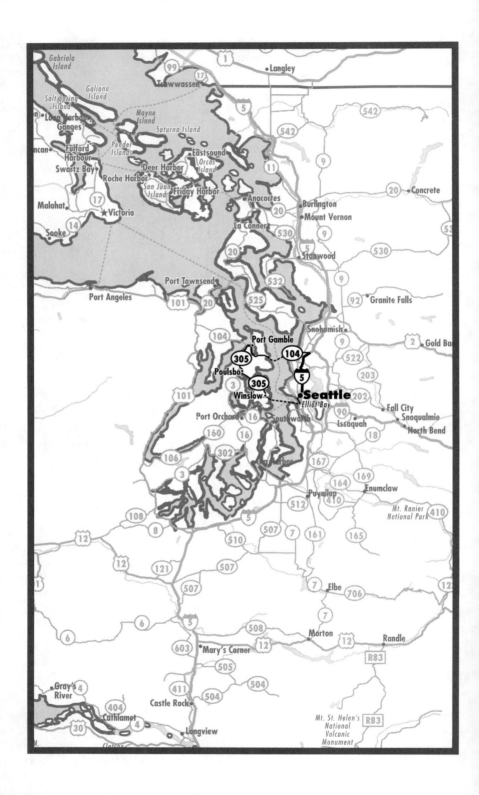

After paying homage to the man who sought peace between his people and the white settlers, the man who said that "the very dust under your feet . . . is the ashes of our ancestors," visit nearby **Old Man House State Park** (signs clearly mark the way). This shady hillside park above the bay was the site of a native communal home, the "Old Man House," built of cedar and 900 feet long.

Learn more about the culture of these Native Americans at the **Suquamish Museum,** named by the Smithsonian as the best Native American museum in the Northwest. Follow Route 305 west; the museum is just off the highway on the **Port Madison Indian Reservation.** Near the entrance, under a shelter, you may see carvers patiently forming a long, dugout canoe from a huge log of cedar. The excellent, sometimes poignant museum artifacts and photographs depict native life as it was for thousands of years before white settlement and the results after it.

Continue west on Route 305 as it curves up toward Liberty Bay and **Poulsbo.** Turn left on Lincoln Road, which ends at the waterfront. When you see painted murals on downtown buildings and signs reading VELKOMMEN TIL POULSBO, you know you're deep into Scandinavian country.

The little town was settled in the late 1880s by fishers, loggers, and farmers, many of them from Norway; *Poulsbo* means "Paul's Place" in Norwegian. Liberty Bay, then called Dogfish Bay, and its inlets reminded the settlers of the fjords of their native land. The town's tie to the water remains strong today, with three marinas on the bay's waterfront.

The people of Poulsbo take pride in their rich heritage. They hold several traditional festivals to honor their roots, and numerous shops sell Scandinavian handicrafts, jewelry, and foods.

LUNCH: Benson's Restaurant, Olympic Square on Front Street in Poulsbo. (360) 697–3449. Upscale establishment offering Northwest cuisine. Lamb, fish, and pasta dishes, along with hard-to-resist desserts. Another good lunch choice is **New Day Seafood,** on Front Street overlooking the water. (360) 697–3183. With both a restaurant and a fishing boat in the family, you know the seafood is fresh.

Afternoon

Visit **Verksted,** Olympic Square on Front Street, an artist coop stocked with wood carvings, leather work, hand-painted shirts, chocolate sculpture, and cribbage boards made from elk horn. (360) 697–4470.

Chief Seattle's grave lies under a frame of dugout canoes.

Stroll **Liberty Bay Park,** which is connected by a wooden causeway over the water to American Legion Park, to soak up the maritime flavor of this engaging town. Pennants snap in the wind on fishing and pleasure boats as they come and go in the busy harbor. Liberty Bay has a picnic area and a covered pavilion used during the summer for dancing, concerts, and arts festivals. At the **Poulsbo Marine Science Center** on Liberty Bay, you can examine sea life under microscopes, touch anemones, see ghost shrimp, and watch videos and documentaries.

Raab Park, at Caldart Avenue off Hostmark Street, is Poulsbo's largest park. On its fourteen acres are grassy slopes, covered picnic facilities, barbecue grills, a playground, horseshoe pits, a sand volleyball court, and an outdoor stage.

Browse the shops along **Front Street** for unusual souvenirs, such as the brass and nautical items in Cargo Hold and merchandise imported from Norway at Five Swans. The fragrance wafting from Sluy's Bakery will draw you to this famous shop, where fresh-baked breads and toothsome pastries are sold.

Leaving Poulsbo, take Bond Road west to Big Valley Road and turn left. Drive 4 miles through idyllic countryside, where forested hills back green fields, to the **Manor Farm Inn.** Arrive by 3:30 P.M. and you'll be in time for tea, a regular ritual at this country estate.

After tea, stroll around the farm and reacquaint yourself with tranquility. In this setting, right from *All Creatures Great and Small,* Manor Farm Inn offers an opportunity to experience a slower pace. Horses and dairy cows graze in the pastures, and lambs gambol in the fields. Walk to the trout-stocked pond in back, or sit on the veranda and admire the flower-filled courtyard.

DINNER: Molly Ward Gardens, 27462 Big Valley Road, near your night's lodging. (360) 779–4471. Reserve a table in this small restaurant, where you are surrounded by dried flowers and fine food.

LODGING: The Manor Farm Inn, 26069 Big Valley Road NE, Poulsbo, WA 98370. (360) 779–4628. French country-style farmhouse with seven rooms in two wings. Masses of flowers, luxurious rooms, enthusiastic hospitality. Full breakfast everyday for guests; breakfast available to public on weekends.

DAY 2

Morning

BREAKFAST: The Manor Farm Inn. Hot scones and juice in your room begin the day. Then comes breakfast in the dining hall. Full country breakfast at 9:00 A.M. is included in your room cost.

Spend the morning at the farm petting the animals or reading on the veranda, or borrow a bicycle and explore the winding country roads.

Kitsap State Memorial Park is less than 2 miles from the inn.

LUNCH: After the morning's bountiful meal, most guests prefer to skip lunch or snack at the restored 1853 trading post in Port Gamble.

Afternoon

Follow Big Valley Road to State Route 3, and turn north toward **Port Gamble.** This historic, picturesque village, which lies across an inlet from the eastern, and northernmost, tip of Kitsap Peninsula, is one of the last company towns still in existence. Port Gamble is owned by Pope and Talbot, one of the world's major timber companies.

The founders of Port Gamble came from New England in the midnineteenth century and built the new town to resemble the one they'd left—East Machias, Maine. Today Port Gamble has been restored to its turn-of-the-century appearance, with neat Victorian homes, a steepled church, and a general store.

The 1856 **Port Gamble Cemetery,** burial site of the first U.S. Navy man killed in action in the Pacific Northwest, draws a lot of people to this town.

Main Street is lined with elm trees brought around Cape Horn from Maine in 1872. The entire town is on the National Register of Historic Places. The **Port Gamble Historical Museum** explains the area's history. **Of Sea and Shore Museum** holds a collection of more than 14,000 species of shells and marine life. For information on the town, call (360) 297–2426.

From Port Gamble turn south on State Route 104, along the wooded bluff above Port Gamble inlet to Port Gamble–Suqaumish Road. You're headed back to the village of Suquamish.

Take Suquamish Way to Route 305 and recross Agate Passage. Drive again through the woodlands and pastoral countryside of Bainbridge Island, and at Winslow catch the ferry back to Seattle.

THERE'S MORE

Clearwater Casino has been a big hit since it opened on the Port Madison Reservation in Suquamish in 1990. Gaming tables, no slot machines.

Old Schoolhouse. Brick two-story school at Kola-Kola Park, Kingston.

Point No Point Lighthouse. White, square tower in Hansville, at the tip of Kitsap Peninsula. Lighthouse established in 1879; present structure built in 1900.

SPECIAL EVENTS

Mid–May. Viking Fest, Poulsbo. In honor of Norway's Independence Day, a Sons of Norway luncheon, pancake breakfast, arts-and-crafts show, fun run, carnival, food booth, parade.

Mid-June. Skandia Midsommarfest, Poulsbo. Skandia Folk Dance Society performs in costume. Midsummer pole raising and dance.

Mid-August. Chief Seattle Days, Suquamish. Native American dancing, canoe races, food stands, softball games.

September. September-Fest, Poulsbo. Classic yacht show, food booths, wine tasting, beer garden, live music. Live animals and a petting zoo for the little ones.

December. Yule Fest, Poulsbo. Scandinavian legends and storytelling, lighting of the Yule Log, Sons of Norway bazaar, Lucia Bride, strolling musicians.

OTHER RECOMMENDED RESTAURANTS AND LODGINGS

Seaback

Willcox House, 2390 Tekiu Road. (360) 830–4492. Bed-and-breakfast inn in former private waterside mansion. Five rooms, marble fireplaces, pool, view of Hood Canal, Olympic Mountains. Full breakfast served; dinner available by reservation is not included in price of guest room.

FOR MORE INFORMATION

Greater Poulsbo Chamber of Commerce, 19131 Eighth Avenue, P.O. Box 1063, Poulsbo, WA 98370. (360) 779–4848.

Kitsap Chamber of Commerce, P.O. Box 1790, Silverdale, WA 98383. (360) 692–6800 or (800) 416–5615.

Suquamish Tribal Center, Route 305, Suquamish, WA 98392. (360) 598–3311.

Washington State Ferries, 801 Alaskan Way, Pier 52 Colman Dock, Seattle, WA 98104. (360) 464–6400; within Washington, (800) 84–FERRY.

Skagit County

SPRING FLOWERS BY THE SEA

1 NIGHT

*Fields of spring flowers • Quaint waterfront • Boutiques
Art galleries • Historical museum • Wildlife refuge
Antiques shops • Jetboat ride*

Here's a two-day sojourn into the country, a brief escape that's full of color and activity. Have fun with this one—maybe do your gift shopping for the year in La Conner's myriad shops, where you may find unexpected treasures.

The route suggested allows time to stroll La Conner's busy downtown area (packed with tourists on summer weekends and during the tulip festival), but it takes you to quiet byways, too, where you can observe wildlife, smell the flowers, and revel in rural serenity.

DAY 1

Morning

Drive north on I–5, past Mount Vernon and over the **Skagit River** to State Route 20 (about 60 miles), and turn west. When you see the EDISON-BOW sign, where Best Road turns left, turn right; it may be unsigned, but you are on Farm to Market Road. Follow signs left down Josh Wilson Road and right down Bayview-Edison Road to **Padilla Bay National Estuarine Research Reserve,** which offers hands-on learning about the adjacent estuary. Bayview-Edison Road edges the shore of **Padilla Bay,** a body of water well protected by a circling group of islands: Fidalgo, Guemes, and Samish.

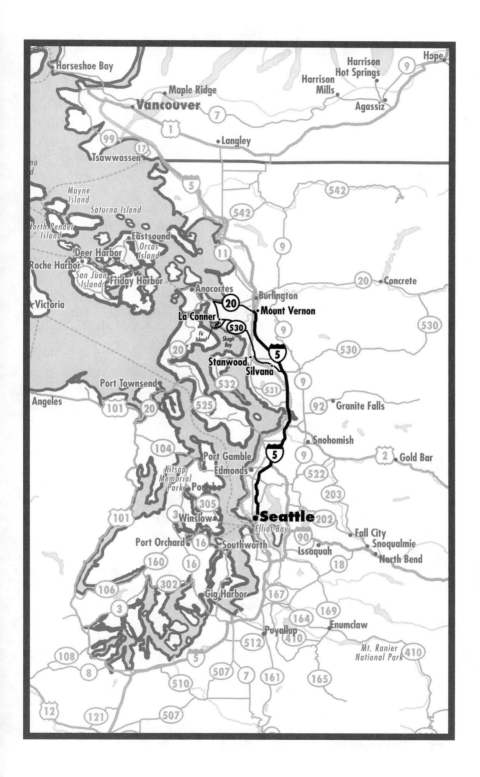

The reserve is one in a nationwide system that teaches visitors about estuaries—mixes of salt- and freshwater—that teem with life. Walk the uplands nature trail, view aquatic displays and Padilla Bay, and, if you're still curious, learn more in the center's research library. (360) 428–1558. Hours vary seasonally.

Retrace your steps and cross Highway 20. You are now on Best Road, in the heart of the tulip, iris, and daffodil fields of the **Skagit Valley,** where great swaths of springtime color draw hordes of admirers. The world's greatest volume of tulips comes from the fertile farmlands of Skagit County.

In other seasons the valley is equally beautiful, if not as brightly colored, with its tawny summer fields and autumn mists and leaf and harvest fragrances. **Mount Baker** stands on the far horizon, a high, snow-mantled cone.

When you come to **La Conner Flats,** 15920 Best Road (360–466–3190), stop for a tour of this English country garden. Eleven acres bloom with color March through October, from the daffodils and rhododendrons of March to June's roses, August's dahlias, and the brilliant foliage of fall. In addition to the array of flowers are savory-scented herb gardens and vegetable and berry gardens.

LUNCH: The Granary, La Conner Flats. (360) 466–3190. Homemade soup, salads, sandwiches, desserts, served in a rustic former granary near the entrance to the gardens. (High tea served 2:00 to 5:00 P.M. Open March through October; closed Mondays.) Lunch is available by reservation only.

Afternoon

Continue on Best Road to Chilberg Road, and turn west toward **La Conner** proper. The historic, picturesque little town had its beginnings in 1867 as a trading post. A few years later, John Conner, from Olympia, bought the store and town and seventy additional acres for the sum of $500. In 1872 he named the settlement after his wife, Louisa Ann Conner, using her initials.

La Conner, perched on the edge of **Swinomish Channel,** which lies between the mainland and Fidalgo Island, grew into an active port and fishing community. But when the Great Depression brought business to a standstill, La Conner began to fade.

In the 1970s energetic townsfolk decided to make some changes to encourage tourism. Their efforts succeeded beyond all expectation. La Conner has not only been discovered; it has gained fame for its charming waterfront and turn-of-the-century architecture, its numerous shops and art galleries.

On your way to the downtown district, stop at **Tillinghast Seed Company,** 623 Morris Street. (360) 466–3329. The wooden porch overflows with flowers at this old-fashioned store, the oldest mail-order seed company in the Northwest. Inside you'll find seeds, plants, kitchen tools, country gifts, and spicy scents; upstairs there's a Christmas shop, and out in back a nursery in the shade of a one hundred-year-old tree—the largest European beech on the West Coast.

First and Second Streets, above the harbor, are lined with **antiques shops, boutiques, and art galleries.** A sampling: Earthenworks, showing top-quality Northwest ceramics, fabrics, watercolors, and photographs; La Conner Gallery, a channel-side showroom with crystal and jewelry; The Wood Merchant, for finely carved sculptures and tools; Homespun Market, where European laces, handwoven throws, and homespun fabrics are sold; and The Scott Collection, with Northwest pottery and porcelains, jewelry, bronze and brass sculpture, and soapstone carvings.

As you explore the town you'll see, just off Second Street, one of La Conner's oldest landmarks—a bank built in 1886, now City Hall, a triangular-shaped building. Near it is the **Magnus Anderson Cabin,** a pioneer home constructed in 1869 by a Swedish immigrant.

The **Gaches Mansion,** also on Second Street, is a twenty-two-room structure that dates from 1891. Once used as a hospital, the mansion has been restored and is open for tours on weekend afternoons.

The **Museum of Northwest Art** is in a striking contemporary building at 121 South First Street. (360) 466–4078.

Skagit County Museum is on Fourth Street. Its exhibits show life as it was in a previous century, and its windows frame views of the valley's fields with Mount Baker behind them.

DINNER: Palmers, 205 East Washington Street in La Conner. (360) 466–4261. The town's consistently best restaurant, serving Northwest and French cuisine. Fresh local seafoods, pastas, wines. Tables upstairs, cozy booths in the downstairs pub.

LODGING: The Channel Lodge, P.O. Box 573, La Conner, WA 98257. (360) 466–1500. Stylish inn with country-contemporary decor. Forty rooms, all with fireplaces, most with harbor views.

DAY 2

Morning

BREAKFAST: The Channel Lodge.

You might rent a bicycle and take a ride in the country, passing fields green or ablaze with color; perhaps you'll see swans gliding through the marshes in the morning mist.

Alternatively, check the shops you missed yesterday. If you're interested in **antiques,** La Conner has plenty to offer. Cameo Antiques showcases Victorian and American primitives in oak and pine, Creighton's Quilts is known for its Amish quilts, and Morris Street Antique Mall carries a wide range of furniture, glassware, toys, and books. Nasty Jack's has a large selection of oak furniture.

LUNCH: Legends, 708 South First Street. (360) 466–5240. Barbecued salmon and fry bread, prepared and eaten outdoors on a deck overlooking the water from late March through Labor Day.

Afternoon

Leaving La Conner, take Chilberg Road south to Fir Island. Less than a mile after you cross the bridge, the toasty scent of freshly baked waffles will draw you to **Snow Goose Produce.** The open market sells produce, flowers, fresh seafood, and, most important, huge and delicious ice cream cones. The hot waffle cones are baked as you watch.

The Fir Island coast, along Skagit Bay, is ragged with islands and waterways, as the Skagit flows into the bay in a dozen places. Take Fir Island Road to Game Range Road, about 1½ miles west of Conway, and you'll come to **Skagit Wildlife Recreation Area.** In this 12,000-acre preserve you'll see hundreds of waterfowl and, in winter, Siberian snow geese.

Back on Fir Island Road, head east across the Skagit to Route 530 and turn south. It's a few miles down the road to **Stanwood,** a small farming community. **Scandia Bakery,** on 3-block-long Main Street, is a good place to stop for a coffee break and pastry. Lace curtains and Norwegian rosemaling decorative trim emphasize the Scandinavian theme of the bakery (along with the sign by the coffeepot that reads NORWEGIAN GASOLINE).

From Stanwood, drive to Silvana on State Route 531. The pastoral valley is far more picturesque and relaxing than the freeway ride, and it doesn't add much time. You'll pass sprawling green fields and tidy plots, a red barn half-submerged in ivy and a gray one with a moss-covered roof. A flag flies from the porch of an old-fashioned farmhouse, behind the lilacs.

About 7 miles from Stanwood, you'll see a small white church on a hill. **Peace Lutheran Church,** built in 1884, is now a historic site, still in use and a favored location for weddings.

Blink as you enter the village of Silvana, on your way to join I–5, and you may miss it. You left the Fir Island turnoff just 23 miles ago.

Drive south on I–5 for the return to Seattle.

THERE'S MORE

Cruises. *Viking Star,* 101 North First Street. (360) 466–2639. Forty-nine passengers; variety of cruises, including three-hour whale-watching and nature cruise to San Juan Islands, May to September.

RoozenGaarde, 15867 Beaver Marsh Road, Mount Vernon. (360) 424–8531. Display garden and gift shop, open daily.

Skagit Gardens, 1695 Johnson Road, Mount Vernon. One of the oldest public display gardens in Skagit County. Year-round botanical garden: thousands of tulips, crocuses, daffodils in spring; brilliant annuals in August; poinsettias in November. Visitors welcome; bring a lunch to the gazebo and picnic table.

Skagit Valley Bulb Farms, Memorial Highway and Young Road. (206) 424–8152. Picnic facilities; walk in fields of flowers.

Westshore Acres Bulb Farm and Display Garden, 956 Downey Road, Mount Vernon. (360) 466–3158.

SPECIAL EVENTS

April. Skagit Valley Tulip Festival. Major Northwest festival, with parades, flower shows, street fair, pancake breakfast, salmon barbecues, dances, pick-your-own and display flower fields, food fair, sports events (gymnastics, Slug Run). Park and ride to avoid traffic congestion. Go early, preferably on a Tuesday or Wednesday.

OTHER RECOMMENDED RESTAURANTS AND LODGINGS

La Conner

Calico Cupboard, 701 South First Street. (360) 466–4451. Cafe that's famous for cinnamon rolls, muffins, breads, biscuits. Eat here, or take pastry to go and eat by the water. Coffee drinks, too. (Crowded in the busy season.)

Hotel Planter, 715 First Street. (360) 466–4710. Twelve guest rooms in renovated building. Inexpensive. Private hot tub in garden.

La Conner Country Inn, 107 South Second Street. (360) 466–3101. Attractive, twenty-eight-room inn with theme of a country guest house. In the heart of town. Continental breakfast.

Ridgeway Bed-and-Breakfast, 14914 McLean Road, P.O. Box 475. (360) 428–8068 or (800) 428–8068. Dutch Colonial farm home on two acres. Tulip fields, six guest rooms, homemade desserts, full breakfast.

White Swan Guest House, 15872 Moore Road, Mount Vernon. (360) 445–6805. Storybook Victorian farmhouse 6 miles from La Conner. Three guest rooms, garden cottage. Lovely gardens.

Wild Iris, 121 Maple Avenue. (360) 466–1400. Nineteen-room, two-story hotel in Victorian style. Guest and public dining Sunday through Wednesday.

FOR MORE INFORMATION

La Conner Chamber of Commerce, P.O. Box 1610, La Conner, WA 98257. (360) 466–4778.

Mount Vernon Chamber of Commerce, 325 East College Way, P.O. Box 1007, Mount Vernon, WA 98273. (360) 428–8547.

Gig Harbor

IN AND AROUND THE WATER

1 NIGHT

Ferry ride on Puget Sound • Views of Seattle skyline
Antiques shops • Quiet country roads • Waterfront village
Fishing boats • Pleasure boats • Intriguing shops
Hiking • Boating

All these attractions in one overnight getaway? Yes, a quick trip to Gig Harbor can seem like a full vacation, with its variety of things to see and do. You can simply stroll the shop-lined streets and watch the sailboats, if you prefer total relaxation, or you can fill the time with action.

The sleepy fishing village that was Gig Harbor is rapidly disappearing, with new housing developments and even a sizable shopping center, complete with McDonald's, going in. But residents are struggling to retain the small-town atmosphere and slower pace that give the place its charm. Despite its discovery by tourists, Gig Harbor remains a boat-centered community with a focus on commercial fishing.

DAY 1

Morning

Ride the ferry from Fauntleroy Cove across Puget Sound to **Southworth.** Head west across Kitsap Peninsula to the waterside town of **Port Orchard,** where you can search for treasures in the many antiques shops, browse through the art galleries, and shop for handicrafts. Stroll by the busy marina, tour the

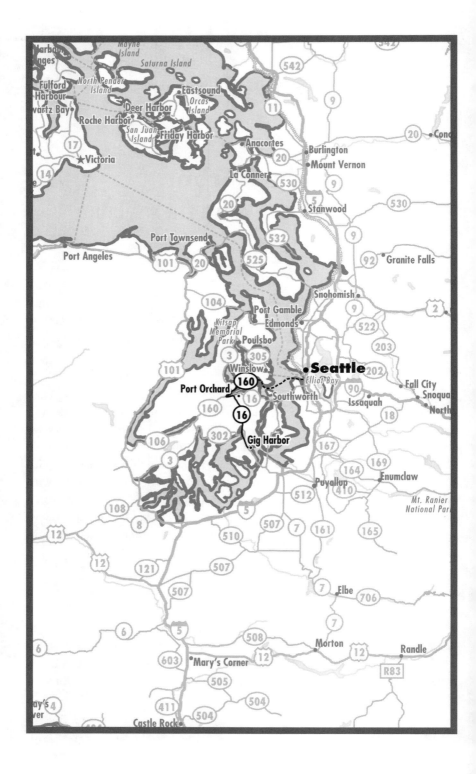

Log Cabin Museum, and, on summer Saturdays, buy fresh produce at the farmers market. (For more details on Port Orchard, see Seattle Escape Three.)

LUNCH: Bay Coffee Company and Espresso, 807-B Bay Street. (360) 895–2115. The name describes it: coffee, espresso, sandwiches, and pastries in a small, casual cafe near the water.

Afternoon

Take Bethel Road from Port Orchard, and head east on Sedgwick to Banner Road; then turn south. This country road passes through the woodlands, fields, and homes along **Colvos Passage,** with green **Vashon Island** lying on the east.

Passing Olalla, you'll see the Carl Nelson home, a Victorian estate still owned by descendants of the sea captain who built it. Continue south on Crescent Valley Drive, driving by Canterwood, a security-conscious, planned country-club community with luxurious residences, townhouses, a golf course, a swimming pool, tennis courts, and stables.

Turn right on Vernhardson and left on Peacock Hill, and you will reach the heart of **Gig Harbor:** Harborview Drive. The road edging the little bay is lined with specialty shops, some offering souvenirs of the T-shirt-and-coffee-mug variety, others with original art, stylish clothing, and antiques. Intermingled with the boutiques are marina offices, a yacht sales broker, and a wholesaler of smoked herring. Wharves and boats dot the protected inlet.

Nisqually Indians were the only human inhabitants of Gig Harbor until 1841, when the Wilkes expedition stumbled upon it. One of the party's small boats, a captain's gig, took shelter in the bay during a storm; hence the name Gig Harbor. After that discovery, settlers and fishers, many from Yugoslavia, immigrated and began a still-active fishing fleet.

Stop at the chamber of commerce office on Judson Street for maps and brochures, then amble back to the waterfront and stroll the new walkway that edges the harbor. Life loses its sometimes-hectic quality here, as you watch the gulls swoop and shriek above the pilings and the boats bob gently on the waves. Dream over the luxurious vessels pictured at the yacht sales office or afloat in the bay.

Check in at your lodgings.

DINNER: Shorline Steak & Seafood, 8827 Harborview Drive, Gig Harbor. (253) 853–6353. Great location above the inner harbor, with high, angled windows overlooking the water. Specializing in seafood and steak entrees. Extensive Northwest wine list. Dine outdoors and ducks will come begging.

LODGING: The Pillars Bed and Breakfast, 6606 Soundview Drive, Gig Harbor, WA 98335. (253) 851–6644. Gracious home on a hillside, offering views of Colvos Passage, Vashon Island, and Mount Rainier. Three large, comfortable rooms, two with water and mountain views.

DAY 2

Morning

BREAKFAST: Juice, fresh fruit, cereals, and freshly baked sticky buns are served every day at The Pillars. If you want an omelet or other egg dish, the agreeable hosts, Alma and Bill Boge, are happy to prepare it.

Work your way along Harborview Drive, browsing through the dozens of shops and boutiques as you go. At **Mariners Museum,** 3311 Harborview Drive, you can see nautical artifacts displayed.

Next buy picnic makings and drive Rosedale Street west about 5 miles to **Kopachuck State Park.** On the way, you might like to stop at **Rosedale Gardens** to see the greenhouse and nursery under the cedar trees.

Kopachuck is a popular park for its location and amenities. Roads are paved, and campsites are numerous, wooded, and well maintained. Pass the camping section and head for the parking lot in the picnic area. From here you can walk the sloping path to the rocky beach or take one of the side trails that lead to nooks with picnic tables and grills under the trees. On sunny days, dappled light filters through the maple and cedar branches. The view across Carr Inlet to the snow-mantled Olympic Mountains is outstanding.

LUNCH: Picnic in Kopachuck State Park.

Afternoon

Enjoy the woodlands and beaches at Kopachuck; then return to Gig Harbor, and drive to the dock at Shorline Steak & Seafood for your **boat ride.** 8827 Harborview Drive, Gig Harbor. (253) 853–6353. You can rent powerboats, sailboats, and sea kayaks by the hour, or for a half or full day. Instructions provided as requested. Boat around the harbor for an hour, or, if you're feeling ambitious, sail east to **Point Defiance,** near **Tacoma.** You'll find good fishing in these waters.

Back at the Gig Harbor dock, turn in your boat and head for **The Tides Tavern** for a late-afternoon drink on the deck overlooking the water. You can't say you've truly seen Gig Harbor if you haven't stopped at least once at the local gathering place. The convivial tavern on Harborview Drive serves pizza, beer, good chowder, and desserts made at a local bakery.

Drive Route 16 toward Tacoma and connect with I–5 north for the one-hour trip to Seattle.

THERE'S MORE

Gig Harbor Peninsula Historical Society and Museum. 4218 Harborview Drive. (253) 858–6722. Web site address: www.peninsula-art. com/ghphsm/ghphsm.html. Artifacts and photos show the history and development of Gig Harbor Peninsula.

Golf. Gig Harbor Golf Club, 6909 Artondale Drive NW, Gig Harbor. (253) 851–2378. Nine-hole course.

Madrona Links, 3604 Twenty-second Avenue NW, Gig Harbor. (253) 851–5193. Eighteen-hole course.

Performance Circle Theater. Evening theatrical events, outdoors in summer at 9916 Peacock Hill Avenue, Gig Harbor. (253) 851–PLAY.

SPECIAL EVENTS

Early June. Maritime Gig, downtown Gig Harbor. Theme parade, bike rodeo, baked salmon dinner in waterside park.

Mid-July. Gig Harbor Art Festival, Judson Street. Display of regional artworks: oils, pottery, stained glass, watercolors.

Mid-August. Gig Harbor Jazz Festival. Nationally acclaimed jazz performers entertain all weekend.

Early December. Tide Fest. Tree lighting, boat parade, arts-and-crafts sale.

OTHER RECOMMENDED RESTAURANTS AND LODGINGS

Gig Harbor

Harbor Inn Restaurant, 3111 Harborview Drive. (253) 851–5454. Waterfront dining overlooking the bay.

Inn at Gig Harbor, 3211 Fifty-sixth Street NW. (253) 851–6665. Friendly, completely refurbished hotel with lounge and upscale restaurant serving Northwest cuisine, steaks, seafood.

Water's Edge Bed and Breakfast, 8610 Goodman Drive NW. (253) 851–3890. Waterfront suite, downstairs with deck, dock, and private entrance, across the harbor from town. Full breakfast.

FOR MORE INFORMATION

Gig Harbor/Peninsula Area Chamber of Commerce, 3125 Judson Street, Gig Harbor, WA 98335. (253) 851–6865.

Washington State Ferries, 801 Alaskan Way, Pier 52 Colman Dock, Seattle, WA 98104. (206) 464–6400; within Washington, (800) 84–FERRY.

VANCOUVER
ESCAPES

Explore the Fraser Valley

FARM AND GARDEN ROUTE

BETWEEN THE MOUNTAINS

2 NIGHTS

Fraser River • Westminster Abbey • Harrison Hot Springs
Scenic lakes and mountains • Minter Gardens
Picturesque village • Historic Fort Langley • Fur traders

Fur trader Simon Fraser explored the 850-mile-long Fraser River from its source in the Rocky Mountains to the Fraser Canyon, then down the fertile Fraser Valley to the delta where the city of Vancouver now stands. He built fur-trading posts for the Hudson's Bay Company along the way.

When prospectors struck gold in the Fraser Valley in 1858, the traffic came from the opposite direction, with hordes of would-be miners going up the Fraser in search of their fortunes. The Colony of British Columbia was proclaimed from Fort Langley, on the Fraser. The river city of New Westminster is still called the Royal City because Queen Victoria named it the first provincial capital.

All of those "treasures," except the gold strikes, are still there in the 80-mile-long Fraser Valley, whose fruit and vegetable farms have fed city folk for generations. The glorious lakes and mountains are still the backdrop to every valley scene, as they were in the days of the fur traders. Living history sites tell the old stories. Fruit farms, show gardens, and hot springs tempt you to stop along the way.

This escape follows the north side of the Fraser River to the glorious lake-and-mountain setting of Harrison Hot Springs and comes back down the

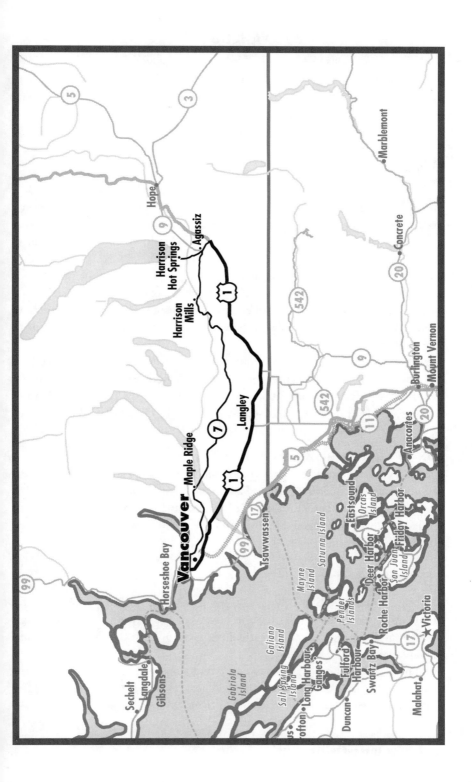

south side, past Minter Gardens and Historic Fort Langley to the Royal City of New Westminster.

DAY 1

Morning

Follow Highway 7A east as Hastings Street becomes Inlet Drive and then Barnet Road. Turn left at **Port Moody,** and find yourself on Highway 7, known to all and sundry as the Lougheed Highway. Several miles of roadside commerce lead you over the Pitt River into **Pitt Meadows** and **Maple Ridge,** where our tour begins.

This was a lively riverboat town a century ago when people and goods came downriver, picking up produce and other freight for the cities of Vancouver and New Westminster. Pick up a **Heritage River Walk** brochure from the InfoCentre at 22238 Lougheed, and follow directions downhill to the **Fraser River.**

The restored Port Haney buildings are on River Road. The old Bank of Montreal building is now the popular **Billy Miner Pub.** Walk out on the rebuilt **Port Haney Wharf;** then join the Haney bypass road to see **Haney House,** the **Maple Ridge Museum,** and the old **CP Rail Caboose.**

Rejoin Highway 7 and head for **Mission.**

LUNCH: The **Norma Kinney House,** located in the Fraser River Heritage Park, serves homemade soups and sandwiches in an old log cabin and offers stunning views of the Fraser River Valley. Open May 1 through September 30. A good year-round choice is **Fogg 'n' Suds** at the Best Western Mission City Lodge, 32281 Loughheed Highway, which features an international lunch menu (640–820–5577).

Afternoon

Railway Avenue loops you back east along the river to Highway 7, and the signboard directs you uphill on Stave Lake Road to **Fraser River Heritage Regional Park.** You'll get a breathtaking view of both the Fraser River and Mount Baker.

There may be kite flyers on the grass and a seasonal event in the Kinsmen bandstand or on Rotary Club Plaza. Check out the two log cabins, the **Norma Kenney House,** and the ruins of **St. Mary's Mission.** In summer, locals will be having a light lunch or tea, and buying homemade jams, in the **Raspberry Kitchen.**

Continue up Stave Lake Road and turn right on Dewdney Trunk Road to **Westminster Abbey,** part of a Benedictine monastery and Seminary of Christ the King. The complex crowns a grassy hill with spectacular views at 34224 Dewdney Trunk Road. The abbey was named after the city of New Westminster and is not related to the famous abbey in London, England.

The slender columns of the contemporary abbey create a beautiful modern echo of the ancient cross-shaped cathedrals of Europe. Tour buses bring visitors from the United States and Canada to enjoy the sanctuary and the light coming through the stained-glass windows. Services are open to visitors, and the monastery is used as a retreat.

Follow Dewdney Trunk Road downhill, and take Highway 7 east across the bridge at Hatzic, then turn immediately left into the **Longhouse Interpretive Centre** at **XA:YTEM,** pronounced "hay-tem." The Sto:lo Nation honors a large rock on an ancient river terrace, sacred site of their ancestors.

You will pass general stores at Dewdney and Deroche and waterfront cottages at Lake Errock before following the shore of Harrison Bay into **Harrison Mills,** where lumber mills once thrived on the timber floated down Harrison Lake.

The family of Charles Pretty owned large tracts here. His sons created a hunting lodge and a home that now offer unusual lodging choices to those who turn left up Morris Valley Road and follow signs to historic, rustic **Fenn Lodge** or the elegant **Rowena's Inn on the River.** (See "There's More.")

When Highway 7 crosses the Harrison River, follow signs right to **Kilby Historic Store and Farm,** a 1920s living history site taken over by the Province of British Columbia to preserve the old general store, post office, milk house, log cabin, and tearoom in farm country near the Harrison River.

It is about a fifteen-minute drive from there on Highways 7 and 9 to **Harrison Hot Springs.** When the road dead-ends at the lake, turn left and check in at the Harrison Hot Springs Hotel.

DINNER: Dine and dance in the elegant Copper Room, or watch the view from the Lakeview Terrace in the **Harrison Hot Springs Hotel.**

LODGING: Harrison Hot Springs Hotel, Harrison Hot Springs, B.C. V0M 1K0. (604) 796–2244 or (800) 663–2266. This resort complex has always dominated the center of town, overlooking Harrison Lake and its surrounding mountains. Take one of the nicely restored rooms in the historic original building, or stay in the 1950s addition on one side or the new brick high-rise on the other side.

DAY 2

Morning

BREAKFAST: Lakeview Terrace, Harrison Hot Springs Hotel.

From your breakfast terrace you can enjoy the mountains that embrace Harrison Hot Springs on every side, the lake that shimmers away to **Echo Island,** and the distant **Breckinridge Mountains.** Below you, people walk the **esplanade** to the left, along the shore to the original hot springs, or to the right, past the boat docks and the grassy playgrounds, to the enclosed lagoon. The town stretches only a few blocks along the lake and is only a few blocks wide.

The hot springs were known to the Coast Salish people for centuries. According to legend, three 1850s gold-rush miners discovered the springs when one miner fell in the water and discovered it was warm. The St. Alice Hotel was famous on this spot after 1885, and the water rights to the hot springs are still held by its successor, the Harrison Hot Springs Hotel. The springs are piped straight into the hotel pools; nonguests can use the public pool at Hot Springs Road and Esplanade.

Spend your morning exploring the pools and the town. Rock hounds explore for jade, garnets, agates, fossils, and even gold in the surrounding hills. Or join the search for the legendary apelike Sasquatch, twice the size of a man. His huge footprints are supposed to have been sighted for years here in Sasquatch country.

LUNCH: Picnic on the sand beach at Harrison Hot Springs.

Afternoon

Buy tickets at the hotel and cruise 40-mile-long **Harrison Lake** aboard the *Lady Harrison.* You'll wind among the beautiful islands and between the mountains that soar out of the lake.

If you feel ambitious, drive Highway 7 east for 22 scenic miles (38 km) along the north side of the Fraser River to the town of **Hope,** where a Hudson's Bay fort once stood at the entrance to the Fraser Canyon.

Walk through the **Othello Quintette** tunnels once used by the Kettle Valley Railway. Ten miles east of Hope on Highway 3, you can see the results of the 1965 **Hope Slide,** 45-meter-deep rock rubble created by the collapse of one side of Johnson Peak. Return on Highway 7 or along the south side of the river on Highway 1, and follow the signs to Harrison Hot Springs.

DINNER: Auberge La Cote d'Azur, 310 Hot Springs Road. (604) 796–8422. Joyce and Eddie Cordes had a restaurant on Robson Street in Vancouver for twenty years before they started serving duck, rabbit, and other French-style foods in Harrison Hot Springs.

LODGING: Harrison Hot Springs Hotel.

DAY 3

Morning

BREAKFAST: Lakeview Restaurant, 150 Esplanade. (604) 796–9888. Great view.

Follow Highway 9 through **Agassiz** and across the Rosedale Bridge to **Minter Gardens,** 52892 Bunker Road, Rosedale. (604) 794–7191. Toll-free in Canada, (800) 661–3919. You will find twenty-seven acres (eleven hectares) of showcase gardens set against the Coast Range at the foot of Mount Cheam. Paved wheelchair-accessible paths wind through eleven themed garden settings that change with the season.

Allow at least an hour, especially during tour-bus season, to salute the flowered flag, photograph the flowered peacock, and say hello to the bush ladies, their skirts covered with flowers grown on moss, who peak out under the trees in their summer hats.

Continue south on Highway 9 across Highway 1 (the Trans-Canada Highway) and follow the signs to **Bridal Veil Falls.** You can picnic in **Bridal Falls Provincial Park,** but you must park and climb fifteen minutes uphill to see the falls tumbling down 7,000-foot-high Mount Cheam.

If you have children in the backseat, they may not let you go past the two kid-popular attractions on Bridal Falls Road: **Dinotown** and the better-known **Trans-Canada Water Slides.**

Join Highway 1, the Trans-Canada Highway, going west. Divert to the commercial services available in **Chilliwack,** the main town of the Fraser Valley, or continue west to exit 73 and turn south a few blocks on 264th Street to another popular family attraction: the **Greater Vancouver Zoological Centre,** 5048 264th Street, Aldergrove. (604) 856–6825. This 119-acre (forty-eight-hectare) game farm takes you on foot and aboard a small red train around large paddocks that are home to rhinoceroses, giraffes, llamas, tigers, and other species.

Continue on Highway 1 to exit 66, and follow signs to the picturesque and historic village of **Fort Langley.**

LUNCH: Lamplighter Gallery Cafe, 9213 Glover Road. (604) 888–6464. Locals fill the tables noon to 1:00 P.M., but after that you can sit inside or out in a cozy setting on the main street of town. Ask about the well-known chicken-and-everything sandwich, known as "The Clucker."

Afternoon

The village is only a few streets wide and a few streets long, so plan to walk the picturesque streets, explore the shops, and visit the historic sites. The Province of British Columbia was born in **Historic Fort Langley,** so start your tour by picking up a walking map at the InfoCentre, which is in the old green-and-white railway station at the corner of Glover and Mavis.

Two blocks down Mavis you'll find the rebuilt fort that was born as a fur-trading post and became famous as the place where Governor James Douglas proclaimed the creation of the Colony of British Columbia.

Watch the short film and walk through the palisaded walls into the old fort, where "fur traders" still live and work every day as part of the fort's living history program. During its many special events, "fur traders" at the **Fort Langley National Historic Site** paddle the old *canoes du nord,* bundle skins for their journey east, and put on social events in the Big House.

This part of British Columbia is known for its horse ranches, so ask about any special events or horseback pleasures available at the moment. For example, **Campbell Valley Regional Park** may be offering Pub Rides: You ride to the pub, tie up for a burger and brew, and ride back.

You can follow Glover Road until it dead-ends a few blocks from town at the ferry terminal. A tiny car ferry crosses the Fraser River to Maple Ridge and the north shore. It carries only a few cars at a time, so prepare to wait during busy periods.

From Fort Langley it is only a forty-five-minute drive back to Vancouver. Consider diverting to **Westminster Quay** in the Royal City of **New Westminster.** Buy fish, fruit, vegetables, and flowers in the market. Follow the river walk. Dine upstairs or down while the boats struggle upriver and coast down. (See Seattle Escape One.)

THERE'S MORE

Golden Ears Provincial Park. Turn north off Highway 7, 2 miles east of Maple Ridge, for a day trip or a one-hour diversion into scenic lake and mountain country.

The **West Coast Express,** a commuter train, runs several times a day between Vancouver and the communities on the north side of the Fraser River to Mission. Call (604) 683–7245 or (604) 689–3641 to speak to a service representative.

SPECIAL EVENTS

May. Dixieland Festival, Chilliwack.

Mid–May. Country Living Festival, Chilliwack.

Early June. Kite Festival, Harrison Hot Springs.

Early July. Mission Pow Wow.

July. Festival of the Arts, Harrison Hot Springs.

Early August. Fur Brigade Days and Fort Festival, Fort Langley National Historic Site, Fort Langley.

September. World Championship Sand Sculpture Competition, a well-known event at Harrison Hot Springs.

September. Agassiz Fall Fair and Corn Festival.

OTHER RECOMMENDED RESTAURANTS AND LODGING

Fort Langley

Marr House, 9090 Glover Road. (604) 888–6455. Highly recommended for its food; a historic house setting. Lunch, dinner. Afternoon tea available 3:00 to 5:00 P.M.

Spill the Beans, 9124 Glover Road. (604) 888–3434. A great little coffeehouse for cappuccino, tea, and fresh-baked goods at small tables on the main street.

Harrison Hot Springs

The Black Forest Restaurant, 180 Esplanade. (604) 796–9343. German specialties in a fine setting inside or on a terrace overlooking Lake Harrison in summer.

Conca D'Oro, 234 Esplanade. (604) 796–2695. Pasta and a terrace view on the lakefront.

Little House on the Lake Bed and Breakfast, 6305 Rockwell Drive. (800) 939–1116. Beautiful contemporary log house on a bluff overlooking Lake Harrison. Deck, hot tub, dock. Five minutes from town.

Old Settler Pub, 222 Cedar Avenue. (604) 796–9722. This is where locals go for a casual dinner and a drink in a comfortable setting.

Quality Inn, 190 Lillooet Avenue. This new establishment, which broke ground in spring 1997, will be a good choice as one of the town's few mid-range business hotels. It's part of Choice Hotels Canada. Call (888) 265–1155 for reservations, or (604) 796–5555 for general hotel information.

Harrison Mills

Fen Lodge Bed and Breakfast, 15500 Morris Valley Road. (604) 796–9798. Former hunting lodge of wealthy pioneer Charles Pretty. Rustic but very interesting lodging in forested setting near Harrison River.

Rowena's Inn on the River, 14282 Morris Valley Road. (604) 796–0234 or (800) 661–5108. An elegant, large home on a sweep of grass between cedar groves and the Harrison River. Large, beautiful guest rooms and public dining room in the house; luxurious cabins nearby.

FOR MORE INFORMATION

British Columbia Travel Information. (800) 663–6000.

Coast and Mountain Tourism. (604) 739–9011 or (800) 667–3306.

Fort Langley Chamber of Commerce, 8790 204th Street, #5, Fort Langely, B.C. V1M 2R4. (604) 888–1477.

Harrison Hot Springs Chamber of Commerce, 499 Hot Springs Road, Harrison Hot Springs, B.C. V0M 1K0. (604) 796–3425.

Maple Ridge InfoCentre, 22238 Lougheed Highway, Maple Ridge, B.C. V2X 2T2. (604) 463–2202.

Mission Regional Chamber of Commerce, 34033 Lougheed Highway, Mission, B.C. V2V 5X8. (604) 826–6914.

Mountain/Canyon Circle

HIGH COUNTRY AND THE GOLD RUSH

2 NIGHTS

Mountain splendor • *Lakes and rivers* • *Gold Rush*
Caribou Road • *Ranches* • *Hell's Gate* • *Fraser Canyon*

There are often more European than Canadian travelers on this circular mountain route, which winds through the high ranch country of the Pemberton Valley and down the mighty Fraser River to the terror of Hell's Canyon.

They come to see glacier-green lakes and roaring rivers amid uninhabited mountain splendor. They come to relive legends about fur traders and gold prospectors and especially the Caribou Trail. They come to raft wild rivers, hike mountain trails, and ride horses into glorious places that have never seen roads.

This escape is for you if you like long stretches of scenic open road between funky little towns, where you bed down in bed-and-breakfast accommodations, roadside motels, or small historic hotels.

DAY 1

Morning

Pack a picnic lunch and follow Highway 99 to Horseshoe Bay and up Howe Sound toward Whistler. Start early and you will have time to stop at the **British Columbia Museum of Mining** at **Britannia Beach, Shannon Falls Provincial Park** near Squamish, and the entrance to **Garibaldi Provincial Park.**

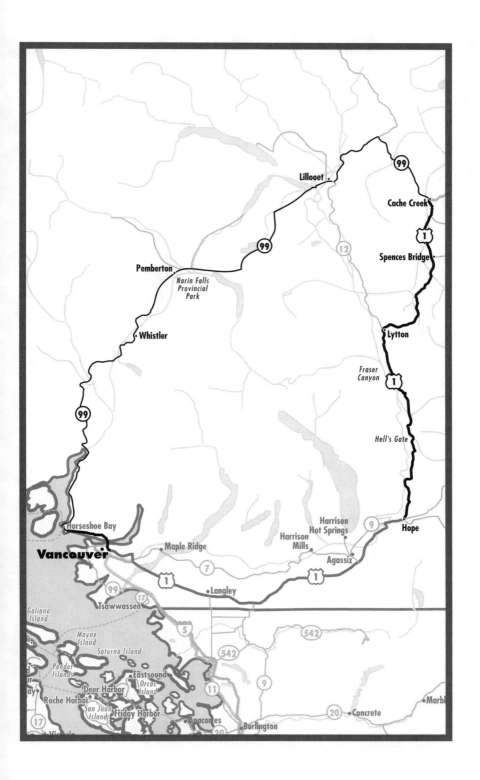

Commercialism ends where our route begins, just beyond Whistler. We leave condominiums behind and drive toward snowcapped mountains silhouetted against a blue sky to the east. Turn into **Nairn Falls Provincial Park.** You will hear the roar of the **Green River** when you open your car door. Follow the path cut like a ledge against the side of a forested hill high above the river, and clamber over smooth rocks to a fenced view of the 196-foot (60-m) falls. About a mile round trip.

LUNCH: Picnic at Nairn Falls Provincial Park.

Afternoon

Highway 99 bursts out of the mountains into the **Pemberton Valley,** a plateau of ranches and farmland where the Lillooet River rushes into Lake Lillooet. The valley is surrounded by tree-covered mountains, stony ridges, and ice-capped peaks. The black rock ridge of Mount Currie rises above **Pemberton Village.**

A path and boardwalk encircle **One–Mile Lake** at the entrance to the village. Turn right at the stop sign and right again into **Pemberton Adventure Ranch,** where Steve and Susan Anderson are waiting to take you for a ride.

Steve will take you jet-boating up to the bottom of Nairn Falls in spring or white-water rafting or kayaking anytime on the Lillooet River or other class 3 waterways. Susan will lead you on horseback down valley or mountain trails. (604) 932–3532.

There are three other Pemberton attractions on this side road: **Big Sky Golf and Country Club,** a community course called **Pemberton Valley Golf and Country Club,** and the terminal building that opened in 1996 at **Pemberton Airport. Prime Air** flies in from the coast.

Turn left out of this airport road into the village of 500 people, and check into your bed-and-breakfast.

You might consider the scenic 20-mile (35-km) drive northeast to **D'Arcy,** at the south end of Anderson Lake, with a side trip to the canoeing and fishing pleasures of Birkenhead Lake; a drive along the Lillooet River to **Meager Creek Hot Springs;** or a trip along a gravel road to the old gold-mining towns of **Bralorne** and **Gold Bridge.** Check road conditions, as some require four-wheel drive.

It is only a five-minute walk from anywhere in Pemberton Village to the heritage log buildings of **Pemberton Museum.**

DINNER: Santa Fe Station, across the road from the museum at 7458 Prospect Street. (604) 894–1500. Southwestern and West Coast food in an attractive light-wood setting.

LODGING: Cedars Bed and Breakfast, 7414 Pioneer Street (604) 938–6468. Don and Monique Boulanger will welcome you into their home at the edge of town, serve a great breakfast, give you touring advice, and lead you personally on mountain biking or hiking trips at your request. (Alternative: Log House Bed and Breakfast Inn; see "There's More.")

DAY 2

Morning

BREAKFAST: Cedars Bed and Breakfast

Cross the Lillooet River to the village of **Mount Currie,** in the Mount Currie Indian Reserve. Stop at the **Spirit Circle,** a cafe and crafts shop that schedules produce and crafts fairs on summer Saturdays. There are no gas stations or other commercial buildings between here and Lillooet.

When you pass the north end of Lake Lillooet, there is nothing to indicate what this historic waterway meant during the gold rush of the 1860s. While the Royal Engineers were chipping their way inch by inch through the Fraser Canyon to provide access to the gold camps in the north, other enterprising explorers found a water passage north from Harrison Lake to Lillooet Lake and on through Anderson and Seton Lakes to Lillooet. Port Pemberton lived briefly where Highway 99 passes Lake Lillooet.

From there, Highway 99 climbs steeply up the mountain. Watch for the B.C. PARKS sign to **Joffre Lake.** Park and walk five minutes down a groomed trail to a tiny jewel of a lake and a full-face view of **Joffre Glacier.**

The highway swings in wide loops uphill and down, with the silver gleam of **Duffy Lake** visible between the mountains ahead. **Duffy Lake Road** was a gravel road used only by the locals and a few intrepid drivers until it was paved in the mid-1990s. It follows the rushing green-and-white waters of **Cayoosh Creek** past gleaming white waterfalls as the treed mountains of the valley give way to drier slopes around Lillooet.

Turn left at the B.C. HYDRO sign, and park in the recreation area above **Seton Lake.** Photograph the glorious green lake spreading away between mountains to the horizon and read the interpretive signs. Steamships carried prospectors north via a chain of lakes from Harrison Lake to the landing spot below on the Harrison-Lillooet Trail. You can turn left to picnic and swim in the kid-friendly shallows at **Second Beach,** or go right to **First Beach,** on Sta'atl'imc Nation land, where the water drops off sharply and boat tours are available from the dock.

Stop at the **spawning channel,** especially during September in odd-numbered years, when the great run of salmon comes upstream. There are three single-lane bridges between Seton Lake and Lillooet. Stop at the second one and watch for mountain goats on the bluff ahead.

Lillooet is where the chain of lakes meets the **Fraser River.** Turn right on Main Street and park where the street turns right again. You are at the Lillooet Infocentre, the **Lillooet Museum,** and the **Mile 0 Cairn.** The Caribou Trail, which led north to places like 100 Mile House, measured all distances from this spot.

Lillooet was the biggest little boomtown in the territory until the lake-and-river route was made obsolete by the Caribou Wagon Road through Fraser Canyon. Main Street is wide enough to turn around a double-freight wagon hauled by ten yoke-spans of oxen; that's what was needed to pull twenty tons over 5,000-foot Pavilion Mountain on the trail ahead.

Pick up a **walking-tour** booklet and see the sights, including the 1890s **Miyazaki Residence** and the nearby **Hanging Tree,** an old ponderosa pine used by Matthew Begbie, the "hanging judge."

LUNCH: Elaine's Coffee Garden, 842 Main, where you can enjoy espresso or tea with sandwiches and baked goods, inside or out.

Afternoon

There are two routes south from here. Highway 12 follows the river 40 miles (64 km) along the Fraser River directly to Lytton. We will stay on Highway 99 and travel just over 100 miles via Cache Creek and Spences Bridge to Lytton. Either way you leave Lillooet across the **Bridge of the 23 Camels,** which commemorates camels brought in during the gold rush and abandoned.

Highway 99 circles north and east from here, passing through **Marble Canyon Park** and past three lakes: **Pavilion, Crown,** and **Turquoise.** Just before reaching Highway 97, which goes north into Caribou country and the gold-mining town of Barkerville, follow the signs to **Hat Creek Ranch,** a privately managed B.C. Parks attraction with an admission fee.

Swimmers and boaters have replaced steamships full of gold prospectors on Seton Lake.

There is still a piece of the **Caribou Wagon Road** in front of the old hotel on the ranch, where passengers and mining supplies stopped on their way to the goldfields. Stop at the Reception Centre, with its gift shop, tearoom, and video.

Teamster Fred Paige will help you aboard the old freight wagon for a tour of the grounds. Walk over to the **Native Interpretive Site,** where a member of the Bonaparte Indian Band will lead you into a kekuli, a circular pit house traditionally used by the Interior Salish.

Take a guided tour of **Hat Creek House,** one of the stagecoach stops on the Caribou Wagon Road between Yale and Barkerville.

It is 7 miles (11 km) south to the town of **Cache Creek.** Rock hounds should check out **Caribou Jade and Gifts,** where owner Ben Roy will tell you how Chinese railway workers recognized the value of British Columbia jade and sent shiploads of it home as "ballast" before North Americans caught on.

This is the junction of Highway 97 and Highway 1 (the Trans-Canada Highway). **Ashcroft Manor and Teahouse** is 6 miles (10 km) south. Kim and Audrey Jenner own the Manor, which was one of the original roadhouses on the Caribou Wagon Road, and now offer panabode "log" cabin accommodations and a teahouse-restaurant.

Follow Highway 1 through dry sagebrush-covered mountains to Spences Bridge, where a toll bridge was built across the **Thompson River** to hasten supplies to the goldfields. In this narrow section of the Thompson Valley, where the river bends briefly east-west, there is just room between two barren mountains for the wide, strong river bracketed on either side by a road, a railroad, and a strip of houses.

DINNER: Steelhead Inn, where Mavourneen and Jack Ryan serve meals outside on a patio or inside at a window overlooking the river.

LODGING: Steelhead Inn, Box 100, Spences Bridge, B.C. V0K 2L0. (604) 458–2398 or (800) 665–7926. There are seven clean, renovated, simple rooms upstairs in the old two-story hotel, which stands on this spot in very early photographs of the area.

DAY 3

Morning

BREAKFAST: Sit at a window at Steelhead Inn's small, popular dining room and watch the action on the river.

The Ryans have been leading class 3 white-water rafting trips down the Thompson to the Fraser River for ten years from a grassy campsite on the river below the hotel. Last year they bought the inn as a logical accompaniment. Rafters often camp overnight on the grassy bank before launching into the strong current of the river.

The Thompson River is 50 to 100 yards wide and beginning to whitewater as you follow it downstream. Campers sit on a ledge of grass beside the river in **Skihist Provincial Park.** It is 23 miles (37 km) downriver to **Lytton,** where the Thompson flows into the mighty Fraser at the north end of **Fraser Canyon.** Native fishers once harvested tons of salmon from this junction of two big rivers. Their trail became the supply trail for the gold rush and is now Highway 12. Several white-water rafting companies begin or end their rafting trips here, prompting the name "Rafting Capital of Canada." The area has also been called the "hot spot of Canada" because of high summer temperatures.

Cross the bridge above the river junction, and take the first left, Ferry Street, downhill to the Fraser River. You can ride the tiny orange-and-white ferry free across the river and back. It is called a "reaction ferry": Two men spin the wheel furiously at take-off to change the direction of underwater paddles that use the power of the river current to move the ferry to the other side. There is no schedule. The ferry moves to pick up whatever automotive or foot passengers are waiting for it.

Join Highway 1 high above the river, and begin your journey south through Fraser Canyon, which runs from Lytton for about 60 miles (100 km) south to Yale. This canyon was the setting for one of the most difficult road-building jobs in the world.

The interior of British Columbia was untouched except for native villages and fur brigades when the 1858 cry of "Gold!" lured 25,000 prospectors into impassable mountains and terrifying canyons on their trek north to the Caribou goldfields.

James Douglas, who had ruled the Hudson's Bay Company from Vancouver Island, brought the uninhabited mainland into what is now British Columbia. He ordered the impossible: Chip a trail, then a mule track, and finally a wagon road into cliffs high above the Fraser River to supply the gold camps. Most of the towns on our route exist today because of the gold rush and the Caribou Trail.

The most difficult part of the canyon is between Boston Bar and Yale. Boston Bar is just a scattering of houses today. Seven miles (11.25 km) south you see a red line above the river far below, which means you are approaching **Hell's Gate.**

Turn right into the parking lot. You can hike down the steep hill, cross the bridge free, and make the steep climb back, but most people pay to ride the **Hell's Gate Airtram.** You can ride one way and hike the other if you like.

The original wagon road is just below the deck where the tram begins its 502-foot (153-m) descent toward the roaring waters. The river is only 110 feet wide here, but the water is 150 feet deep in spring. Two million salmon swim up through the Hell's Gate Fishways every year. See the video, the fishery exhibits, and the gift shop on the landing below. Two river-rafting companies actually bring their motorized rafts through that boil of water (see "There's More").

LUNCH: Salmon House, at the base of the air tram. Try the salmon chowder.

Afternoon

Drive south on Highway 1 a very short distance to the provincial park at **Alexandra Bridge.** The first bridge across the raging river was built here to access the Caribou Road. It was washed away, but you can walk across a second bridge preserved intact within the park.

Highway 1 crosses a newer bridge to **Spuzzum,** two gas stations and a restaurant at the spot where men and mules were once ferried across the river.

When you drive into **Yale** today, you see a small, typical Canadian town, with only a little brown church and a few other historic mementos of the days when fur brigades, gold miners, and settlers made this strategic spot, at the foot of the canyon, the jumping-off place for destinations north. The Caribou Wagon Road began here, as did every attempt to tame the canyon as a transportation route. Visit the **Anglican Church of St. John the Divine,** the oldest church in mainland British Columbia.

It is only a short drive from here—past **Emory Creek Provincial Park,** where prospectors once struck gold on **Emory's Bar**—to **Hope,** where the Fraser turns west toward the Pacific Ocean. Stop for a coffee at the Euro Cafe, 243 Commission Street, and enjoy this small town at the eastern end of the Fraser Valley.

Hope calls itself the "Chainsaw Carving Capitol." You can see the work of wood-carver Jack Ryan in **Memorial Park,** behind the District Hall, where families picnic and play in the block between Park and Wallace streets.

The **Othello Tunnels** are west of town; they were built for the old Kettle Valley Railroad and are now part of a scenic walking tour. You can park and walk half an hour or do the full circle, which has steep parts, in an hour. Carry a flashlight for the tunnels.

It is almost 100 miles (150 km) back to Vancouver; the trip takes less than two hours along the Trans-Canada Highway, Highway 1. The gold miners came up the Fraser River, through this lush valley, to the end of navigation at Yale. Imagine the relief of settlers who later came downstream out of Fraser Canyon into this wide green valley, with mountains rising on either side only as scenery.

THERE'S MORE

Fishing. Fraser River Sturgeon Charters, Box 739, Lillooet. (250) 256–7355. Half-day, full-day, or overnight charters, May through September. Also Fraser River boat tours, Lillooet to Bridge River Junction.

Gliding. Pemberton Soaring Centre, Box 725, Pemberton. (604) 894–6656 or (800) 831–2611. The Pembertown Valley, surrounded by mountains, creates thermals that are excellent for gliding.

Rafting. Kumsheen Raft Adventures, 281 Main Street, Lytton. (250) 455–2296 or (800) 663–6667. Offers half-day to three-day rafting trips on the Thompson and Fraser rivers, combined with climbing and mountain-biking tours on request. Motorized raft tours through Hell's Gate.

Fraser Rafting Expeditions, a kilometer south of Yale on Highway 1, offers paddling and motorized tours on the Fraser (including Hell's Gate), the Thompson, and other places. Also eight-day float trips, and half-hour and one-hour Zodiac (a twelve-person, rigid-hull rubber craft) rides. (604) 863–2336 or (800) 363–7238.

Ryan's Rapid Rafting, Box 129, Spences Bridge. (250) 458–2479 or (800) 665–RYAN. Launches inflatable rafts into the Thompson River in front of the Steelhead Inn and rides the white water to the junction of the Fraser River at Lytton. The company also rafts and floats the Nicola.

Train. B.C. Rail runs daily from Vancouver through Pemberton and Lillooet and on north. You can ride from Pemberton to Lillooet, stay a few hours, and ride back. Reservations suggested. (604) 984–5246 or (800) 663–8238.

SPECIAL EVENTS

Late May. Lytton Days.

Late June. Canada Week Festival, Pemberton. Marching bands, classic cars, and wagon parades.

Early November. Remembrance Day Pow Wow, Lytton. A festival of dance and music to recognize Native Canadians who fought in the Canadian armed forces.

OTHER RECOMMENDED RESTAURANTS AND LODGING

Lytton

Totem Motel, 320 Fraser Street, Box 580, Lytton. (250) 455–2321. E-mail: vdbos @wkpowerlink.com. Nicely decorated rooms in an old two-story house or in red-and-white cabins, with kitchens, overlooking the Fraser River.

Pemberton

Log House Bed and Breakfast Inn, 1357 Elmwood. (800) 894–6002. Margaret and Bill Scott have six rooms opening onto a balcony overlooking a spacious sitting room. Approved by Tourism British Columbia. Listed in several Northwest guidebooks.

FOR MORE INFORMATION

British Columbia Travel Information. (800) 663–6000.

Coast and Mountain Tourism Association, 205-1755 West Broadway, Vancouver, B.C. V6J 4S5. (604) 739–9011 or (800) 667–3306.

Gold Country, 301 Brink Street, P.O. Box 1239, Ashcroft, B.C. V0R 1H0. (250) 453–9467. E-mail: Gold@Goldcountry.bc.ca.

Lillooet Chamber of Commerce, 930 Main Street, P.O. Box 650, Lillooet, B.C. V0K 1Z0. (250) 256–4364.

Lytton and District Chamber of Commerce, 400 Fraser Street, Box 460, Dept. RC3, Lytton, B.C. V0K 1Z0. (250) 455–2523.

Vancouver Island: West Shore
THE WILD PACIFIC COAST

2 NIGHTS

Spectacular waterfalls • Pristine wilderness
Ancient forests • Native art
Whale watching • Beaches • Boat rides • Scenic hikes

The western coast of Vancouver Island holds some of the world's most dramatic wilderness scenery. In this temperate, wet climate, where rainfall is 160 inches a year, vegetation grows in lush profusion; dense jungles of ferns, mosses, and shrubbery grow under the tall evergreen trees. This is logging country, but some of the wilderness is almost untouched, allowing visitors to gain a sense of the primeval forests that once covered the entire island.

An abundance of water makes for lush, verdant growth, and Vancouver Island has plenty of both. The coast is fringed with fjordlike inlets, bays, and coves, while dozens of lakes and rivers are scattered throughout the inland regions. It's a recreational wonderland, waiting to be explored.

DAY 1

Morning

Pack a picnic lunch and take the ferry from Horseshoe Bay west on its two-hour run across the Georgia Strait to Nanaimo, on **Vancouver Island.** Drive north 21 miles (35 km) on Route 19 to Parksville.

When you reach the Route 4 junction, turn west and travel 3 miles (5 km) to Errington Road. Head south to **Errington,** a small farming community;

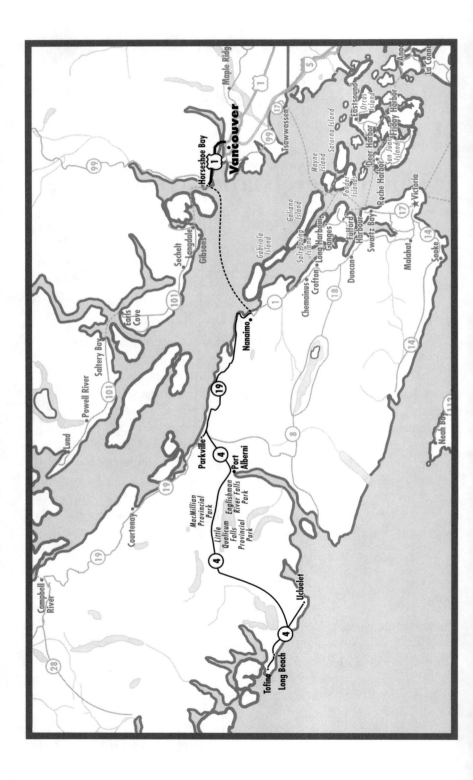

you'll pass the general store, a log complex with a cafe, post office, laundromat, and video store. Across the street is the **Farmers' Market.** Stop here for fresh fruits and produce in season.

From the highway it's 5 miles (8 km) to **Englishman River Falls Provincial Park.** The road travels through rolling rural countryside dotted with horse ranches and enormous old barns before entering the cool, dense forest of the park.

Tall cedars, firs, and hemlocks form green canopies over fern-filled hollows and mossy boulders in this scenic retreat. Walk the easy trail to **Englishman Falls,** a roaring torrent of water that pours into a narrow chasm between two wide rock ledges. The park contains picnic tables, a shelter, fireplaces, firewood, drinking water, and campsites.

LUNCH: Picnic at Englishman River Falls.

Afternoon

Continue west on Highway 4, with a possible stop at the gift and craft shops in Coombs, to **MacMillan Provincial Park** and **Cathedral Grove.** In this awe-inspiring ancient forest, giant hemlock trees and Douglas firs stand in silent, shadowed splendor. Some of the oldest trees in British Columbia, they've been living for up to 800 years. Trails wind through the virgin grove, crossing weathered wooden bridges and logs with chinked steps. Interpretive signs explain the trees' long cycle of growth and decay.

Continue to **Port Alberni,** a logging community at the tip of a long fjord. The port is named after a Spanish explorer, Don Pedro Alberni, whose expedition came to the West Coast in 1791. The area's first sawmill was built here in 1860; now the MacMillan-Bloedel Company maintains a large complex that includes two sawmills and a pulp-and-paper mill.

Fishing is another significant industry, with 320 commercial vessels operating from Port Alberni's harbor. Recreational fishers are lured to the area during the peak salmon runs of August and September. The famous *M. V. Lady Rose,* a stout packet freighter and passenger ferry, leaves from the Harbour Quay, steaming down the scenic fjord to the **Broken Group Islands** and the coast, 30 miles (48 km) west Monday, Wednesday, and Friday. It cruises to Ucluelet, a picturesque fishing village, on Tuesday, Thursday, and Saturday. Both are day-long trips leaving early in the morning.

From Port Alberni, Highway 4 winds along the Taylor and Kennedy rivers, passing thickly forested ridges and logged-off slopes, on its way to the ocean shore. **Pacific Rim National Park,** established in 1970, borders this untamed coast, stretching along the shoreline from **Tofino** to Port Renfrew. The park has three divisions: the rugged **West Coast Trail** to the south; Broken Group Islands, one hundred picturesque islands dotting Barkley Sound; and **Long Beach,** a 7-mile (12-km) stretch of surf-washed sand and rocky headlands north of Ucluelet.

At Long Beach, 2 miles (3½ km) off Route 4, is **Wickaninnish Centre,** just above the beach. Tour the center to learn about marine life and wave action, enter a replica of the *Explorer 10* submersible, see a native whaling canoe, and watch a presentation on humpback whales. The inn that adjoins the interpretive center serves excellent food and has a panoramic view of the ocean and the long sweep of beach directly below. This is a good spot for a coffee break.

After a brisk walk in the briny air of Long Beach, return to the highway and drive on to the **Shorepine Bog Trail.** A boardwalk trail rests upon the surface of this fascinating, soggy forest of stunted trees and sphagnum moss. Pick up a pamphlet from the box at the trail entrance for an explanation of the delicate, colorful ecosystem.

Continue on Highway 4 to check in at **Pacific Sands Beach Resort.**

Drive 4 miles (7 km) more to Tofino for a stroll around town before dinner. Surrounded on three sides by water, this quaint village at the end of the road has unparalleled views of **Clayoquot Sound,** the moody ocean, and the thick forests of fir, pine, cedar, and hemlock that rise from the shore.

Cafes, shops, and galleries line the main street, quiet in the off-season and jammed in summer. The population of 1,000 swells when visitors flock to the cool coast for recreation and natural beauty.

DINNER: The Blue Heron, at Weigh West Marine Resort, 634 Campbell Street, Tofino. (250) 725–3277. Attractive restaurant above a busy marina; views of Clayoquot Sound and Strawberry Island. Steak, chicken, and seafood; the fresh crab is best.

LODGING: Pacific Sands Beach Resort, P.O. Box 237, Tofino, B.C. V0R 2Z0. (250) 725–3322 or (800) 565–BEACH from 9:00 A.M. to 8:00 P.M. Sixty-five ocean-facing rooms on lovely Cox Bay. Lodge rooms, housekeeping units, cabins. Spacious and clean, with balconies and some fireplaces.

Long Beach, on Vancouver Island's west shore, is part of Pacific Rim National Park.

DAY 2

Morning

BREAKFAST: If you are lodging in a housekeeping unit, you can prepare your own morning repast; or drive into Tofino and enjoy a healthful breakfast at **Common Loaf Bake Shop** on First Street. (250) 725–3915. The cozy, off-beat cafe serves good home-baked breads and pastries and will stoke you up for the morning's adventure.

After breakfast, go to **Meare's Landing,** 71 Wharf Street (beside the Coast Guard dock) for your whale-watching trip. Phone (250) 725–3330 or toll-free, from B.C., (800) 666–9833. (Cost of tour: $35 per adult. Trip available March through October only.) **Remote Passages** will supply you with boots, a hat, and a full-length, waterproof flotation outfit. At a nearby wharf, you'll board a 24-foot Zodiac (a twelve-person, rigid-hull rubber craft) and ride twenty-five minutes to the feeding grounds of the gray whales.

An experienced skipper will provide commentary on the sights, as well as a safe, exhilarating journey through flying, salty spray. High mountains and glaciers are the backdrop as the zippy Zodiac winds through Clayoquot Sound, passing native villages, sea lion rookeries, and a reserve where tufted puffins reside. Seals, otters, and occasionally orca whales may be seen.

On a two-and-a-half-hour expedition, you'll watch the 50-foot grays spout and dive, and maybe, if you're lucky, see one of these magnificent, gentle mammals breach or "spy-hop."

On the return trip, your skipper may run the boat past **Strawberry Island** for a close view of **Weeping Cedar Woman,** a figure carved in 1984 as a protest against logging the virgin forests of **Meares Island.** This issue is still unresolved; Tofino residents are fighting to preserve some of the last of the old-growth forests.

An interesting feature on little Strawberry is the ferry that perches on dry land like a wide brown ark. The boat was used as transportation in Vancouver before the Lion's Gate Bridge was constructed over Burrard Inlet. Now it's a private home.

On land again, return your borrowed gear and cross the street to **The Loft.**

LUNCH: The Loft, Campbell and Second Streets. (250) 725–4241. Pleasant, low-key restaurant frequented by locals and visitors alike. Praiseworthy sandwiches, salads, fish-and-chips, hamburgers.

Afternoon

One of Tofino's greatest attractions is its collection of art galleries showing native works. Not to be missed is the **Eagle Aerie Gallery,** where Roy Vickers's paintings and books are strikingly displayed.

House of Himwitsa, 300 Main Street, sells limited-edition prints, silver jewelry, weavings, carvings, and pottery.

Stop in at **Alley Way Cafe** for a cup of tea or coffee and a rich, sweet pastry.

Buy a batch of fresh crab at **The Crab Bar** and a bottle of white wine and return to Pacific Sands Resort. Spend the rest of the afternoon relaxing on the beach at Cox Bay or exploring the long stretches of driftwood-covered sand beaches for which this coast is famous, especially **Combers Beach** and Long Beach. Photograph the great view from the top of **Radar Hill.** The best places to spot whales from land are in Grice Bay, where whales sometimes move in for the summer, or from the beach at Florencia Bay at the south end of the park.

DINNER: Picnic on the Cox Bay beach or on your balcony as you watch the sunset.

LODGING: Pacific Sands Beach Resort.

DAY 3

Morning

BREAKFAST: Prepare your own, or breakfast at The Blue Heron, Weigh West Marina.

This is a good day to stroll on the beach, take a hike in the rain forest, or go bird-watching. Some 250 species of birds live in the area. You're likely to see blue herons, bald eagles, osprey, cormorants, tufted puffins, and swans, plus several varieties of gulls. You might ask if a trip to Meares Island is available.

Meares is a place of legends and ancient tradition. Rootlets from the towering spruce were once used by the Clayoquot Indians to make stout ropes, the yew made harpoon shafts, and cedar was the material of daily goods: clothing, utensils, homes, baskets. Salal berries and herbs were gathered for food and medicinal uses.

Drive south to the village of Ucluelet and the lighthouse that sits on a headland where the road ends. Walk the wooden boardwalk just south of the lighthouse at He Tin Kush Park. Return to walk the picturesque streets of the village, which looks across a scenic inlet to the mountains.

LUNCH: Eagle's Nest Pub, foot of Bay Street on the waterfront. (250) 726–7570. Marine pub and RV site. Good lunches, pub food. Open daily.

Afternoon

Drive north back to Route 4. Follow the road as it turns east. You'll pass the steep slopes of the heavily logged MacKenzie Range on your way back toward Port Alberni and the island's east coast. Nearing **Parksville,** stop at **Little Qualicum Falls,** where white cascades foam into the rushing green **Little Qualicum River.** Woodsy trails wind through the park, leading to overlooks.

About a ½ mile (1 km) west of Coombs is **Butterfly World.** (250) 248–7026. In this unusual, tropical greenhouse garden a thousand butterflies live and fly freely. It's a unique opportunity to photograph exotic species and see the colorful creatures at close hand. Wheelchair accessible, Butterfly World is open from 10:00 A.M. to 6:00 P.M., April through October.

Coombs is known for its **Old Country Market.** The picturesque landmark has a turf roof; many a visitor has halted in surprise at the sight of goats
placidly walking on the roof and nibbling the grass.

At Parksville, turn south on Route 19.

DINNER: The Mahle House, Cedar and Heemer Roads, Nanaimo. (250)
722–3621. Web site address: www.island.net/~mahle. (Closed Monday and
Tuesday.) Country-home-turned-restaurant, serving excellent Northwest cuisine. Fresh seafood and produce, pastas, homemade desserts, daily specials.

From Nanaimo, catch the ferry east to Horseshoe Bay and Vancouver.

THERE'S MORE

Amphitrite Point, Ucluelet. Rhododendrons, ferns, and coastal pines grow
profusely near paved paths leading to the coast guard station and lighthouse. Watch the surf crash against jagged rocks.

Diving. Barkley Sound's clear, quiet waters make it a popular divers' destination. It has rich marine life, reefs, and 200-year-old shipwrecks to explore.

Fishing. Weigh West Marine Resort, Tofino. (250) 725–3277. Boat rentals,
guided charters at marina.

Canadian Princess Resort, Ucluelet. (250) 726–7771. Fishing and sight-
seeing charters.

Golf. Long Beach Golf Course, Tofino. (250) 725–3332. Nine-hole scenic
course, narrow and challenging.

He Tin Kush Park, Ucluelet. A fifteen-minute hike on the boardwalk takes
you to the beach or up to a viewing point above the sea. Secluded coves,
tide pools.

Hot Springs Cove. A natural geothermal hot springs lies in a sheltered inlet
north of Tofino, inaccessible by road. Its steaming pools, sea caves, and
abundant marine life and wildlife make it an appealing side trip. (Bring
sneakers; there are sharp rocks.)

Kayaking. Tofino Sea Kayaking Company, 320 Main Street, P.O. Box 620,
Tofino, B.C. V0R 2Z0. (250) 725–4222 or (800) TOFINO–4. Kayak rentals
and guided trips around Clayoquot Sound offer some of the best sea kayaking in the Pacific Northwest. In the same building, you can browse in a

well-stocked retail store filled with kayaking supplies. A large bookstore offers more plesant distraction, and the adjoining The Paddlers Inn provides overnight accomodations to individuals and groups.

M. V. Lady Rose. Passenger and cargo freighter makes daily runs from Port Alberni to Broken Group Islands and Ucluelet. Riders return by boat or bus from Ucluelet. (250) 723–8313.

West Coast Trail. This notoriously rugged wilderness trail, 48 miles (78 km) long, was originally built as a lifesaving trail for shipwreck survivors. It comprises one of three sections of Pacific Rim National Park and lies between Bamfield and Port Renfrew, south of Barkley Sound.

SPECIAL EVENTS

March through May. Pacific Rim Whale Festival, Tofino and Ucluelet. Films, displays, exhibits, whale-watching excursions, and hikes.

July. Pacific Rim Summer Festival, Tofino and Ucluelet. Chamber music, multicultural concerts.

Late July. Ukee Daze, Ucluelet. Fishing derby, arts-and-crafts displays, music, dances, crab and salmon feeds.

Early September. Salmon Derby, Port Alberni. Fishing competition with cash prizes up to $20,000. Other events: children's bullhead derby, horse rides, bed race, entertainment, boat raffle, fireworks, salmon barbecue.

OTHER RECOMMENDED RESTAURANTS AND LODGINGS

Tofino

Ocean Village Beach Resort, Box 490, Helleson Drive. (250) 725–3755. Two-story duplex chalets with kitchens, on the beach 2 miles south of town.

Ucluelet

Canadian Princess Resort, P.O. Box 939. (250) 726–7771 or (800) 663–7090. Moored survey ship with lodgings and nautical restaurant and lounge. Small berths on board, larger units in modern hotel section on shore. Open March through September.

Little Beach Resort, Box 376. (250) 726–4202. White, 1930s-style duplex cottages overlooking a small, protected cove where newer accommodations have been built. Good view, moderate prices, great for families.

Matterson Tea House, 1682 Peninsula Road. (250) 726–2200. Historic house, fresh bread, good lunch or dinner.

Wickaninnish Inn, in Wickaninnish Centre, Osprey Lane at Chesterman Beach, P.O. Box 250, Tofino, B.C. V0R 2Z0. (250) 725–3100 or (800) 333–4604. Web site address: www.wickinn.com. Seaside location, admirable food. Tender, crisply battered fish-and-chips; savory salad with raspberry vinaigrette and lightly smoked salmon.

FOR MORE INFORMATION

Alberni Valley Chamber of Commerce, Highway 4, RR 2, Site 214, Port Alberni, B.C. V9Y 7L6. (250) 724–6535.

BC Ferries, 1112 Fort Street, Victoria, B.C. V8V 4V2. Vancouver (888) 223–3779, Victoria (250) 386–3431.

British Columbia Travel Information. (800) 663–6000.

Pacific Rim National Park, Box 280, Ucluelet, B.C. V0R 3A0. (250) 726–4212 mid-March to October; year-round (250) 726–7721.

Tofino Chamber of Commerce, Box 249, Tofino, B.C. V0R 2Z0. (250) 725–3414.

Ucluelet Tourist Information, P.O. Box 428, Ucluelet, B.C. V0R 3A0. (250) 726–4641.

South Vancouver Island

HIGH TEA AND HIGH SEAS

1 OR 2 NIGHTS

Ferry rides • Scenic water views • World-renowned museums
Provincial capital • Antiques shopping • Native crafts
Heritage sites • Beaches • Fine cuisine

The southern end of Vancouver Island is rich with contrast and beauty. It has pastoral farmlands and rugged wilderness, clear streams and ocean whitecaps, quiet villages and a city known for its shopping and dining. This itinerary will give you a taste of them all, as you curve from east to west, sampling some of the best a lovely land has to offer.

DAY 1

Morning

Board the ferry at Tsawassen, crossing the **Strait of Georgia** to **Swartz Bay,** on Vancouver Island. The scenic ride across the strait's blue waters takes about ninety minutes.

From here it's 13 miles (21 km) south to **Victoria,** the province's capital city, where British traditions and Canadian breeziness meet on the Pacific shore.

If you've never visited Victoria, start with a stroll around the lively **Inner Harbour** to soak in the atmosphere. Sailboats bob on the water, and ferries nose against the wharves; bagpipers play on the corners under hanging baskets of flowers, while tourists climb into double-decker buses. The venerable **Empress Hotel,** the **Parliament Buildings,** the wax museum, the undersea

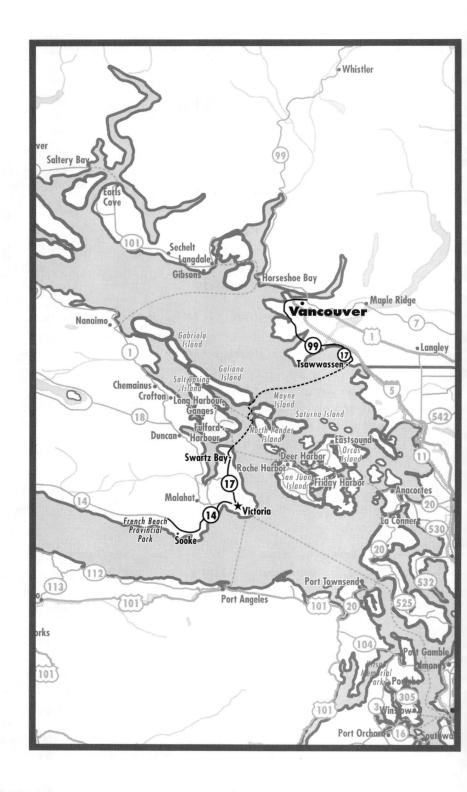

garden, and the **Royal British Columbia Museum** cluster around these harbor streets. The atmosphere is festive.

LUNCH: Early tea (12:30) at the Empress Hotel, 721 Government Street. (250) 384–8111; reservations recommended. Sandwiches, tea, and scones in a historic landmark. The grand old ivy-covered hotel, facing the harbor, has been renovated with style. If you want a heartier lunch in the Victorian mode, try the curry special in the Empress Bengal Lounge.

Afternoon

Cross the street to one of the world's great museums, the Royal British Columbia Museum, which has undergone a major renovation. It traces Vancouver Island's story from the Ice Age to the present day. Indian totems and masks, the lives of early trappers and settlers, explorers' ships, homes of the early twentieth century—all these and more are brilliantly presented to allow visitors a sense of participation.

Outside, totem poles are grouped in **Thunderbird Park,** eloquent reminders of a rich past and a living form of expression.

Poking about in the intriguing shops is a must for visitors to downtown Victoria. You'll find dozens of antiques shops and specialty stores selling woolens, tweeds, china, and chocolates. In **Bastion Square** you'll see how the city began. James Douglas, a British explorer, established a Hudson's Bay Company fort on this site in 1843. The complex of nineteenth-century buildings now houses restaurants, shops, art galleries, and the **Maritime Museum of British Columbia,** which has an outstanding collection of marine artifacts.

Check **Eaton's Department Store** for the best finds in inexpensive souvenirs of good quality.

Drive about ½ mile from downtown to **Craigdorrach Castle** on Joan Crescent off Fort Street. The baronial stone manor, built by a coal magnate in 1887, is open for tours. Lavishly furnished, the thirty-nine-room home exemplifies Victorian opulence.

Travel east to **Oak Bay,** a bayside district of gracious homes and well-kept gardens, and check in at your hotel.

Sealand of the Pacific is nearby, on Marine Drive (250–598–3373). Canada's largest oceanarium, Sealand offers a close look at Pacific Northwest marine life. Watch orca whales and sea lions perform, and see octopus grottoes and wolf-eel dens in underwater galleries. (Open daily.)

Back at the **Oak Bay Beach Hotel,** enjoy a pint of ale in the Snug. Weather permitting, take a table on the terrace and enjoy the view.

DINNER: Bentley's on the Bay, Oak Bay Beach Hotel, Victoria. (250) 598–1134. West Coast cuisine with a view of the bay.

LODGING: Oak Bay Beach Hotel, 1175 Beach Drive, Victoria, B.C. V8S 2N2. (250) 598–4556. Tudor-style, very British in tone, overlooking Oak Bay. Colorful gardens slope to the sea.

DAY 2

Morning

BREAKFAST: The Demitasse, 1320 Blanshard Street, Victoria. (250) 386–4442. This tiny cafe serves commendable croissants with scrambled eggs and coffee.

Cross the **Johnson Street Bridge** to **Esquimault.** On Lampson Street you'll find a bit of England that predates the Victorian era by 400 years. Cyril Lane, owner of the **Olde England Inn,** has painstakingly built a replica of **Anne Hathaway's Cottage,** a reproduction of William Shakespeare's wife's home and an authentic example of a sixteenth-century residence. The guided tours are well informed and interesting.

From here, join Route 1A (Island Highway) traveling west to Ocean Boulevard. Follow the signs to **Fort Rodd Hill National Historic Park.** On its peaceful, grassy grounds are bunkers and gun batteries erected between 1878 and 1956.

Cross the Causeway to tour **Fisgard Lighthouse,** the first lighthouse on Canada's west coast. It has been restored to its 1859 condition. Looking east from the lighthouse, your view is of the Victoria skyline across Esquimault Harbour.

Continue on Route 1A to **Mill Hill Park** in Langford for a short walk to the summit observation point or a hike in **Galloping Goose Regional Park**. The park, opened in 1988, follows an old railbed for 26 miles (42 km).

Take Route 14 west, and when you reach **Sooke** (46 miles, or 60 km, from Victoria), stop at the **Sooke Region Museum.** It's a treasure of a find, with handsome displays of pioneer and native artifacts. On the property is a pioneer homestead that shows how life was lived here a century ago.

Sooke, the home of Salish Indians for centuries, has a comparatively mild climate and bountiful supplies of fish, fowl, berries, and produce.

If this is a one-night trip, turn back on Route 14 toward Victoria. Join Route 17 for the drive north to Swarz Bay; from there a ferry will take you back to the Tsawassen terminal near Vancouver.

If you are continuing your travels, drive to **Sooke Harbour.** Board a charter boat that will take you out to sea for some of the best salmon fishing on the coast. (Whale-watching cruises are available, too, March through October.) As you sail past the rugged cliffs and green forests of the island and head for deeper waters, you may see bald eagles, whales, and sea lions.

For a fishing cruise, contact **Sooke Charter Boat Association,** 8760 West Coast Road, Sooke, B.C. V0S 1N0. (250) 642–7783. Tackle and bait are supplied. Boats are 17 to 30 feet long.

Afternoon

DINNER: Sooke Harbour House. (250) 386–1244. One of the finest restaurants in British Columbia, with innovative cuisine featuring local fresh seafood (probably caught that morning by the owner). Herbs, vegetables, and edible flowers are grown in gardens on the premises. Incomparable setting and atmosphere.

LODGING: Sooke Harbour House, 1528 Whiffen Spit Road, Sooke, B.C. V0S 1N0. (250) 642–3421. Exquisite inn on two waterfront acres. Beautifully furnished rooms with views of well-tended gardens and the sea.

DAY 3

Morning

BREAKFAST: Sooke Harbour House. Breakfast included in room rate.

From the inn, drive northwest on Route 14 to surf-washed shores. Waves toss high, and spindrift streams in the wind on blustery days. The coast has seen storms so wild, and has had so many shipwrecks, that sailors call it the graveyard of the Pacific. On mild days, however, the coast is benign, and you may see divers and surfers catching the waves.

A majestic rain forest grows in green splendor on the east. In this forest stand the largest Douglas fir tree, 41 feet (13 m) around, and the tallest Sitka spruce, 310 feet (95 m), in Canada. Environmental controversy rages around the spruce and its tall companions.

Stop at **French Beach Provincial Park** to watch for birds and orca and gray whales.

Ten miles (16 km) past **Point No Point,** a fifteen-minute walk through the forest will lead you to **China Beach,** a lovely, protected cove of white sand. You might see black bears in this park.

Another pretty spot on the coast is **Sandcut Beach.** A short trail provides access to the beach, which has small waterfalls and sandstone formations.

Revel in the expansive ocean views; then head back toward Sooke.

LUNCH: Included in your room rate at Sooke Harbour House.

Afternoon

Stroll through the inn's gardens, with their forty varieties of geraniums and 300 types of herbs; then hike out **Whiffen Spit** for a last view of the far southwest corner of Canada and the Strait of Juan de Fuca.

Take Route 14 to Victoria and Route 17 north to Swartz Bay and the Tsawassen ferry.

THERE'S MORE

Afternoon tea. You'll find Victoria's best afternoon teas at the Empress Hotel, Blethering Place, and Oak Bay Beach Hotel.

Golf. The Greater Victoria area has numerous eighteen-hole golf courses, most of them open all year. A sampling of public courses:

Cedar Hill Municipal Golf Course, 1400 Derby Road. (250) 595–2823.

Cordova Bay Golf Course, 5333 Cordova Bay Road. (250) 658–4444.

Olympic View Golf Course, 643 Latoria Road. (250) 474–3671.

Sooke Potholes Provincial Park, Sooke. Off Sooke River Road, a forested park with waterfalls, hiking trails, swimming in river.

West Coast Trail. This rugged wilderness path, originally constructed to assist shipwrecked sailors, begins at Port Renfrew, 50 miles (80 km) west of Sooke. Hikers take a water taxi across the inlet to the southern end of the trail, which extends 48 miles (78 km) north. It's part of Pacific Rim National Park and has been overcrowded, so you must reserve. (250) 726–4212 mid-March to October; (250) 726–7721 year-round.

SPECIAL EVENTS

May. Swiftsure Yacht Race, Victoria. World-class regatta.

Late May. Victoria Day, huge parade, teacup races, and the launch of the Victoria Exhibition on the birthday of city's namesake, Queen Victoria.

June. Oak Bay Tea Party, Victoria.

Third Saturday of July. All Sooke Day, Sooke. Grilled salmon, barbecued beef feast, loggers' sports.

OTHER RECOMMENDED RESTAURANTS AND LODGINGS

Sooke

Margison House, 6605 Sooke Road. (250) 642–3620. Bed-and-breakfast with one room and one cottage in a charming home with sea and garden views. Full breakfast.

Point-No-Point Resort, R.R. 2, West Coast Road. (250) 646–2020. Rustic cabins in an expensive, spectacular cliff-top setting in the woods, above the island's western shore.

Victoria

Clarion Hotel Grand Pacific, 450 Quebec Street. (250) 386–0450 or (800) 663–7550. Luxury hotel in the center of Victoria. Swimming pool, athletic club, attractive restaurant, 149 rooms and suites.

Dashwood Manor, 1 Cook Street. (250) 385–5517. Bed-and-breakfast mansion near Beacon Hill Park, overlooking the water. Suites have fireplaces and kitchens.

The Empress Hotel, 721 Government Street. (250) 384–8111. Grand old ivy-covered hotel, renovated, with stylish and comfortable rooms. A major tourist attraction, facing Inner Harbour.

Olde England Inn, 429 Lampson Street. (250) 388–4353. Antiques-furnished rooms and restaurant in British manor house and village. Colorful gardens.

Paprika Bistro, 252 Estevan Avenue. (250) 592–7424. Small Hungarian restaurant serving perfectly prepared classic dishes with a few innovations.

Pounder's Restaurant, 535 Yates Street. (250) 388–3181. Mongolian stir-fry. Select items ranging from prawns and vegetables to rattlesnakes, and pay by the pound.

ReBar, 50 Bastion Square. (250) 361–9223. Affordable vegetarian food; a local favorite. The ReBar serves "Grass," a pureed green grass beverage.

Swans, 506 Pandora Avenue. (250) 361–3310. Charming hotel and pub in one of Victoria's oldest buildings, beautifully restored. Rooms are former condos with kitchens.

The Victoria Regent Hotel, 1234 Wharf Street. (250) 386–2211 or (800) 663–7472. Downtown waterfront hotel with suites, kitchens, fireplaces, balconies.

FOR MORE INFORMATION

BC Ferries, 1112 Fort Street, Victoria, B.C. V8V 4V2. Vancouver. (250) 669–1211, Victoria (250) 386–3431.

British Columbia Travel Information. (800) 663–6000.

Tourism Association of Vancouver Island, Suite 302, 45 Bastion Square, Victoria, B.C. V8W 1J1. (250) 382–3551.

Tourism Victoria, 812 Wharf Street, Victoria, B.C. V8W 1T3. Information, (250) 953–2033; reservations, (800) 663–3883.

West Shore Chamber of Commerce, 697 Goldstream Avenue, Victoria, B.C. V9B 2X2. (250) 478–1130.

The Gulf Islands

ISLAND HOPPING

IN THE GEORGIA STRAIT

3 NIGHTS

*Picturesque landscapes • Ocean views • Mild climate • Wildlife
Whale watching • Tranquil setting • Evergreen forests
Hiking trails • Secluded beaches • Fine dining*

Between British Columbia's mainland and Vancouver Island lies the Strait of Georgia, its waters sprinkled with lumpy green hummocks called the Gulf Islands. Some are tiny and uninhabited, but several are populated year-round and draw tourists for the outdoor recreation, natural beauty, and pebble-strewn beaches.

This itinerary will introduce you to three islands: Galiano, North and South Pender, and Mayne. Each has a distinct character and much to offer the curious traveler.

(The largest and most densely populated island, Salt Spring, is described in Vancouver Escape Seven.)

A note about riding the ferries: You can reserve space on Canadian ferries from Tsawwassen to the Gulf Islands and back, and it will be held for you until thirty minutes before departure. This is a boon to line-weary travelers, especially on busy summer weekends when long waits are common. Fares to Gulf Islands are the same as to Victoria, while traveling interisland costs much less.

There are many routes and schedules you can follow in touring the islands. This itinerary is just one example, designed for a Friday-through-Monday

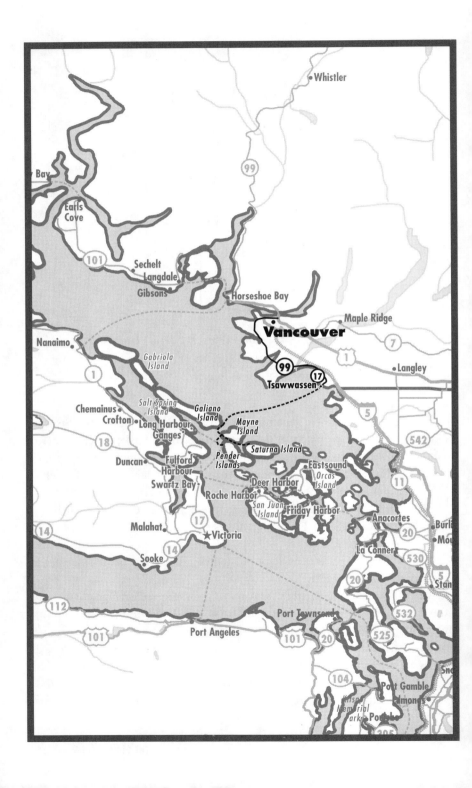

getaway and based on current ferry schedules for those days. Those schedules may change without notice; be sure to consult an up-to-date one.

DAY 1

Morning

From the Tsawassen docks, south of Vancouver off Route 17, board the ferry to the **Pender Islands.** With a mighty blast of its whistle, the great white behemoth will ease into the channel and plow its way past densely forested islands. Seabirds wheel and call, clouds scud across the sky, and your tensions begin to slip away.

After a stop at **Mayne Island,** the ferry continues to **North Pender,** arriving at **Otter Bay.** North and South Pender are divided by a channel and connected by a narrow bridge. A rock isthmus once joined them, but it was blasted out in 1903 to allow boats through. The little bridge was built in 1950.

While housing development has increased rapidly in recent years, the Penders have retained much of their wild charm. There are several coves, lakes, and parks where you can enjoy the natural surroundings, and country roads that are fine for bicycling.

From Otter Bay, head south on Otter Bay and Bedwell Harbour roads toward **Port Browning.** The sheltered harbor bustles with action in summer, as boats enter and depart the marina. Walk the rocky beach here, watch the sailboats, and bask in the islanders' friendly welcome at the pub.

LUNCH: Port Browning Cafe or **Pub** on the east coast of North Pender, off Hamilton Road. (250) 629–3493. The pub is known for its English-style fish-and-chips and native decor; the masks and totems are part of a private collection. You can eat on the deck overlooking the marina. The cafe on a shaded slope around the corner also offers outdoor tables.

Afternoon

Heading south, take Canal Road and cross the bridge to **South Pender.** Take Canal Road and Spalding to Gowlland Point Road, and proceed to the end. From the unmarked beach here, you have a good chance of observing orca whales. Perch on the boulders and watch the water's surface for spouts and the distinctive flukes of the great black-and-white mammals. You may see them swimming in pods of fifteen or so, an awesome sight. Another good whale-watching site is from the cove at the end of Higgs Road, also off Gowlland Point Road. You'll hear the steady moan of offshore buoys and the shrieks of seabirds as you search for whales.

A private path at the end of Higgs Road allows access to the beach and cove. Visitors are permitted to use it, as is often the case on the islands. Local residents know which landowners have granted permission for their trails to be used, and most will be happy to tell you where those trails are.

After you've sighted the orcas and relaxed in the sun, retrace your route to the bridge and North Pender. Drive to **Hope Bay** and one of the best lodgings in the islands, **Cliffside Inn On-the-Sea.** Ask about packages here; some have a minimum stay of two nights.

DINNER: Cliffside Inn On-the-Sea. Penny Tomlin serves a four-course dinner in The Conservatory, a glass-walled dining room in her inn for guests only, by arrangement. The candlelighted tables, superb food, and view across the water make this an evening to remember.

LODGING: Cliffside Inn On-the-Sea, North Pender Island, B.C. V0N 2M0. (250) 629–6691. A four-room inn of great charm and a hospitable hostess. Serene setting viewing Plumper Sound, Mayne and Saturna Islands, and the Washington mainland with Mount Baker on the horizon.

DAY 2

Morning

Rise early, and you may see the river otter that nests at the bottom of the cliff, the shorebirds of dawn, and the bald eagles that frequent the area.

BREAKFAST: Cliffside Inn On-the-Sea serves a full breakfast that includes fruits and berries from the garden, smoked salmon omelets, and giant muffins.

This is a morning for relaxing in your island hideaway. You can rent a boat or mountain bike at Bromley's Otter Bay marina, take a whale and wildlife tour, picnic at Penny's private ten-acre "Sahhalla," or watch her feed the eagles.

Leave Cliffside for Otter Bay (2 miles) in time to catch the ferry bound for Sturdies Bay on **Galiano Island.**

Galiano's distinctive feature is its dense greenery. The island is 75 percent forest-zoned land so has both logged-off areas and miles of Douglas fir forest. With 950 permanent residents, it's less developed and less pastoral than Pender.

Galiano Island has numerous driftwood-strewn, secluded beaches.

LUNCH: The **Hummingbird,** Sturdies Bay Road, Galiano Island. (250) 539–5472. A friendly, open pub with windows overlooking a grassy picnic area. Good soups and salads, several kinds of beers. Dart boards and a casual atmosphere.

Afternoon

A new road, which was finished but still unopened when this book went to press, has caused a lot of controversy on the island. There is presently only water access to the driftwood-strewn beaches of Dionisio Point Provincial Park and Porlier Pass Channel, which separates Galiano and Valdes Islands.

Landlubbers follow Porlier Pass Road north from the ferry for about 10 miles and turn right on Cottage Way, which ends at Bodega Ridge Provincial Park. You can walk for several miles on a park footpath that follows a cliff 800 feet above the sea.

Go south again on Porlier Road to Clanton Road and turn right to **Montague Harbour Provincial Marine Park.** (250) 539–5733. You can make campground reservations at (800) 689–9025. Montague offers boat rentals, groceries, fishing and camping equipment, and an espresso–ice cream cafe.

DINNER: Woodstone Country Inn. Fine dining in a small hotel restaurant.

LODGING: Woodstone Country Inn, R.R. 1, Georgeson Bay Road. (250) 539–2022. Twelve light, airy guest rooms furnished with wicker and antiques. Some fireplaces. Scenic setting.

DAY 3

Morning

BREAKFAST: A hearty breakfast is included in the room rate at Woodstone Country Inn.

Drive to Sturdies Bay in time to board the ferry to **Village Bay, Mayne Island.**

Mayne, 4 miles (7 km) across, is the smallest of the islands on your brief tour, and it's the sweetest. Less developed than Pender, less forested than Galiano, its tone is softly pastoral. Open green fields and gardens surrounded with high wire fences (to keep the numerous deer out) characterize much of Mayne's landscape. Along the roadsides, Scotch broom bursts a brilliant yellow in spring, followed by summer's foxglove and lupine. As on the other islands, you'll see groves of madrona trees, with their distinctive, peeling red bark, along with towering firs.

Take Village Bay Road to **Miners Bay,** the local gathering spot and the island's commercial center. The picturesque bay was named after the many miners who stopped here in the mid-1800s on their way to the Fraser River/Cariboo gold rush.

Pick up picnic foods at the grocery store in Mayne Mall or at **Miner's Bay Trading Post.** Hike up Mount Parke, in the center of the island, for a spectacular view of sea and islands.

LUNCH: Picnic at Mount Parke.

Afternoon

Hike back down the mountain and head southwest to Dinner Road. You'll be just in time for tea and check-in at **Oceanwood Country Inn.**

Williams Place is a short street off Dinner Road, ending in eleven-acre **Dinner Bay Community Park** and beach. After tea you might like to visit the sandy beach to search for shells, watch for bald eagles, and breathe the fresh, briny air.

DINNER: Oceanwood Country Inn. Prix fixe menu of continental dishes, specializing in fresh seafood and local ingredients imaginatively prepared. British Columbia house wines.

LODGING: Oceanwood Country Inn, 63D Dinner Bay Pond, Mayne Island, B.C. V0N 2J0. (250) 539–5074. Spacious, renovated Tudor-style inn overlooking a small bay. Gracious hosts Marilyn and Jonathan Chilvers welcome guests to rooms furnished with verve and style. Three have fireplaces and whirlpool tubs.

DAY 4

Morning

BREAKFAST: The Chilvers serve a full breakfast—fruit, eggs, bacon, coffee, juice—in the pink stucco dining room at Oceanwood Country Inn.

Head for Miners Bay and gather picnic supplies. You might stop at **Mayne Street Mall** and go to the Manna Bakery Cafe, where sandwiches, soups, and baked goods are offered, as well as espresso and capuccino.

From Fernhill Road, turn northeast on Campbell Bay Road. As the road curves toward **Campbell Bay,** you'll see a grassy meadow and just beyond it a parking turnout. An unmarked trail borders the meadow. Walk this trail about ¼ mile, and you'll come to a wide, serene, protected beach, just right for sunbathing, beachcombing, and exploring the sandstone shelves that shelter brilliantly colored starfish.

Mayne Island has many attractive beaches, but Campbell Bay, with its deep, fjordlike bay, is one of the most appealing. It's the most popular swimming area on the island and a good, safe place to bring children.

LUNCH: Picnic on the beach at Campbell Bay.

Afternoon

Take Campbell Bay Road to Waugh Road and follow it to Georgina Point Road, headed toward **Oyster Bay.** At the tip of **Georgina Point,** on a grassy field with gnarled apple trees, is a lighthouse that is open to the public daily from 1:00 to 3:00 P.M. Originally built in 1885, **Active Pass Light Station** was replaced by the present structure in 1940, with a new tower opened in 1969.

After your lighthouse tour, take Georgina Point Road back toward Miners Bay. On the way you'll pass little **St. Mary Magdalene Church,** a historic structure built about 1898, and several turn-of-the-century homes.

In "downtown Mayne," see **Plumper Pass Lockup,** a minuscule jail that was built in 1896 to accommodate rowdy miners. (The story goes that it housed only one inmate—and he escaped.) Now it's a museum.

Overlooking the waterfront at the bottom of the hill is **Springwater Lodge.** Built in the 1890s, it's the oldest continuously operating hotel in British Columbia. The pub is a favorite local hangout, but the place to be on a sunny afternoon is the hillside deck. From your umbrella-shaded table, watch the boats and tourists go by as you quench your thirst.

After a few days of relaxing on "island time," your watch may seem irrelevant. But don't miss the late-afternoon ferry back to Tsawassen. The 10-mile (16-km) ride will get you to the mainland in about an hour and a half.

THERE'S MORE

Archeology dig. On North Pender, a Salish Indian dig dating back 10,000 years. Occasionally open for summer tours.

Arts and crafts. Artery Studio, Oyster Bay, Mayne Island. Paintings and prints by Frances Faminow and other artists. Open afternoons.

Charterhouse, Charter Road near Bennett Bay, Mayne Island. Heather Maxey's home studio. Quilts, fine woolens, and enamels-on-copper. Open afternoons in summer, weekends in winter.

Greenhouse Studio, Village Bay, Mayne Island. Weavings and woodcrafts at studio of Ann and Brenan Simpson.

Beaches and picnic sites. Montague Harbour Provincial Park, Galiano Island. Waterside park; site of ancient tribal village. Sandy beach, picnic and camping sites.

Bluff Park, Galiano Island, 650 feet (200 m) above Active Pass. Grand view of Gulf and San Juan islands. Good spot for sighting eagles and orca whales.

Magic Lake Walk, southern end of North Pender Island. Loop path leading from Shingle Bay to Buck Lake and pretty Magic Lake.

Boating. Canadian Gulf Islands, Galiano Island, B.C. V0N 1P0. (250) 539–2930. Catamaran, kayak, and sailing tours and rentals. Picnic cruises aboard a 46-foot catamaran, *Great White Cloud.* Lunch includes smoked salmon, fruit, French bread, and wine.

Gulf Islands Kayaking, Galiano Island. (250) 539–2442. Guided sea-kayak trips available. No experience necessary. Office at ferry landing.

Mayne Island Kayak and Canoe Rentals, Seal Beach. (250) 539–2667. Ferry landing pickup and dropoff. Camping and showers available.

Diving. Galiano Island Diving Services. (250) 539–3109.

Farmers' market. Driftwood Centre, North Pender Island. Fresh local produce sold every summer weekend.

Fishing. Mel-n-I Fishing Charters, Galiano. (250) 539–3171.

Golf. Galiano Golf and Country Club, Ellis Road, Galiano Island. (250) 539–5533. PGA-rated nine-hole course, in quiet, wooded setting. (Tennis also available; rent rackets at clubhouse.)

Horseback riding. Bodega Resort, Galiano. (250) 539–2677. Experienced guides at the farm/resort offer one- and two-hour horseback rides on trails and logging roads. The well-trained horses carry you through sun-dappled valleys and along ridge tops that afford magnificent views of Georgia Strait and Trincomali Channel.

SPECIAL EVENTS

June. Galiano Weavers Exhibit and Sale, Galiano Island.

July. Salmon barbecue and fish derby, Pender Islands.

Mid-July. Artists Guild Exhibition and Sale, Galiano Island.

Early August. Music Festival, Mayne Island.

August. Art Show and Fall Fair, Pender Islands.

Mid-August. Fall Fair, Mayne Island. Arts, crafts, photography, needlework, baking, canning, flowers, honey, wine, and produce exhibited in booths near the Agricultural Hall.

Early September. Lions Club Salmon Barbeque, Mayne Island.

November. Christmas Craft Fair, Mayne Island.

OTHER RECOMMENDED RESTAURANTS AND LODGINGS

Galiano Island

Bodega Resort, Box 115. (250) 539–2677. Log cottages with kitchens on twenty-five pastoral acres of meadows and trees. Horses, sheep, hiking trails.

Galiano Golf and Country Club off Ellis Road. (250) 539–5533. Home-style cooking in a cafe setting; fixed menu of three-course dinners.

La Berengerie, Montague Harbour Road. (250) 539–5392. Restaurant nestled under the trees, serving continental cuisine with an experimental (and expert) twist. Open nightly in summer, weekends in winter.

Madrona Lodge, R.R. 2, Galiano Island, B.C.V0N 1P0. (250) 539–2926. Cottage resort in treed setting by the sea. Fireplaces. Complimentary bikes and boats.

Max and Mortiz Spicy Island Food House. (250) 539–5888. Gourmet German hot dogs and Indonesian nasi goreng.

Sutil Lodge, 637 Southwind Road. (250) 539–2930. Renovated 1929 lodge, main house, and cabins, Montague Harbour near provincial park.

Mayne Island

Fernhill Lodge, Box 140. (250) 539–2544. Outstanding inn on a wooded hilltop. Gracious service, comfortable rooms, enchanting gardens, dinners geared to historical themes. Full breakfast included.

Pender Island

Cutlass Court Bed-and-Breakfast, Lot 8, 3816 Cutlass Court Road. (250) 629–6141. Log home with four guest rooms. Owner Doug Heath rents mountain bikes, canoes, and kayaks, and he skippers a 21-foot sailboat.

FOR MORE INFORMATION

BC Ferries, 1112 Fort Street, Victoria, B.C. V8V 4V2. Vancouver (604) 669–1211, Victoria (250) 386–3431.

British Columbia Travel Information. (800) 663–6000.

Galiano Island Travel InfoCentre, P.O. Box 73, Galiano Island, B.C. V0N 1P0. (250) 539–2233.

Tourism Association of Vancouver Island, Suite 302, 45 Bastion Square, Victoria, B.C. V8W 1J1. (250) 382–3551.

Langdale to Lund

THE SUNSHINE COAST

2 NIGHTS

Ferry rides • Scenic water views • Coastal villages
Unspoiled wilderness • Boat cruises • Fishing
Hiking • Beaches • Native arts

The 100-mile (160-km) stretch of British Columbia coastline between Howe Sound and Desolation Sound is said to bask under more sunny days than anywhere else in western British Columbia. The stretch lives up to its nickname, the Sunshine Coast, drawing visitors who are lured not only by the weather but by a wealth of outdoor recreation.

This itinerary provides a taste of the wilderness and seaside relaxation in a three-day escape to sheltered bays, fir-scented forests, and fish-filled waters.

DAY 1

Morning

Board an early morning ferry at Horseshoe Bay, and travel north across Howe Sound to **Langdale,** a forty-minute ride. Under blue skies, the sea sparkles; if it's cloudy, with pewter skies and gray water, you feel that you're floating in a dream world of liquid silver.

Nearing the steep coastline, backed by massive, snow-cloaked mountains, you'll see private piers and cottages dotting the inlets.

From the Langdale ferry landing, it's a 2½-mile (4-km) drive into the village of **Gibsons,** where you can join hard-hatted workers for breakfast at

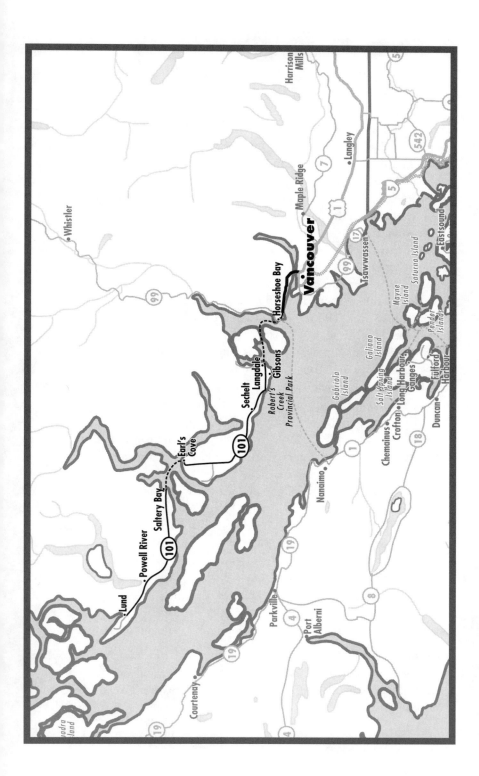

Harbour Cafe. In this bustling local gathering place, the coffee pot is never empty and the pancakes and omelets satisfy the heartiest appetites.

Gibsons faces Shoal Channel and the Strait of Georgia. **Molly's Reach,** at the top of the stairs leading to the boardwalk beside the government wharf, was the setting for the televison series *Beachcombers* and is now a restaurant. Shops line nearby **Molly's Lane.** Descend the steps toward Gibsons Wharf, and you'll see a path edging the waterfront. This easy, level walk will provide you with a pleasant, ten-minute stroll and view of the boat traffic and sloping green hills around the harbor. Plaques posted along the route tell about Gibsons' founders.

Elphinstone Pioneer Museum, on Winn Road, houses Canada's largest shell collection as well as outstanding displays of historical items. Native stone hammers, spear points, cedar root baskets, knives, and arrowheads are on display, along with artifacts from pioneer life and the early logging, fishing, and canning industries. The museum is open daily in summer, and Sundays only from September through February.

Soames Hill, locally known as The Knob, lies off Bridgeman Road, between Gibsons and Langdale. A walk up this steep, 800-foot (245-m) hill will test your leg muscles with its many log steps, but it's a short hike (forty minutes round-trip) and presents you with a glorious view of Gibsons, Howe Sound, Gambier and Bowen Islands, and the Squamish Mountains.

Return to Highway 101, the Sunshine Coast Highway, and drive north to **Sechelt.** You'll pass **Roberts Creek Provincial Park,** a waterside dell of dark cedars, sword fern, and bracken.

From the highway you seldom glimpse the water, since the view is blocked by forests so dense they form a virtually impenetrable wall. To enjoy the real flavor of this scenic country, you have to get out on the water—your suggested afternoon excursion.

At the entrance to Sechelt, just off the highway, is the **Sechelt Indian Band's House of Hewhiwus** (hay-háy-wus), including a small museum, a gift shop, and the **Raven's Cry Theatre.** Standing like sentinels before the hall are twelve totem poles, each carved to record major events in recent Sechelt Indian culture. The tribe's carving house is open to the public.

LUNCH: Pebbles Restaurant in the Driftwood Inn, Trail Avenue, Sechelt. (604) 885–5811. Savory seafood chowder, quiche, and salads served in an attractive dining room with a cheery atmosphere, overlooking the Strait of Georgia.

Afternoon

Follow the signs up Sechelt Inlet to picnic, swim, or canoe at **Porpoise Bay,** or hire experienced guides to take you sea kayaking or on an afternoon sight-seeing excursion around nearby islands. You'll see the waterways and coastline from a different, dramatic perspective. Cruises include a five-hour trip to the tidal rapids at **Skookumchuk Narrows** and an evening ride in **Sechelt Inlet.** Any fish you catch will be smoked and canned for you to take home. (See "There's More.")

DINNER: Blue Heron Inn, East Porpoise Bay Road, Sechelt. Quiet, romantic dining room with water view. Blue herons feed on the salt flats, while osprey and kingfishers swoop above. Fresh seafood includes lobster from the traps at the end of the inn's pier. (800) 818–8977 or (604) 885–3847.

LODGING: Driftwood Inn, 5454 Trail Avenue, Sechelt, B.C. V0N 3A0. (604) 885–5811. Modern hotel with twenty-eight suites, some with water views and kitchenettes.

DAY 2

Morning

BREAKFAST: Driftwood Inn.

Follow the highway north, passing moss-covered boulders, rocky outcrop-pings, and arbutus trees that twist at improbable angles over the sea bluffs. Scotch broom borders the roadside, its flowers bright yellow in spring.

Pass by the charms of **Half Moon Bay** and pretty **Secret Cove** and continue to **Madeira Park.** Stop at **Lowe's Resort** (604–883–2456), and board the boat for your scenic tour or fishing venture in **Pender Harbour.** Guides at this family resort are fishing experts. (You can rent a boat if you prefer.)

LUNCH: Box lunch on your charter trip, provided (at additional charge) by Lowe's Resort. Sandwiches, fruit, dessert, beverage.

Afternoon

The salmon or cod you catch will be frozen and packed at Lowe's Resort.

North of Madeira Park, take Garden Bay Road to **Mount Daniel** trail. The former logging road ascends about 1½ miles (2 km) to the western peak of the 1,545-foot (470-m) mountain, highest in the Pender Harbour area.

Allow about an hour for the hike to the top. When you reach the summit, you'll have a panoramic view of lakes, islands, inlets, and Pender Harbour.

One of the lakes is **Garden Bay Lake,** which was considered sacred by the coast Salish Indians. Young girls, when they reached the age of puberty, would climb the eastern side of the mountain and spend four months there, communicating with the moon through circles of stone. When they returned to the tribe they were considered adult women. Evidence of their traditional rituals can still be seen on Mount Daniel.

Back on the highway again, drive to **Earl's Cove** and board the late-afternoon ferry to **Saltery Bay.** The ride around the tip of Nelson Island and across Jervis Inlet takes fifty minutes.

Drive another 18½ miles (30 km) to **Powell River,** through thick forests interrupted by narrow, shady side roads that wind enticingly down to the sea and private homes. The town is dominated by an immense pulp-and-paper mill, one of the world's largest. Signs at an overlook along the highway list events in the history of Powell River and the harborside mill that created it.

DINNER: Beach Gardens Resort. Comfortable dining room with a fine view and excellent food: tender salmon, spicy Cajun prawns, several seafood dishes, sizable salad bar.

LODGING: Beach Gardens Resort, 7074 Westminster Street, Powell River, B.C. V8A 1C5. (604) 485–6267 or (800) 663–7070. Cabins and sixty-six rooms with private balconies overlooking the marina. Stone-and-cedar buildings under the trees. Indoor pool, sauna, tennis courts, boat rentals.

DAY 3

Morning

BREAKFAST: Restaurant at Beach Gardens Resort.

In Powell River, stop in at the historical museum, across from **Willingdon Beach.** The exhibit explains Powell River's origins as a logging town and displays offbeat artifacts, such as the first piano in the district, a vest made of fishnet, a mastodon bone, and a reconstruction of the unique cabin lived in by an eccentric hermit, Billy Goat Smith.

There are several art galleries along Marina Avenue. **Gallery Tantalus,** 3 blocks north of the ferry terminal, shows paintings, limited-edition prints, pottery, native carvings, jewelry, and glass works. **Paperworks Gallery** features hand-painted silk scarves, jewelry, and kites.

Visit **Cranberry Pottery,** in Cranberry, on the outskirts of Powell River. Cranberry is the starting point for an easy hike up Valentine Mountain. It is also the beginning of a road to Inland Lake, where an 8-mile (13-km) wheelchair-accessible trail circles the lake.

On the southern shore of **Powell Lake, Pacific Coastal Air** keeps float-planes available for business and tourist flights. For breathtaking views of the 30-mile (49-km) lake, the steep green slopes of **Goat Island** (inhabited by mountain goats), the untracked wilderness and its multitude of lakes, and the rugged mountains that surround them, an airplane tour is ideal.

A half-hour flight will buzz you over the cove-scalloped lake and forests, fish farms and log booms, to **Desolation Sound,** British Columbia's largest marine park. The area was named by Captain George Vancouver in 1792, when he explored here and was unimpressed, finding "not a single prospect that was pleasing to the eye." Today the sound and its many islands and inlets are considered jewels among the province's parks. The clear waters and rich undersea life make the area a favorite diving destination.

The plane flies above **Savary Island,** with its summer homes and miles of white sand beaches, passes the smoking sawmill, and circles back to land on Powell Lake.

LUNCH: Shinglemill Restaurant Pub and Bistro, 6233 Powell Plaza, Powell River, B.C. V8A 4S6. (604) 483–2001. Bistro and pub. Good chowder, pasta, sandwiches, seafood, and ambrosial desserts. Open, bright setting on lakeshore, near float-plane docks.

Afternoon

Take the Sunshine Coast Highway as far as it will go, and you'll arrive in the outpost of **Lund,** about 17 miles (28 km) from Powell River. You've reached the northern end of Highway 101, a ribbon of road that stretches 10,000 miles from Lund to Puerto Montt, Chile.

Established in 1889 by the Thulin brothers, who named it after the Swedish town, Lund is a relaxed, friendly community, favored by boaters and lovers of peace and quiet.

Stop at **Carver's Coffee House** for espresso and cookies. The quaint cafe stands at the end of a boardwalk that extends over the water when the tide is in. Anne Steblyk and Keith Matthison, the owners, are hospitable folk who welcome visitors to their warm, inviting shop. Take your coffee to the deck, and watch for the nesting eagles in the trees above.

The renowned Jackie Timothy, a local native artist, may be carving above the dock at the Lund Hotel, a large white hotel that has dominated the village for a century. Prawn boats dock in front of the hotel with their catch in the afternoon.

Turn south now for the four-hour trip back to Vancouver. (The last summer ferry on Sundays and holiday Mondays departs from Langdale at 10:10 P.M. Check your ferry schedule for changes.) If there's time on the return trip, stop at one of the attractions you missed on the way up (see "There's More" for suggestions).

As you wend your way south on Highway 101 to Horseshoe Bay, it's a certainty that you'll be planning your next trip to the splendid Sunshine Coast.

There's More

Canoeing, kayaking. Powell Forest Canoe Route travels a chain of eight wilderness lakes linked by portage trails with canoe resting racks and tent sites.

Ocean canoeing and kayaking are favorable in Jervis Inlet, Malaspina Inlet, and Desolation Sound Marine Park.

Rising Sun Kayaks. (604) 883–2062 or (800) 632–0722. Kayak above Skookumchuck Narrows from Egmont, at the top of Sechelt Inlet.

Pender Harbour and Three Lakes Circle Route is a 7½-mile (12-km) trip through Garden Bay, Mixal, and Lower Sakinaw Lakes. You can see pictographs at Sakinaw Lake.

Pedals and Paddles, Sechelt Inlet. (604) 885–6440. E-mail: pedals_paddles@ sunshine.net. Web site address: www.sunshine.net/paddle. Sea kayak and canoe rentals.

Diving. Powell River, considered the diving capital of Canada, has numerous diving spots with colorful marine life and intriguing shipwrecks. Mermaid Cove, the "Iron Mines" on Texada Island, Saltery Bay, Scotch Fir Point, and Okeover Arm are favorites.

Dive packages, Beach Garden Resort. Featuring the Emerald Maiden, a 9-foot-high bronze statue submerged off Saltery Beach Provincial Park.

Fishing and boating charters. Sunshine Coast Tours and Charters, R.R. 1, S9 C1 Garden Bay, B.C. V0N 1S0. (604) 883–2280 or (800) 870–9055 for bookings. E-mail: sunshine_coast_tours@sunshine.net. Web site address: www.sunshinecoasttours.bc.ca. Scheduled marine tours. Also offers transportation to scuba divers.

Coho Fishing Charters, 104 East Forty-ninth Avenue, Vancouver, B.C. V5W 2G2. (604) 324–8214. Fishing trips from Secret Cove, on 28- and 32-foot Fairlines. Yacht rentals available.

Sunshine Coast Charter Boat Association, Box 316, Madeira Park, B.C. V0N 2H0. (604) 883–9362. Half- and full-day fishing charters; all gear supplied.

Golf. Sunshine Coast Golf and Country Club, 3206 Highway 101, Gibsons. (604) 885–9212 or (800) 667–5022. Hillside nine-hole course above water. Nonmembers after 1:00 P.M. weekdays, after 3:00 P.M. weekends.

Pender Harbour Golf Course, Highway 101, south side of Pender Harbour. (604) 883–9541. Nine holes. (Open daily.)

Myrtle Point Golf Club, Powell River. (604) 487–GOLF. Eighteen-hole championship course.

Hunter Gallery, Marine Drive, Gibsons. Art gallery showing the works of more than one hundred local artists. Paintings, pottery, jewelry, scarves. (Open daily in summer.)

Inland Lake. Unique to Powell River, Inland Lake is encircled by a wheelchair-accessible, 8-mile (13-km) trail. A wide, level, graveled path winds through cedar, fir, and dogwood and around a lake that contains native cutthroat trout. Log cabins, fishing piers, picnic tables, and overlooks are all designed for wheelchair use. (Open mid-April to mid-October.)

Powell River Recreation and Cultural Centre. This remarkable, top-quality community facility holds a 25-meter pool, sauna, whirlpool, leisure pool, exercise room, two regulation arenas, meeting rooms, and a 725-seat theater.

Princess Louisa Inlet. This fjord lies in a majestic, glacier-carved gorge, with more than sixty waterfalls cascading down precipitous cliffs into placid inlet waters. Chatterbox Falls, at the head of the inlet, tumbles 120 feet (37 m); it's accessible only by sea.

Pulp-and-paper mill tours. Daily tours in summer of MacMillan-Bloedel pulp-and-paper mill, Powell River, are available. The minimum age is twelve.

Raven's Coast Expeditions. Guided Alpine hikes and other excursions. Rob Higgin, (604) 487–9444.

Saltery Bay Provincial Park. Sixteen miles (26 km) south of Powell River, this green park features ocean views, marine life, beaches, and campsites. You can swim, snorkel, and dive at Mermaid Cove, where a bronze mermaid rests 60 feet (19 m) beneath the surface.

Skookumchuk Narrows. This is one of the West Coast's largest saltwater rapids. East of Earl's Cove, the tide turns in a narrow channel. There are cavernous whirlpools; on a 10-foot (3-m) tide, 200 billion gallons of water churn through the channel.

Wilderness Camping. Tzoonie Outdoor Adventures, Box 157, Sechelt, B.C. V0N 3A0. (604) 885–9802. Tour boat up Sechelt Inlet, overnight camping, kayaking, mountain biking, scuba diving, fishing, access to Skookumchuk Narrows.

SPECIAL EVENTS

Mid–March. Powell River Music Festival, Powell River.

July. Sea Cavalcade, Gibsons. Salmon barbecues, parades, dances, log burling, boat races, long-distance swims.

Early July (biannual, in even-numbered years). Kathaumixw, Powell River. Week-long choral festival with choirs from around the world.

Mid–July. Texada Sandcastle Days, Powell River. Sandcastle competition.

Late July. Sea Fair, Powell River. Parade, ethnic foods, pancake breakfast, outdoor music, folk dancing, Indian dancers, canoe jousting, navy ship tours.

Mid–August. Blackberry Festival, Powell River. Week-long celebration honoring the ubiquitous blackberry: baking contest, wine tastings, desserts, pancake feeds.

Mid–August. Sea Fair, Powell River. Bathtub races, entertainment, fireworks, parade, and food booths.

August. Festival of the Written Arts, Sechelt. Nationally renowned three-day gathering of authors, booksellers, journalists. Centered in Rockwood Lodge, restored heritage building with open-air pavilion.

Early September (Labor Day weekend). Sunshine Folk Festival, Powell River. Arts and crafts and music on outdoor stage.

OTHER RECOMMENDED RESTAURANTS AND LODGINGS

Gibsons

Bonniebrook Lodge, R.R. 4, S10 C34. (604) 886–2887. Former boarding lodge 3 miles (5 km) north of Gibsons, on Gower Point. Newly restored as small inn and fine restaurant, Chez Phillipe. French cuisine with West Coast influences.

Cedars Inn, 895 Sunshine Coast Highway, P.O. Box 739, Gibsons Beach 0N1V0. (604) 886–3008. Modern motel near shopping center, forty-five rooms, outdoor pool, sauna, meeting rooms.

Half Moon Bay

Jolly Roger Inn, R.R. 1, P.O. Box 7. (604) 885–7184. Fully equipped townhouses; kitchen, fireplace, television. Heated pool, views of beautiful little cove.

Lord Jim's, a coast resort, on Secret Cove. R.R. 1, Ole's Cove Site, C-1, Half Moon Bay, B.C. V0N 1Y0. (604) 681–6168 or (800) 663–1144. Rustic cabins and lodge with popular fine dining on a hill over the sea.

Madeira Park

Lowe's Resort, Box 153. (604) 883–2456. Housekeeping cottages with one to three bedrooms, on cove of Pender Harbour.

Powell River

Beacon B&B, 3750 Marine Avenue. (604) 485–5563. Centrally located across highway from beach. Three rooms, private baths, hot tub. Full breakfast. Great view.

Herondell Bed and Breakfast, R.R. 1, Black Point 29. (604) 587–9528. Country home on forty wooded acres with creek, pond, and river, 8 miles (13 km) south of Powell River. Comfortable rooms, full breakfast.

ESCAPE SIX

VANCOUVER

FOR MORE INFORMATION

BC Ferries, 1112 Fort Street, Victoria, B.C. V8V 4V2. Vancouver (604) 669–1211, Victoria (250) 386–3431.

British Columbia Travel Information. (800) 663–6000.

Powell River Travel InfoCentre, 6807 Wharf Street, Powell River, B.C. V8A 1T9. (604) 485–4051.

Sechelt Chamber of Commerce, Box 360, Sechelt, B.C. V0N 3A0. (604) 885–0662.

Tourism Association of Southwestern B.C., Suite 204, 1755 West Broadway, Vancouver, B.C. V6J 455. (604) 739–9011.

Salt Spring Island
IDYLLIC ISLAND RETREAT

2 NIGHTS

Scenic ferry rides • Panoramic views
Hiking • Horseback riding • Art galleries
Boutique shopping • Fine dining
Wooded seaside park

It's the largest, most populated, most visited island in the Strait of Georgia, but Salt Spring retains its rural ambience and woodsy charm. This island is different from the others in many ways, beginning with its early history. Unlike most Gulf Islands, Salt Spring had no native villages, though weddings and other important events were celebrated on its shores. The white shell beaches attest to centuries of shellfish feasting.

The first immigrants, who arrived in 1859, were black slaves from the United States, fleeing persecution. They were joined by pioneers of British, Portuguese, German, Japanese, and Hawaiian descent, the start of a multicultural community. As the island was more settled, agriculture became its mainstay, then logging. Now, although orchards, dairies, and sheep farms can still be seen, Salt Spring's fame rests upon art and tourism.

Dozens of artists and craftspeople make their homes on the hilly, green island in a blue sea. Tourists come for the outdoor recreation, scenic beauty, and gallery browsing. All three are a part of this three-day visit to an extraordinary corner of Canada.

Avoid the summer crowds by visiting in spring or fall, if possible. The weather is warm, sailing winds are up, and there's far less traffic.

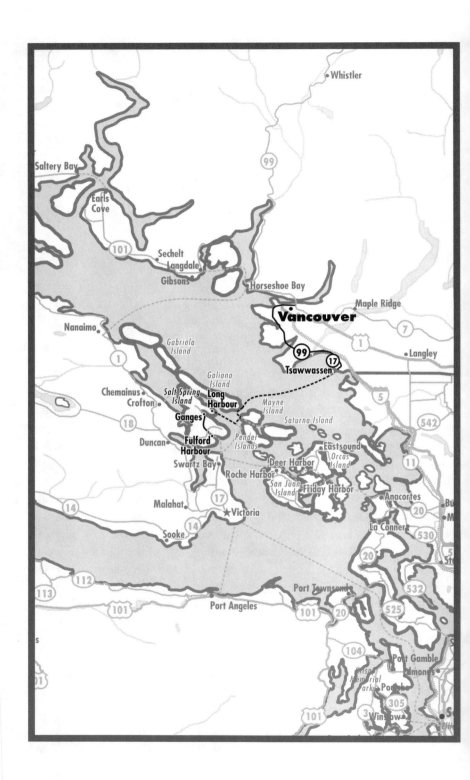

DAY 1

Morning

In Tsawassen, south of Vancouver, board the ferry bound for the **Gulf Islands.** You're headed for **Long Harbour,** on **Salt Spring,** by way of Galiano, Mayne, and Pender Islands. The trip takes about two and a half hours, a journey from mainland bustle into a world of calm beauty as you glide over the Strait of Georgia. The stillness is broken by the cries of gulls and the occasional bellow from the ferry's horn.

Cars, passengers, and bicycles are unloaded and loaded at each stop, until at last the ferry bumps against the splintered, barnacle-encrusted pilings of Long Harbour and you are on Salt Spring.

A ferry route that takes less time and has more daily sailings is from Tsawassen to Swartz Bay, on Vancouver Island; transfer ferries for the ride to **Fulford Harbor,** Salt Spring. (There's no additional charge for a transfer if you request it at Tsawassen.)

When you disembark, if you've taken an afternoon ferry, drive to your lodgings and check in. If you arrive earlier, drive to **Ganges,** a pedestrian-oriented village that is the island's major community. It's a festive place, full of shops and cafes, bobbing boats in the harbor, and an open-air **farmers' market** on Saturdays from late April to October—all within easy walking distance.

At **The Fat Rascal,** on Fulford-Ganges Road, choose picnic items from the array of deli foods. Then head toward Cranberry Road and Maxwell Road (partially unpaved), which will take you up **Mount Maxwell** for a panoramic view of the island and its surroundings—a pleasant way to get your bearings. From the summit, the outlook encompasses the mountains of Vancouver Island, across Sansum Narrows, and the San Juan archipelago on the south. You'll see a log-sorting operation directly below, in **Burgoyne Bay.**

LUNCH: Picnic on Mount Maxwell.

Afternoon

Descend from Mount Maxwell and drive to **Ruckle Provincial Park,** at the far-southeast corner of the island. The park has an interesting history: Settled in 1872 by Henry Ruckle, the land was purchased by the province in 1974, but Ruckle's descendants still live on the site. They run a 200-acre farm.

Several historic farm buildings in various states of repair stand in the park. One is the Ruckles' quaint, Victorian home, which can be seen from the road but is not open to the public.

Beyond the homestead is a campground with picnic tables and 6 miles (10 km) of hiking paths that wind through the thick forest of Douglas fir, cedar, maple, and ferns to secluded beaches. Walk the trails and you may see deer, raccoons, quail, and grouse.

A 2-mile (3⁄10-km) trail along the shore leads from the campground to the Ruckle farmhouse.

From the beach you may spot orca whales in **Swanson Channel** and sea lions basking on the rocks. Cormorants, guillemots, and eagles fly above. The tide pools are full of mussels, oysters, crabs, anemones, and starfish.

Return to Ganges and purchase picnic foods for the next day. In Creekside, a complex of shops, you'll find rolls and other baked goods in Barb's Buns, and cheeses, produce, and organically grown foods in Mobile Market. Ganges' new Thrifty Market offers standard groceries.

DINNER: House Piccolo, 108 Hereford Avenue, Salt Spring Island. (250) 537–1844. Wide range of fine continental and Scandinavian cuisine in a small house on a side street. Known for asparagus, prawns, lamb, seafood platter. Open 5:00 to 10:00 P.M.

LODGING: Weston Lake Inn, 813 Beaver Point Road, Salt Spring Island, B.C. V8K 1X9. (250) 653–4311 or (888) 820–7174. E-mail: westonlake@ saltspring.com. Web site address: www.saltspring.com/westonlake. Bed-and-breakfast on a ten-acre farm with lake views. Country charm, fireside lounge, three rooms with private baths, hot tub. Day and overnight sails on 36-foot sailboat. Instruction also provided.

DAY 2

Morning

BREAKFAST: Susan Evans serves a full breakfast at Weston Lake Inn.

Pack a picnic and drive out North End Road, passing the eastern shore of **St. Mary Lake,** to Southey Point Road, at the northern end of Salt Spring. Park your car near Sunset Drive, where you see a driveway blocked by a chain. Across the road there's a public access footpath to the beach.

A walk through the woods will take you to a pretty beach. At low tide, you can stroll the sand for several miles, beachcombing, relaxing, and enjoying the view of Trincomali Channel and Galiano Island.

For another pleasant country hike, park at the intersection of North End Road and Fernwood. Walk Fernwood to North Beach Road and turn north. The road above the shore proffers views of the beach and forests of Galiano, across the water. On the inland side are quaint cabins and large new homes.

Continue to North End Road; follow this road south to make the loop back to your car.

LUNCH: Picnic on the beach.

Afternoon

Follow Sunset Drive, the shoreside route to **Vesuvius Bay.** This is a region both pastoral and woodsy, with sheep grazing in open fields, stands of dark green firs, and madrona (arbutus) growing rusty red against the hills. The ferry to Crofton, Vancouver Island, sails from Vesuvius. There's a nice beach near the ferry terminal (though parking is limited). Like most Salt Spring beaches, it's accessible only when the tide is out. Tides reach 12 to 15 feet (4 to 5 m) on the island, so beaches are often under water at high tide. Consult a tides table, printed in the local newspaper, as you make your plans.

Visit **Gordon Wales Pottery,** on Sunset Drive near Vesuvius, to see and purchase the artist's handiwork.

DINNER: Vesuvius Inn, at Vesuvius Ferry Dock, Vesuvius Bay. (250) 537–2312. Good food served in a pub with a convivial atmosphere.

LODGING: Weston Lake Inn.

DAY 3

Morning

BREAKFAST: Weston Lake Inn.

See Salt Spring on horseback this morning, riding the wooded paths of the Mount Maxwell area. Make your arrangements through Salt Spring Trail Rides (250–537–5761). For an enjoyable alternative, arrange with Weston Lake Inn for a sailboat ride.

LUNCH: Tides Inn, 132 Lower Ganges Road. (250) 537–1097. From fish-and-chips and pub-style finger food to entrees such as salmon Wellington with Stilton cheese. One of Ganges' best eateries.

Afternoon

Many of the island's 9,000 residents live in Ganges, a popular boating destination. Stroll by the busy harbor, watching the people and boats come and go, and browse through the town's interesting shops.

Mouat's Mall, in a 1912-vintage white-and-green frame building, has expanded and is linked by waterfront boardwalk to the renovated Harbour Building. Mouat's shops sell hardware, fashions, foods, toys, jewelry, and more, with the mall's lower floor devoted to thrift shops. Near the mall is Grace Point Square, a retail development and condos on the water.

Pegasus Gallery is one of the many **art galleries** on Salt Spring. Located in Mouat's Mall, it features the jewelry, carvings, and basketry of native artists.

ArtCraft at Mahon Hall showcases the works of more than 200 artists in every imaginable medium: Weavings, paintings, jewelry, and batik work are a few. ArtCraft is open daily from June to September. Ewart Gallery displays fine art that includes oil paintings, watercolors, and sculptures by Canadian artists.

The Tufted Puffin, northeast of Ganges near the Long Harbour ferry terminal, shows David Jackson's wildlife sculptures.

Leave Long Harbour on the ferry in the late afternoon for the ride back to Tsawassen or take the ferry from Fulford Harbour to Swartz Bay, Vancouver Island, which runs much more often. From Swartz Bay you would ride another ferry to return to Tsawassen.

THERE'S MORE

Fishing. The island's lakes are stocked with trout and bass.

Hiking. The Visitor InfoCentre has information on dozens of hiking trails. An easy walk is Beaver Point Park trail, starting next to the community center on Beaver Point Road. Old-growth forest, a rolling landscape, birds, and a pretty pond are among its attractions.

Kayaking. Rentals available at Salt Spring Kayaking, Fulford Harbour (250) 653–4222, and Sea Otter Kayaking, Ganges (250) 537–5678. Numerous small harbors and 77 miles (124 km) of shoreline offer interesting kayak ventures, such as this one:

Fulford Harbour to Musgrave Landing, an 18-mile (29-km) trip. Put in at the dock by the ferry terminal, and paddle down the bay and around Isabella Point. Pass Cape Keppel and continue northwest toward Musgrave Point and the little cove behind it. Fish for salmon, watch for seals and orca whales, and bask in tranquility.

SPECIAL EVENTS

Late May. Sheep to Shawl, Ganges. Exhibition of wool process: sheep shearing, wool washing, spinning, dyeing.

Mid-June. Sea Capers, Ganges. Parade, clowns, dance, pancake breakfast, log jousting, sand-castle contest, sailboat race, tug-of-war, food stands, children's games, treasure hunt.

July. Festival of the Arts, Ganges. Month-long celebration of the performing arts. Dance and theater productions.

OTHER RECOMMENDED RESTAURANTS AND LODGINGS

Salt Spring Island

Beach House Bed-and-Breakfast, 930 Sunset Drive, Salt Spring Island, B.C. V8K 1E6. (250) 537–2879. E-mail: beachhouse@saltspring.com. Web site address: www.saltspring.com/beachhouse. Three suites and one private cottage in a cove on Sansom Narrows. Three acres of gardens, 400 feet of waterfront, charter boat available for salmon fishing. Full breakfast. Afternoon tea.

Hastings House, 160 Upper Ganges Road, P.O. Box 1110, Salt Spring Island, B.C. (250) 537–2362 or (800) 661–9255. Expensive luxury and charm on a twenty-acre farm estate above Ganges Harbour. Twelve suites in several buildings, English country atmosphere, restaurant, superb service.

The Old Farmhouse, 1077 Northend Road, Salt Spring Island, B.C. V8K 1L9. (250) 537–4113. Restored, century-old farmhouse on three country acres. Idyllic setting, four rooms, full breakfast.

FOR MORE INFORMATION

BC Ferries, 1112 Fort Street, Victoria, B.C. V8V 4V2. Vancouver (604) 669–1211, Victoria (604) 386–3431.

British Columbia Travel Information. (800) 663–6000.

Salt Spring Island Tourist Information, 121 Lower Ganges Road, Ganges, B.C. V08 2T1. (250) 537–5252.

VANCOUVER

The Okanagan

PEACH BLOSSOMS AND WINE

3 NIGHTS

Sunshine • Orchards • Lakes • Wineries
Museums • Stern-wheeler cruise • Luxury resorts

British Columbia's Okanagan country, rich in fertile valleys, clear lakes, and frontier history, has one more enviable attraction: sunshine. People say there are more sunny days in this region than in any other part of Canada. Penticton proudly proclaims that while Tahiti receives 453 hours of sunshine in July and August, and Bermuda basks under 584 hours, the southern Okanagan Valley gets 598.

Thus it's not surprising that fruit orchards and vineyards flourish and oudoor recreation is a way of life in the Okanagan-Similkameen. Much of the area focuses on the water, for Lake Okanagan stretches up the valley for 80 miles (128 km), and there are a hundred more lakes and streams nearby. Three major ski areas draw thousands to the dry powder that falls east of the British Columbia Cascades.

Bicycling, boating, fishing, and sports events make the Okanagan an active vacationer's dream. This four-day itinerary adds other points of interest—such as museum tours, wine tastings, and a tour through ranching country—to the recreational fun.

DAY 1

Morning

Pack a picnic lunch and drive Trans-Canada Highway 1 east from Vancouver

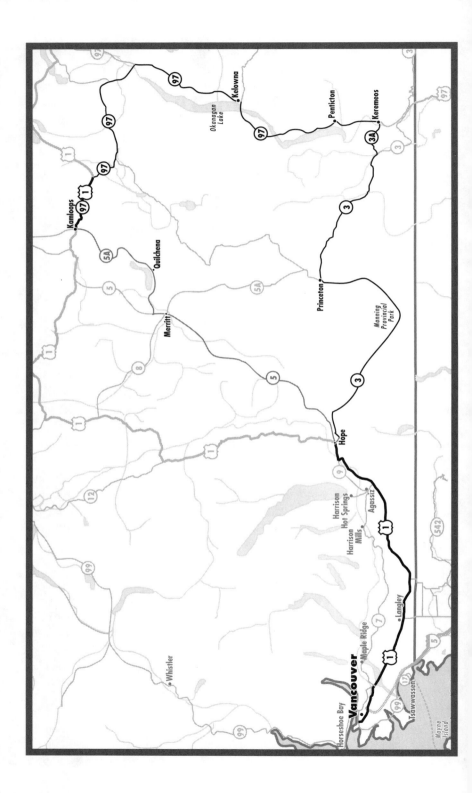

to Hope, 90 miles (144 km). Turn south on Route 3 to **Manning Provincial Park.**

Manning is a vast, green playground for nature lovers. There are boat launches, campsites, hiking trails, calm mountain lakes, wildlife, and wildflowers. Hike into Alpine Meadows in summer, and you'll walk among carpets of colorful blooms.

LUNCH: Picnic in Manning Park.

Afternoon

Continue north on Route 3, along the Similkameen River, to Princeton, where the road turns south toward **Kremeos.** Stop here for a look at the **Kremeos Grist Mill,** on Upper Bench Road (250–499–2888). Built in 1877 and still operating, it's one of the best-preserved waterpowered mills in Canada. Take a tea break in the mill's restaurant, then turn northeast on Route 3A.

You're in the heart of the **Okanagan,** where volcanic mountain ranges shelter a series of valleys, creating a unique microclimate. It ranges from arid desert in the south to a dry and mild environment in the north.

When you reach **Penticton,** on the southern edge of **Lake Okanagan,** check in at **The Penticton Lakeside Resort at Penticton.**

Stretch your legs with a shoreside stroll to the **Rose Garden**, where a miniature golf course full of castles and windmills may tempt you into a game; or take a cruise on the *Casabella Princess.* The fifty-passenger stern-wheeler, which began service in Penticton in 1986, sails daily from the beach at the Penticton Lakeside Resort. Penticton has another stern-wheeler, the SS *Sicamous*, built in 1914, that plied the lake's waters for three decades. Now it rests on dry land, as a museum with displays showing the history of paddlewheelers on the lake.

DINNER: Theo's, 687 Main Street. (250) 492–4019. Greek food in Mediterranean atmosphere. Tables in courtyard with hanging bougainvillea and indoors under open beams and copper pots.

LODGING: The Penticton Lakeside Resort at Penticton, 21 Lakeshore Drive West, Penticton, B.C. V2A 7M5. (250) 493–8221 or (800) 663–9400. Full-service resort at water's edge. Swimming pool, tennis courts, fitness center, sandy beach, restaurants, 204 guest rooms.

DAY 2

Morning

BREAKFAST: Peaches and Cream, The Penticton Lakeside Resort. A cafe off the open, airy white lobby, with lake view.

Drive north on Route 97 along the western shore of Okanagan Lake. On your left are high, eroded cliffs and pillars, while the ground slopes to the blue lake on the right. Small parks dot points of land beside the water. At the sign pointing to the **Summerland Research Station,** turn left and ascend the hill, through vineyards and fruit trees, to the agricultural center, where new varieties of grapes and other fruits are developed. There's a lovely garden here, with flowers identified, and a picnic area.

Continue north on 97 to **Peachland** and **Westbank** and watch for the signs to **Okanagan Butterfly World,** 1190 Stevens Road. This outstanding exhibit, which has a coffee shop and wheelchair access, is well worth a stop. In exotic botanical gardens, hundreds of butterflies flutter. There are streams, birds, and a butterfly breeding area.

From here cross the bridge to **Kelowna,** a town on the east side of Okanagan Lake. Since this is orchard country, where most of British Columbia's apples, peaches, apricots, grapes, and cherries are grown, this is the place to see a working orchard and vineyard.

Drive out KLO Road to Dunster Road and KLO Orchards, 2930 Dunster Road. (250) 763–1091. On this working farm, tours show visitors how orchards are run. Freshly squeezed apple juice is a specialty.

LUNCH: McCullough Station, on McCullough and KLO Roads. (250) 762–8882. The pub/cafe, built to resemble an old-time railway station, is adorned with historic photos of the Kettle Valley Railway. You can sit outside in the orchard or indoors by the fireplace.

Afternoon

Another tour, this time exploring the wine industry, is next on the agenda. Head for **Calona Wines,** 1125 Richter Street. (250) 762–3332. Calona, established in 1932, is the oldest and largest commercial winery in the Okanagan.

With a unique microclimate and soil of volcanic ash and clay loam, vineyards flourish in the region. Calona, known for its riesling, gewürztraminer, and chardonnay wines, has garnered hundreds of medals in international competitions over the past ten years. It's noted for blended table wines. The winery offers tours, tastings, and souvenirs daily in summer and weekdays in winter.

In downtown Kelowna, at the foot of Bernard Avenue, you'll find lakeside symbols illustrating the Okanagan spirit: a soaring sculpture, *Sails,* by Dow Reid; an old-fashioned paddle wheeler, the *M. V. Fintry Queen;* an inviting green park with a public beach; and a whimsical statue of *Ogopogo,* Okanagan Lake's legendary sea serpent. The *Fintry Queen* offers lunch and dinner cruises daily. (250) 763–2780. Beyond this is **Kelowna Waterfront Park,** with lagoons and walkways, adjoining the Grand Okanagan Resort, a large resort complex.

Purchase gifts and boutique items in Kelowna's quaint shops (with names like Teddy Bear Crossing and Scalliwag's) on **Tutt Street.** You might take tea here, in The Gathering Room.

Turn east at this point to Benvoulin Road, where the **Pioneer Country Market and Museum** is located. The old-fashioned market stands where fields of onions once grew, planted by the pioneering Casorso family. The Casorsos grew produce and tobacco and ranched cattle, sheep, and hogs. John Casorso's great-granddaughter now operates the remarkable store, displaying antiques and heritage photos, as well as a wide variety of preserves and country crafts. It's a good place to buy locally made gifts and souvenirs.

Nearby, also on Benvoulin Road, is the **Father Pandosy's Mission.** Father Charles Pandosy was the first white man in the valley. He set up a mission in 1860 and began Okanagan's fruit industry by planting the first apple tree. The home, church, schoolhouse, and blacksmith shop on the carefully maintained heritage site are open for self-guided tours. (250) 860–8369.

Afternoon

DINNER: Hotel Eldorado. Lakeside dining in a light, upbeat atmosphere. Emphasis on seafood prepared with imagination (prawns with fresh papaya, three seafood mousses baked in puff pastry, salmon with saffron). Fresh seafood menu daily. Homemade gelatos and tempting pastries.

LODGING: Hotel Eldorado, 500 Cook Road, Kelowna, B.C.V1W 3G9. (250) 763–7500. Small, elegant country inn with twenty rooms, most with views of Okanagan Lake. Antiques, Jacuzzi tubs, original art, live music in the lounge, and an art deco flavor.

The restored Okanagan Post Office and General Store at O'Keefe Ranch.

DAY 3

Morning

BREAKFAST: In the Hotel Eldorado sun room. Try the toasted brioche with fresh fruit and syrup.

Drive north beside several small lakes for 28 miles (45 km) to Vernon. You'll leave sagebrush-covered ridges to climb green, rolling hills, finally descending to a lush valley with mountains rising in the distance.

Vernon is a small, rural town with lakes on all sides. Okanagan, Kalamalka, and Swan lakes all have beaches and parks and offer good boating, fishing, waterskiing, and swimming.

Seven miles (11 km) north of town, on Highway 97, is **O'Keefe Ranch,** a significant piece of Okanagan history. On the sixty-two-acre site are ten buildings dating from the late 1800s. Each brings the past to life, through outstanding displays, demonstrations, and exhibits.

The General Store holds an array of merchandise from yesteryear: high-button shoes, harnesses, butter churns, bolts of calico. In the blacksmith shop, the big bellows keeps a fire blazing while the blacksmith forges tools (some are for sale in the ranch's gift shop). St. Anne's, a simple wooden church, was the first Catholic church in the Okanagan. Its first service was held in 1889.

The O'Keefe mansion illustrates the opulence of ranch life at the turn of the century, in contrast to the humble log house that was the first home of Cornelius and Mary Ann O'Keefe. The ranch the O'Keefes founded was run by the family until the 1960s.

Take Route 97 west after you leave Vernon. The 48-mile (78-km) drive will lead you to Monte Cristo; from there it's 16 miles (26 km) west to **Kamloops.**

Cool off in **Riverside Park,** a stretch of greenery along the Thompson River near downtown Kamloops. The park has an outdoor pool, a lawn bowling green, several tennis courts, playground equipment, and a long, sandy beach with lifeguard supervision. There are an old steam locomotive on display and a Japanese garden honoring Kamloops's sister city, Uji, Japan.

Back when water transport was used to reach British Columbia's mountainous interior, there were more steam-driven paddleboats on its lakes and rivers than anywhere else in the world, including the Mississippi River. Those days are long gone, but Kamloops has a boat that evokes nostalgic memories. The *Wanda-Sue* is a one-hundred-passenger stern-wheeler, hand built by a local retiree in his backyard several years ago. Two-hour cruises now travel the scenic waters of the Thompson River. (250) 374–7447 or 374–1505.

Take Route 5A south from Kamloops, through a long stretch of rugged, mountainous terrain, to **Quilchena,** on the shore of Nicola Lake.

Afternoon

DINNER: Quilchena Hotel. Hearty ranch food in a quaint country inn.

LODGING: Quilchena Hotel, Quilchena, B.C. V0E 2R0. (250) 378–2611. Hotel built in 1906 on a 66,000-acre cattle ranch. Fourteen rooms share two baths. Victorian parlor, restaurant, peaceful setting. Fishing, sailing, horseback riding, and golf available.

DAY 4

Morning

BREAKFAST: Quilchena Hotel restaurant.

Join the Coquihalla Highway at **Merritt,** and drive south. It's 72 fast miles (120 km) from Merritt to Hope, with one stop at the toll plaza. The freeway drive is both speedy and scenic, with craggy peaks rising high above the forested ridges on either side of the road. Waterfalls stream down steep, rocky ravines, while snowfields glisten on the mountainsides.

THERE'S MORE

British Columbia Falls, Vernon. Off Silver Star Road, a gorgeous waterfall and picnic area.

British Columbia Orchard Industry Museum, 1304 Ellis Street, Kelowna. (250) 763–0433. One hundred-year history of fruit industry in the valley. Open Tuesday through Saturday.

Davison Orchards, west of Vernon off Bella Vista Road. (250) 542–7840. Family farm market selling numerous apple varieties and other produce. Hayrides, self-tours available July through October.

Fishing. Hundreds of lakes in the Okanagan and Shuswap regions offer good fishing for kokanee, Dolly Varden, and the world-famed Kamloops rainbow trout. Ask at Visitors InfoCentres for local information.

Golf. Aberdeen Hills Golf Club, Kamloops. (250) 828–1149. Challenging eighteen-hole course. Hillside views of Kamloops and the river valley.

Gallagher's Canyon Golf Resort, Kelowna. (250) 861–4240. Eighteen-hole course under ponderosa pines, beautiful views.

Predator Ridge Golf Resort, Vernon. (250) 542–3436. Challenging eighteen-hole, world-class course.

Salmon Arm Golf Course, Salmon Arm. (250) 832–4727. Eighteen-hole championship course in Shuswap Lake country.

Kalamalka Lookout, south of Vernon. Hike or bicycle to the lookout for a striking view of Kalamalka, the "Lake of Many Colours," which shimmers in brilliant hues of green and blue.

Kamloops Wildlife Park, Kamloops. (250) 573–3242. Largest nonprofit wildlife park/zoo in British Columbia. Exotic and British Columbia wildlife in natural surroundings, miniature train, picnic areas, concession stand.

Kettle Valley Railway. Hike and cycle on the old railway; rails and ties have been removed between McCullough Lake Resort to Myra Canyon at Kelowna, and through to Penticton. There are fine views from sixteen trestles, all safe to cross.

The Lloyd Gallery, 598 Main Street, Penticton. (250) 492–4484. Centrally located art gallery with more than 2,000 square feet of exhibition space. Works by noted Canadian sculptors and painters.

Munson Mountain, Penticton. Drive up the mountain on the edge of town, and walk the last few yards to the summit for a view of the long lake. It's touted as the "$100 view" because the scene was once depicted on the $100 bill.

Okanagan Game Farm, Penticton. (250) 497–5405. Open daily, 8:00 A.M. to dusk. Exotic animals roam 560 acres of land above Skaha Lake, 5 miles (8 km) south of Penticton.

Penticton Museum, 785 Main Street. (250) 490–2451. Considered to have the largest collection of western Canadiana in the British Columbia interior.

Red Bridge, Kremeos. This 1911-era covered bridge was left from the days of the Great Northern Railway. Mountain goats are sometimes seen nearby.

Sumac Ridge Estate Winery, Summerland. (250) 494–0451. Tours, tastings.

Secwepemc Cultural and Education Society, 355 Yellowhead Highway, Kamloops. (250) 828–9779. Exhibits portraying all aspects of the culture of the Secwepemc Indians (European newcomers abbreviated the name to Shuswap).

Skiing. Apex, Penticton (forty minutes' drive from town). (877) 777–2739. Hilly course for the intermediate and advanced skier. Four lifts, fify-six runs. Condo rentals available.

Big White, Kelowna (forty minutes' drive). (250) 765–8888; in western Canada, (800) 663–2772. Highest ski resort in British Columbia. Warm temperatures, dry powder snow on 7,606-foot (2,319-m) mountain. Sixty-eight runs, eight lifts (three high-speed quads), 25 kilometers of Nordic trails. Numerous accommodations and restaurants.

Holiday Inn Sunspree Resort at Apex. (250) 495–7223.

Silver Star Mountain, Vernon. (250) 542–0224 or (800) 663–4431. Ideal powder conditions, usually sunny November through April. Resort village in Old West style; ski shop, restaurant, saloon, condo rentals. Seven lifts, eighty-four runs. Summer chair lift to summit, 6,280 feet (1,915 m), for wide view of Monashee Mountain Range.

Wineries. Cedar Creek Estate Winery, 9 miles (15 km) south of Kelowna. (250) 764–8866. Landscaped grounds overlooking Okanagan Lake. Tastings daily, tours in summer.

Mission Hill Vineyards, south of Kelowna in Westbank. (250) 768–5125. Daily tours and tastings.

SPECIAL EVENTS

Early February. Vernon Winter Carnival, Vernon. Largest festival of its kind in western Canada, with a parade, dances, sleigh rides, ice sculpture, and stock-car races on ice.

Early May. Spring Wine Festival, Kelowna and Penticton. A celebration of wine and food when new varietals are introduced.

Early June. Creative Chaos, Vernon. Crafts fair offering arts and crafts of regional artists.

Mid-August. Penticton Peach Festival. Ten days of music, contests, carnivals, parades, puppet shows, peach feasts.

Mid-August. Restoration Music Festival, Vernon. A wide array of jazz, country, rock, and rhythm and blues.

Late August. Ironman, Penticton. Qualifying events for Hawaii Triathlon.

Early October. Wine Festival, Okanagan Valley. Twenty-five wineries participate in tastings, special dinners.

OTHER RECOMMENDED RESTAURANTS AND LODGINGS

Hatheume Lake

Hatheume Lake Resort, P.O. Box 490, Peachland, B.C. V0H IX0. (250) 767–2642. Log cabins and new cedar homes on mountain wilderness lake, famous for fly fishing. Caters to cross-country skiers, ice fishers, and snowmobilers.

Kaledan

Ponderosa Point Resort, P.O. Box 106. (250) 497–5354. Twenty-six snug log cottages and A-frames on Skaha Lake. Nicely furnished and immaculately clean. Shaded green lawns, pine trees, peace and quiet.

Kelowna

Earl's on Top, 211 Bernard Avenue. (250) 763–2777. Across the street from the lake and *Fintry Queen* landing. Outstanding food and unique art deco atmosphere, with lots of glass and plants.

Lake Okanagan Resort, 2751 Westside Road. (250) 769–3511. Full-service lakeside resort offering golf, tennis, boating, horseback riding, dining, 193 rooms.

Penticton

Country Squire, Naramata (north of Penticton). (250) 496–5416. An experience in fine dining. Leisurely, multicourse meal, with a walk around the scenic grounds between salad and entree. Set in a heritage house near Okanagan Lake's east shore.

Granny Bogner's, 302 Eckhardt Avenue West, Penticton. (250) 493–2711. Half-timbered former private home on landscaped grounds. Fine cuisine.

Riordan House Bed and Breakfast, 689 Winnipeg Street. (250) 493–5997. Ivy-covered, brick-and-stucco home of charm, with three rooms.

Vernon

Castle on the Mountain, 8227 Silverstar Road, B.C. V1B 3M8. (250) 542–4593. Bed-and-breakfast and art gallery. Three guest rooms, use of kitchen, whirlpool tub on outdoor deck, barbecue area, spectacular view of lakes and valley.

Demetre's, 2705 Thirty-second Street. (250) 549–3442. Steakhouse; well-spiced Greek foods.

Intermezzo Restaurant, 3206 Thirty-fourth Avenue. (250) 542–3853. Small place serving excellent Italian entrees. Veal, pasta, chicken, seafood. Take-out available.

Squires Four Public House, 6301 Stickle Road (off Highway 97 north of Vernon). (250) 549–2144. Multilevel pub with oak trim and hanging plants. Lunch and dinner daily. Traditional English dishes, daily soup-and-sandwich specials, chicken, pizza.

FOR MORE INFORMATION

British Columbia Travel Information. (800) 663–6000.

Kamloops Travel InfoCentre, 10 Tenth Avenue, Kamloops, B.C. V2C 6J7. (250) 374–3377.

Okanagan Similkameen Tourism Association, 1332 Water Street, Kelowna, B.C. V1Y 9P4. (250) 860–5999.

Penticton Information Centre, 888 Westminster Avenue West, Penticton, B.C. V2A 8R2. (250) 493–4055.

Vernon Chamber of Commerce, 701 Highway 97 South, Vernon, B.C. V1V 3W4. (250) 545–0771.

VANCOUVER

Southeast Vancouver Island
NATIVE ART AND EDWARDIAN LUXURY

3 NIGHTS

Ferry rides • Scenic water views • Native art
Intriguing murals • Fine cuisine • Nature trails
World-famous gardens • Country mansions • Luxury lodging

A rich mixture of British Columbia history is clustered around the bays and lakes of Vancouver Island's southeastern shore, in the Duncan/Cowichan region. Here you'll find settlers' farmhouses and rich men's mansions, proud displays of native art, wooded paths by quiet streams, and clear-cut hillsides that once were forest. This itinerary covers them all. Since the area covered is within a 50-mile radius and distances between stops are short, mileage is only occasionally included.

Bring outdoor clothes and a dress-up outfit; this is a journey of contrasts.

DAY 1

Morning

Board a morning ferry at Tsawassen, south of Vancouver, headed for Swartz Bay (there are twenty round trips daily in summer). The 24-mile ride takes an hour and thirty-five minutes, with the ferry cruising through the scenic **Strait of Georgia** and among the **Gulf Islands.** In spring and fall you'll see bald eagles and thousands of shore birds, as well as sea lions and possibly orca whales.

From Swartz Bay terminal, head south on Highway 17 and follow the signs to **Brentwood Bay** and **Butterfly World,** located at the intersection

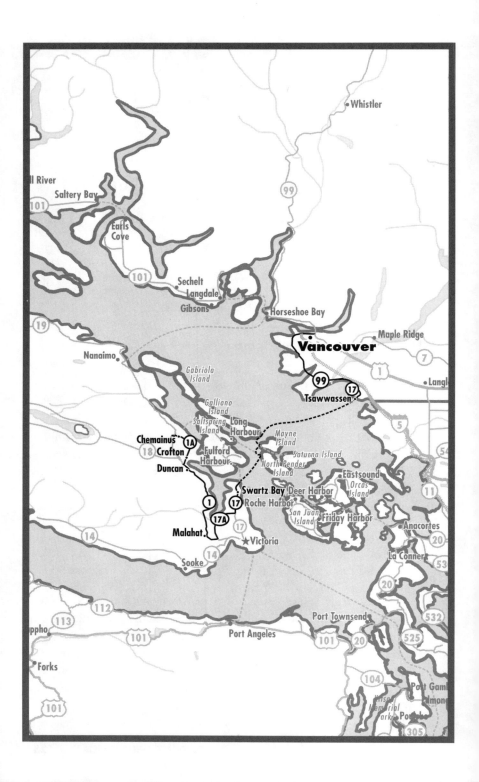

of Highway 17A and Keating Cross Road. When you enter the 12,000-square-foot conservatory that houses Butterfly World, you're in an exotic garden far removed from the Northwest. Here hundreds of multicolored butterflies live in tropical greenery. (Open daily 10:00 A.M. to 5:00 P.M. May through October, 10:00 A.M. to 4:00 P.M. other months; admission charged.)

You might choose to see Butterfly World on your return trip, allowing more time to enjoy the nearby **Butchart Gardens.** It takes at least two hours to explore the gardens, fifty acres of plantings carved from a former limestone quarry. This site is a must for any traveler who appreciates floral beauty and imaginative landscaping.

LUNCH: The Dining Room, Butchart Gardens. (250) 652–5256. A charming restaurant, once the home of the estate's owners, serves lunch, afternoon tea, and dinners in summer. Less expensive meals are offered in the casual, plant-filled Blue Poppy Restaurant.

Afternoon

Catch the Brentwood Bay–Mill Bay ferry that crosses Saanich Inlet. After the twenty-five-minute ride on the little ferry, a contrast to the behemoths that ply the Strait of Georgia, turn north to follow Mill Bay Road, edging to the shore. You'll have views of the water, beaches, and Saanich Peninsula on the east.

When you reach the village of **Mill Bay,** you'll see a shopping complex, Mill Bay Centre, which has several interesting shops. **Asean Imports** sells intricate carvings and puppets from Indonesia, baskets, beaded shoes, and bags. **The Flying Pig,** (250) 743–1324, is filled with whimsical gift and kitchen items, cards, and stationery. Mexican and Guatemalan imports, pottery, and watercolors are displayed in **Excellent Framing Gallery and Handcrafts,** while **Third Addition** is a browser's delight, selling toys, linens, gifts, and cards of high quality. The Centre has a sizable grocery market and an ice-cream shop, **The Creamery,** where you might settle at an outdoor table for coffee or ice cream and dip into the book you purchased at **Volume One Bookstore** in Duncan.

From here take Trans-Canada Highway 1 north to Cowichan Bay Road, turning northeast toward the pretty bay where the Cowichan and Koksilah Rivers join in marshlands at the northern tip of the inlet. The Cowichan Indians gathered here long before Europeans arrived, clamming and fishing for cod and salmon. Fishing is still a major attraction. **The Maritime Centre,** (250) 746–4955, home of the Cowichan Bay Wooden Boat Society and

School, is open for tours. Its cedar buildings, set on a 300-foot pier, have exhibits showing the area's settlement and gradual change from agriculture and fishing to a recreational community.

At the Centre you can watch students build and restore traditional and contemporary wooden boats. The **Marine Ecology Station,** (250) 748–4522, offers marine educational programs to schools and groups. (Open daily in summer, weekends other months.)

Next to the Centre is a tiny art gallery, **The Red Door,** where pottery and weavings are displayed and sold.

Nearby **Hecate Park,** on the waterfront, has a boat ramp and picnic facilities. Look across the harbor and you'll see Mount Tzouhalem, crouching like a huge stone frog—transformed from a living frog, according to a Cowichan legend.

Past Hecate Park on Cowichan Bay Road is Theik Reserve Footpath, a choice place for flowers and birds. It has picnic tables and is close to a shorebird habitat. You may see otters.

Turning inland on Cowichan Bay Road, you'll see myriad birds in the wetlands near the South Cowichan Lawn Tennis Club. In winter they swarm with trumpeter swans and bald eagles.

Continue north on Cowichan Bay Road to Tzouhalem Road, which winds through the Cowichan Indian Reserve. Notice the old stone church on a hill to your left. It's empty and vandalized now, but it retains the quaint look of a stone country church built with care.

At Lakes Road, turn north to check in at **Grove Hall Estate,** where you'll probably arrive in time for tea and appetizers and a walk around the tranquil lakefront grounds.

On your way to dinner, stop at **Art Kinsman Park** on Quamichan Lake to see the flocks of swans, ducks, and Canada geese. The park has a grassy area, playground, and boat launch.

DINNER: Quamichan Inn, 1478 Maple Bay Road. (250) 746–7028. Tudor-style restaurant on the east side of Quamichan Lake, noted for its continental cuisine in a linens-and-candlelight atmosphere.

LODGING: Grove Hall Estate, 6159 Lakes Road, Duncan, B.C. V9L 4J6. (250) 746–6152. Stately, half-timbered manor house on seventeen scenic acres. Three spacious rooms furnished with Asian art and antiques.

DAY 2

Morning

BREAKFAST: Grove Hall serves a full English breakfast in the dining room overlooking the lawn and lake.

Just north of Duncan on Highway 1 is the **Somenos Marsh Wildlife Refuge.** Here you'll see herons, ducks, geese, and other waterfowl in the fall, winter, and spring. There are observation points along the road and more under development.

Continue north and stop at the **British Columbia Forest Museum,** where one hundred acres are dedicated to the history of forestry and logging. You can ride an authentic steam train once used on a logging operation and watch demonstrations of logging skills along the way. (250) 715–1113, open May through September.)

Continue north on Highway 1, turning east on 1A to reach the village of **Chemainus.** The "Little Town That Did" is 1 mile off the main highway and well worth a detour. Thirty-two scenes of the area's history, painted by Canadian, European, and American artists, cover the walls of Chemainus's buildings. In the early 1980s the townsfolk decided to rescue their dying economy by embarking on a program that would attract tourists. They chose historical murals.

Their plan worked. Visitors now flock there to follow the painted yellow footsteps, which guide you past the murals to busy art galleries, quaint gift shops, and ice-cream parlors. See **Waterwheel Park,** the **Chemainus Valley Museum,** century-old **St. Michael and All Angels Church** (open to tourists 1:00 to 4:00 P.M. Wednesday, Friday, and Saturday in summer), and **Locomotive Park.** Kin Park has a beach, a playground, and a boat ramp.

The big sawmill on the edge of town is a reminder of the area's logging history. Tours of the mill are available on Tuesday and Thursday afternoons in summer (250–246–3221).

On Oak Street tour the **Mechanical Music Museum,** with its display of historical music boxes and phonographs. Shop for souvenirs, cards, and kitchen items in the **Chemainiac Shop** on Willow Street (250–246–4621). **Sa-Cinn Native Enterprises, Ltd.,** features jewelry, carvings, pottery, prints, and other fine-quality native arts and crafts. At **Images of the Circle,** a working studio on Chemainus Road, you can watch the artists at work and purchase carvings, paintings, and jewelry.

Afternoon

Drive south on Trans-Canada Highway 1 to **Duncan,** the commercial hub of the region. It's easy to find the **totem poles** for which the city is famous. There are about eighty throughout the city, especially in the downtown district, made by native carvers.

The Totem Pole Project, which began in 1985, honors an ancient Northwest Coast tradition and art form. Guided tours are available; check at the **Travel InfoCentre,** 381 Highway 1, Duncan (250–746–4636). Several totems stand near the Duncan Railway Station, which houses the **Cowichan Valley Museum.** It contains pioneer possessions, a typical turn-of-the-century general store, and a gift and souvenir shop. (Open Monday through Saturday in summer, Thursday through Saturday in winter. Hours vary; phone 250–746–6612.)

On Craig Street, **Judy Hill Gallery** is a small shop with good-quality Native carvings and jewelry. Stop for espresso or cappuccino at Gallows Glass Books on Canada Avenue, near the railway station museum; then take Cowichan Way south to the **Native Heritage Centre,** a complex of buildings where you can see how the famous Cowichan sweaters are made, watch a totem carver at work, and purchase fine native crafts. This is an exceptional visitors attraction, not to be missed. Owned by the Cowichan Indians, the largest tribe in British Columbia, it represents a rich and proud culture.

One mile south of Duncan on Highway 1 is **Hill's Indian Crafts,** one of several Hill's stores selling unique totems, ceremonial masks, leather moccasins, and Cowichan handknit sweaters.

Return to Grove Hall for afternoon tea and a game of tennis or a stroll on the lawn.

DINNER: Bluenose Steak and Seafood House, 1765 Cowichan Bay Road, Cowichan Bay. (250) 748–2841. Prime rib and seafood in a pleasant setting on the water.

LODGING: Grove Hall Estate.

DAY 3

Morning

BREAKFAST: The menu varies daily at Grove Hall. You might have bacon and eggs cooked as you like them, or pancakes with local berry syrup.

From Duncan, take Koksilah Road south to **Bright Angel Provincial Park.** Walk the suspension bridge that hangs above the Koksilah River, hike the trails that wind through fir and cedar trees, and enjoy the rocky, riverside beach. You can swim (a convenient rope swing hangs from a tree limb, over the water) and fish.

Take Koksilah Road east to join Trans-Canada Highway 1 and turn south; past Dougan Lake, branch west on Cobble Hill Road. Driving through this rural area you'll pass a farm selling raspberries and blueberries in season. When you reach the little community of **Cobble Hill,** look for the Crafty Old Lady and Cobble Hill Country Furnishings, antiques and craft shops that have a combination of antiques, collectibles, and locally made handicrafts.

Purchase a picnic lunch at the snack shop in Cobble Hill Country Furnishings and walk across the train tracks that lie at the base of Cobble Hill. Just behind the railroad shelter a trail begins into **Quarry Wilderness Park.** Follow this trail (there are several offshoots; just keep going upward) to the top of the hill, and if it's a clear day you'll enjoy a sweeping view of the countryside. It takes about two hours to climb the hill. There are picnic tables on the summit.

LUNCH: Picnic on Cobble Hill.

Afternoon

After ambling back down Cobble Hill, you might take a refreshment break at the ice-cream bar in Cobble Hill Country Furnishings or in Cobblestone Inn, a Tudor-style pub with a full bar, darts, and evening entertainment on weekends. Then head south on Shawnigan Lake Road.

The country road goes to **Shawnigan Lake Village,** where you can check to see if the **Auld Kirk Gallery** is open. The gallery, in a former church on Wilmot Avenue and Walbank Road, sells the pottery and textiles of local artisans. It's open weekends; weekdays by appointment only. Phone (250) 743–4811.

Continuing on East Shawnigan Lake Road, you'll come to Recreation Road, a right turn. At the end of the road is **Old Mill Community Park,** site of a former sawmill. In the early 1900s, when logging seemed unlimited, the mill handled 80,000 to 100,000 board feet a day. The last mill burned in 1945 and was never rebuilt; now there are few remnants left among the trails that wind through the woods and along the lakeshore.

East Shawnigan Lake Road continues south to join Highway 1. At the juncture, turn north on the highway to Whitaker Road. Travel less than a mile on Whitaker and you'll come to **Spectacle Lake Provincial Park,** a quiet, pretty park centered around a lovely lake. It takes about thirty minutes to walk completely around the lake. Part of the path is wheelchair accessible.

The Aerie is near Spectacle Lake, off Whitaker Road, and is your destination for the night.

DINNER: The Aerie. Expensive, fine cuisine in a spectacular setting with forest, mountain, and water views. Try the pheasant in almond crust or rack of lamb with herbs, and save room for the heavenly chocolate-rum truffles. This is a special place for special occasions.

LODGING: The Aerie, P.O. Box 108, Malahat, B.C. V0R 2L0. (250) 743–7115. Luxurious, Mediterranean-style villa on a hillside above Finlayson Arm, with grand mountain and forest views. Twelve rooms, some with Jacuzzi tubs and fireplaces.

DAY 4

Morning

BREAKFAST: A full breakfast, included in the Aerie's room rate, is served in the dining room with fine china and silver.

Head north on Trans-Canada Highway 1 to the ferry landing south of Mill Bay. If you have time to explore, drive into **Bamberton Provincial Park** for a last walk in the woods.

Catch the ferry to Brentwood Bay. Take Highway 17 north to Swartz Bay and board the ferry bound for Tsawassen.

THERE'S MORE

Boating. Great Northwestern Adventure Company, Pier 66, P.O. Box 57, Cowichan Bay, B.C. V0K 1N0. (250) 748–7374 or (800) 665–7374. Web site address: www.great-northwestern.com. Operates a unique fleet of classic sailing boats and tall ships. Offers a variety of excursions and overnight bed-and-breakfast packages from Cowichan Bay and through the Gulf Islands.

Centennial Park, at the end of First Street in Duncan, has a playground, tennis courts, and lawn bowling.

Chemainus Theatre, Chemainus. (250) 246–9820 or (800) 565–7738. Dinner theater, arts-and-crafts gallery.

Cowichan Lake, west of Route 18. Inland lake with fishing, picnicking, and hiking trails (much of the forest has been logged off, however).

Fishing. Beachcomber Charters, P.O. Box 51, Cowichan Bay, B.C.V0R 1N0. (250) 748–8733. Insured, professional guides offer charters for salmon, steelhead, and bottom fish. All gear supplied.

Golf. Mount Brenton Golf Course, Chemainus. (250) 246–9322. Eighteen-hole course with fir trees and several lakes and creek crossings. Easy to walk but challenging.

Hiking. Cowichan River Footpath follows the scenic, wooded south bank of Cowichan River. The trailhead is shown on the large map at the Community Hall of Glenora, southwest of Duncan, off Indian Road. It's a 6-mile hike in to Sahtlam Lodge (see "Other Recommended Restaurants and Lodgings").

Shawnigan Lake Marina, 2346 East Shawnigan Lake Road. (250) 743–1364. Rents canoes, paddleboats, rowboats, and motorboats. Marina also has jet skis and fishing licenses.

Vigneti Zanatta, in Cowichan Valley, is a farm gate winery, which means that the wine is sold at the farm. (250) 748–2338.

SPECIAL EVENTS

May. Mill Bay Country Music Festival, Mill Bay.

June. Cowichan Wooden Boat Festival, Cowichan Bay.

July. Cowichan Band Canoe Races at Indian Beach.

Mid-July. Duncan-Cowichan Summer Festival.

July through October. Festival of Murals, Chemainus. Outdoor theater, parades, puppetry, street music, folk dancing, food, music, swap meet, and arts-and-crafts demonstrations and sales.

Mid-August. Original Traditions, Chemainus. Weekend celebration of contemporary fine crafts, showcasing artisans from around western Canada.

OTHER RECOMMENDED RESTAURANTS AND LODGINGS

Chemainus

Bird Song Cottage, 9909 Maple Street, Chemainus, B.C. (250) 246–9910. Web site address: www.vancouverisland-bc.com\birdsongcottage. Bed-and-breakfast filled with Victorian whimsy and bird themes. Three suites and a hospitable innkeeper who lets guests try on her fancy hat collection. Cozy sitting room with a grand piano, harp, and pump organ. Full breakfast.

Chemainus Bakery, 2875 Oak Street, Chemainus. (250) 246–4321. Sandwiches and pastries in a bright, cheery space that's flooded with sun on clear days. Good chewy walnut cookies. Closed Sunday and Monday.

Saltair Pub, north of Chemainus on Route 1A. (250) 246–4942. Casual country restaurant in a rural, woodsy setting.

Cobble Hill

Heron Hill Bed-and-Breakfast, 3760 Granfield Place, V0R 1L0. (250) 743–3855. Three bedrooms in a country home with views. Casual, homey, family choice. Guest sitting room with fireplace, refrigerator, and microwave.

Cowichan Bay

The Inn at the Water, 1681 Botwood Lane, V0R 1N0. (250) 748–6222. Waterside hotel with fifty-five one-bedroom suites. Kitchenettes, a pool, and restaurant with ordinary food but great view of the bay.

Masthead Restaurant, 1705 Cowichan Bay Road. (250) 748–3714. Seafood and prime rib in waterside setting.

Rock Cod Cafe, 1759 Cowichan Bay Road. (250) 746–1550. Inexpensive spot with nautical atmosphere and marina views. Fish-and-chips and specials such as honey Dijon halibut with rice and salad.

Duncan

Fairburn Farm Country Manor, 3310 Jackson Road. (250) 746–4637. A working bed-and-breakfast farm with seven rooms, set on 128 secluded acres. Homegrown vegetables, fresh eggs and butter, and freshly baked bread.

Oak and Carriage Neighbourhood Pub, 3287 Lake Cowichan Road, Duncan. (250) 746–4144. English-style pub with comfy couches by the fireplace. A good place for lunch (generous hamburgers) and a game of darts.

Pioneer House, 4675 Trans-Canada Highway. (250) 746–5848. Large log restaurant with friendly, prompt service and well-prepared steak, ribs, seafood, and chicken.

Sahtlam Lodge and Cabins, 5720 Riverbottom Road, Duncan V9L 6H9. (250) 748–7738. Charming, old-fashioned lodge and rustic cabins scattered among woodland and gardens on the Cowichan River. Excellent meals; dinner served to the public, breakfast served to guests in cabins.

Maple Bay

Brigantine Pub, 6777 Beaumont. (250) 746–5422. Eat outdoors on the deck at this friendly pub. A local favorite, it has the usual dart board and television. A good spot for a light, flavorful meal; the mushroom soup is top-notch.

Mill Bay

Friday's, on Highway 1. (250) 743–5533. Lively spot with a youthful clientele. The most popular item is pizza, cooked in open brick ovens.

Pine Lodge Farm, 3191 Mutter Road. (250) 743–4083. Antiques-filled country inn with gardens, pastures, seven guest rooms, and an impressive stone fireplace. Full bacon-and-eggs breakfast included.

Shawigan Lake

Marifield Manor, 2039 Merrifield Lane, V0R 2W0. (250) 743–9930. Spacious Edwardian home with six rooms, lake views, and hospitable hosts. Full breakfast included.

FOR MORE INFORMATION

B.C. Ferries, 1112 Fort Street, Victoria, B.C. V8V 4V2. Vancouver (604) 669–1211, Victoria (250) 386–3431.

British Columbia Travel Information. (800) 663–6000.

Chemainus InfoCentre, Box 575, Chemainus, B.C. V0R 1K0. (250) 246–3944.

Duncan-Cowichan Information Centre, 381 Trans-Canada Highway 1, Duncan, B.C. V9L 3Y2. (250) 746–4636.

Tourism Association of Vancouver Island, Suite 302, 45 Bastion Square, Victoria, B.C. V8W 1J1. (250) 382–3551.

VANCOUVER

Vancouver Island: Northeast Coast

TRACKING SEA LIFE

2 NIGHTS

Sandy beaches • Tidal pools • Marine life
Native art • Secluded island • Luxury lodge
Salmon fishing • Whale watching • Fine dining

In the protected waters of Johnstone Strait, between the British Columbia mainland and the northeast coast of Vancouver Island, life is abundant. Bald eagles, seabirds, fish, and seals are commonly seen. But the animal that most fascinates visitors is the orca, or killer, whale. This three-day itinerary, best taken from late June through October, includes a whale-watching excursion that will take you close to the resident whale population in the strait.

The trip offers a mixture of civilized and rustic pleasures designed to refresh the senses.

DAY 1

Morning

Take the ferry from Horseshoe Bay to Nanaimo, on Vancouver Island. Drive north on Route 19 to **Parksville.**

Stop at **Pipers Lagoon,** northeast of town, to watch the numerous birds circling and soaring above the cliffs that rise from the sandy spit.

Just south of Parksville go to the InfoCentre at 1275 East Island Highway and down the path to the quaint old **Knox Heritage Church** in **Craig**

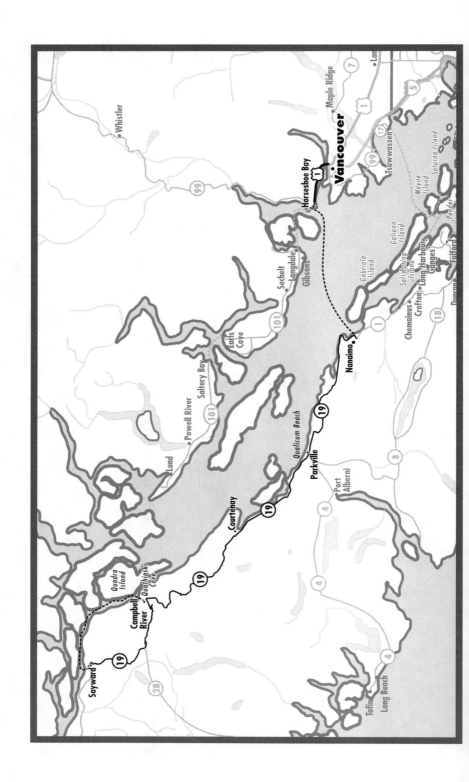

Heritage Museum Park. Weddings are often held here. Proceeds from the wedding fee go toward maintaining the historic park, which has pioneer buildings, the town's original fire hall, and a museum.

LUNCH: Herons, Bayside Inn, 240 Dogwood Street, Parksville. (250) 248–8333. The outdoor terrace above the bay makes a fine setting for a lunch of fresh seafood, a thick sandwich, or a tangy salad.

Afternoon

The Parksville/Qualicum area is known for its scenic hiking trails. Most famous is the path up **Mount Arrowsmith,** which stands 6,000 feet (1,830 m) against the eastern sky. Other wooded paths lead to **Little Qualicum Falls** and **Englishman River Falls** (see Vancouver Escape Three for descriptions).

From Parksville, drive north to **Qualicum Beach,** sometimes referred to as Carmel North for its plethora of artists and craftspeople. Painters, sculptors, weavers, and wood-carvers make their homes here and display their works.

In the **Old School House Gallery and Art Centre,** 122 Fern Road West, numerous artists offer classes and items for sale. **Heritage Pottery and Gallery** carries the creations of more than one hundred Vancouver Island artists.

Pieces done by several island artisans are available in **The Workshop** on Island Highway. Most notable is the finely crafted jewelry of goldsmith John Rhys. At **Hy'emass House** at French Creek, native arts and crafts include murals, button blankets, wood carvings, and prints.

Larry Aguilar Pottery Studio is situated in a lush garden at Good Earth Farm in Little Qualicum. It has a bonsai collection and the largest display of tuberous begonias on Vancouver Island, as well as porcelain, stoneware, and raku.

The **Comox Valley,** north of Qualicum, calls itself the Recreation Capital of Canada with good reason. Fishing, boating, golfing, hiking, surfing, diving, and cycling are a few of the sports easily available. There are four towns in the little valley, centering on **Comox Harbour,** the terminal for the ferry from Powell River.

Drive up the highway, with the shore on your right and rolling rural countryside and high wooded ridges and mountains on your left, to arrive at the Visitors InfoCentre. Stop here for maps, brochures, and a close look at the Kwakiutl-carved **Talking Bear Totem** that graces the grounds.

Enter **Courtenay** (Island Highway skirts the downtown area on the east), and go to the **Native Sons Hall,** which houses **Courtenay and District Museum and Archives,** 360 Cliffe Avenue. The "largest log cabin in the world," it's open daily in summer and Tuesday through Saturday in winter. In 7,000 square feet of exhibit space, the general history museum shows the chronology of the Comox Valley. Permanent displays include native history, exportation, agriculture, logging, and pioneer life.

Alternatively, if you're an aviation buff, you might visit the **Comox Air Force Museum,** across the highway in Comox. The museum, open daily May through September and weekends October through April, focuses on flight in Canada, from the early Silver Dart to the jet age and space technology. Various aircraft are on outdoor display.

Near the Comox Air Force Base is **Kin Beach Provincial Park,** which has a good picnic site with cooking shelters, a playground, a tennis court, a small store, campsites, and beach access. A small breakwater creates a gentle tidal pool.

Don't miss **Comox Marina Park,** the little park with the big view. Tucked against the waterfront, it has a boat launch, picnic shelters, a bandstand, and a magnificent view of the ocean and mountains.

Stop in at **Leeward Pub** on Anderton Road in Comox for a tour of the facility and a taste of the valley's only cottage beer.

Plan to arrive early at the **Old House Restaurant** so that you'll have time to browse through **Dower Cottage,** a fetching country gift shop on the restaurant's grounds.

DINNER: The Old House Restaurant, 1760 Riverside Lane, Courtenay. (250) 338–5406. Lovely old home transformed into a busy two-level restaurant by the river. Lawns, gardens, gazebo, river (and sawmill) view. Formal dining in an inviting lodge atmosphere upstairs, with classic French dishes; casual, less expensive fare on the main level—pastas, salads, sandwiches. Very special.

LODGING: Greystone Manor Bed and Breakfast, 4014 Haas Road, Courtenay, B.C. V9N 8H9. (250) 338–1422. Gracious gray home on one and a half parklike acres above the sea. Three comfortable rooms with private baths. Antique furnishings, hospitable hosts.

DAY 2

Morning

BREAKFAST: Full breakfast in Greystone Manor's dining room. French toast, egg dishes, wild blackberries, light scones studded with raisins, and homemade jams may be served.

Turn north on Route 19 to what's been called Vancouver Island's best-kept secret, **Miracle Beach Provincial Park.** The developed park has miles of sandy beach and warm, shallow water on a protected shore. It's a fine swimming spot on a warm day, and there's a large changing house.

The park's **Nature Centre** has saltwater aquariums, forest displays, and history exhibits. Nature programs are led by park interpreters in summer. Tide pools are full of sea urchins, starfish, crabs, anemones, and other marine life. Nearly 200 campsites are scattered throughout the coastal forest.

LUNCH: Salmon Point Marine Pub and Restaurant, 2158 Salmon Point, Salmon Point. (250) 923–7272. Open, natural-wood restaurant with hanging greenery, native art, and water views. Delectable seafood chowder, good burgers, croissant sandwiches, salads.

Afternoon

Continue north to **Campbell River.** Drive on the main road to **Tyee Plaza** and the Visitors InfoCentre, which has maps, brochures, and information. In the same building is the **Campbell River Museum,** 470 Island Highway, which has exhibits that portray the traditional Kwakiutl, Nuu-Chah-Nulth, and Salish cultures; early coastal exploration; settlement of the area; and industrial development. It's worth a tour just to see the display of carved ceremonial masks.

You can purchase crafts at **Hill's Indian Crafts,** across from the information center on Shoppers Row. Preserving the West Coast heritage, the Hill's outlet sells Cowichan Indian sweaters, wood carvings, souvenirs, and artworks.

This is fishing country, "the salmon capital of the world." Here is your chance to catch the tyee salmon that give the town its claim to fame. Tyee are the big ones: Chinook salmon that weigh more than thirty pounds.

For a dollar a day (free if you're under sixteen or over sixty-five), you can fish from **Discovery Pier,** just south of downtown. Wheelchair accessible, the public pier has won several design awards.

To get out on the water and fish, rent a boat or charter a guide at **Campbell River Sportfishing Rentals** (250–287–7279).

After (or instead of) your fishing trip, board the ferry to **Quadra Island.** It's a ten-minute ride across **Discovery Passage** to the forests of Quadra.

Drive ten minutes to **Quathiaski Cove** and **Cape Mudge,** on the southern tip of the island. The **Kwaguilth Museum and Cultural Centre** in the village here is the heart of the native community, reflecting its revival of a traditional culture. The facility contains historical artifacts and a wealth of carved masks and regalia that were used in potlatches of old.

The potlatch, a ceremony of feasts and gift exchanges, was banned in the late 1800s and the items taken by the government; they were at last returned in the late 1970s and are now on proud display. The museum is open daily in July and August and afternoons Tuesday through Saturday in other months.

In the park across from the museum you can see petroglyphs, a collection of ancient stone carvings. Other petroglyphs are at their original sites along the high-tide line at Wa-Wa-Kie Beach and Francisco Point.

DINNER: April Point Lodge, Quadra Island. Water-facing restaurant serving perfectly prepared classic standards (prime rib, lamb) and salmon and Dungeness crab. Mrs. Peterson's freshly baked desserts are unbeatable.

LODGING: April Point Lodge, P.O. Box 1, Campbell River, B.C. V9W 4Z9. (250) 285–2222. Top-quality resort with lodge rooms and cottages, on 3 miles of waterfront. Some units with fireplaces and kitchens. Stunning views of Discovery Passage, bald eagles, orca whales. Boston whalers available for fishing trips.

DAY 3

Morning

BREAKFAST: Complimentary coffee and muffins in April Point dining room, or order full breakfast from the menu.

Return to Campbell River on the morning ferry and drive 53 miles north on Route 19 to **Sayward.** Mile-high **Mount H'kusam,** capped with snow and often ringed with fog, guards the east side of the **Salmon River Valley,** where the logging town of Sayward nestles. The Indian name for the mountain was *Hiyatsee Saklekum,* meaning "where the breath of the sea lion gathers at the blowhole."

On the east is **Johnstone Strait,** where jagged islands are scattered like puzzle pieces over cold blue waters.

Stop along the way to buy a picnic lunch.

Drive on to the boat launch in **Kelsey Bay,** and join **Robson Bight Charters** for a whale-watching excursion (phone or fax 250–282–3833). You'll board a 56-foot motor yacht, *Le Caique,* for an unforgettable quest to locate and observe the sleek black-and-white orca whales. This is the wilderness habitat of bald eagles, porpoises, harbour seals, Steller sea lions, and other birds and mammals. Be sure to bring a warm jacket.

On an all-day trip, the boat goes to **Robson Bight Ecological Reserve,** a marine sanctuary where the orcas gather to rub against the barnacles on the beach. The resident population of twelve pods has about 135 whales.

LUNCH: Picnic aboard the boat. Coffee, tea, juice, and a fruit basket are provided.

Afternoon

You'll return to Sayward in the late afternoon. With the conclusion of your boat trip, head back to Route 19 and turn south to Parksville.

DINNER: Kalvas Restaurant, 180 North Moilliet, Parksville. (250) 248–6933. Continental cuisine, specializing in fresh seafood.

Drive 21 miles (35 km) south on Route 19 to Nanaimo and board the ferry at Departure Bay, headed for Horseshoe Bay and Vancouver.

THERE'S MORE

Fishing. Blue Goose Fishing, 2608 Willeman Avenue, Courtenay, B.C. V9N 6L2. (250) 338–5485. Sport fishing, diving, sight-seeing cruises aboard the *M. V. Blue Goose,* a 37-foot yacht.

Campbell River District Fishing Guides Assocation, P.O. Box 66, Campbell River, B.C. V9W 4Z9. Organization of professional fishing guides, with boats from 15 to 28 feet. Will refer you to the charter that suits your needs.

Flights. Kenmore, Seattle. (800) 826–1890. Flies from Seattle to Campbell River.

Sound Flight, Renton. (206) 255–6500. Offers flights from Seattle to several British Columbia destinations.

Vancouver Island Air, Ltd., Campbell River. (250) 287–2433. Daily and charter flights to Vancouver.

Golf. Eaglecrest Golf Course, Qualicum Beach. (250) 752–6311. A 3,100-yard course, driving range, restaurant, lounge. Open daily.

Fairwinds Golf Course, Nanoose. (250) 468–7666. Eighteen-hole course; part of hotel and marina resort.

Longlands Par Three, Comox. (250) 339–6363. Manicured eighteen-hole course, easy for the novice but with some challenges.

Nanaimo Golf Club, Nanaimo. (250) 758–6332. Eighteen challenging holes; views of Georgia Strait.

Qualicum Beach Memorial Golf Club, Qualicum Beach. (250) 752–6312. Nine-hole, par 36.

Sequoia Springs, Campbell River. (250) 287–4970. Hillside course with harbor views, eighteen holes.

Storey Creek, Campbell River. (250) 923–3673. Championship eighteen-hole course carved from dense forest. Restaurant, driving range, pro shop.

Sunnydale Golf Course, Courtenay. (250) 334–3232. Eighteen holes, driving range, dining and lounge facilities, mountain view.

Hiking trails. Dalrymple Creek Nature Trail. This self-guided, forest-interpretation trail is in Kelsey Bay Woodlands, 5 miles (8 km) south of the Sayward turnoff on Route 19, 42 miles (68 km) north of Campbell River.

Forbidden Plateau. Several loop trails wind through forests of red cedar, Douglas fir, and western hemlock in this area, leading to lakes and panoramic views. Paradise Meadows is an easy 1½-mile (2⅘-km) walk over carpets of wildflowers. Begin at Mount Washington Nordic ski lodge, 15 miles (24 km) west of Courtenay.

Mitlenatch Island and Bird Sanctuary. This island has unique plant and marine life, history, and climate. There are beaches and picnic areas. Twelve miles (20 km) east of Campbell River, the sanctuary is accessible by plane or boat.

Mount Arrowsmith Trail. This well-marked trail is easy but long. Plan on a six- to nine-hour hike. It starts at Cameron Lake picnic site, 14½ miles (23 km) from Parksville.

Parksville Flats Wildlife Estuary. The 216-acre estuary lies on Englishman River tidal flats. It has hiking paths, birds, wildlife, and trees.

Rathtrevor Park. This park south of Parksville is famous for its long, sandy beach. There's great bird-watching here, with more than 150 species recorded. Nature trails are well marked.

Rebecca Spit Provincial Park, Quadra Island. The park is ideal for picnicking, beachcombing, and swimming.

Seal Bay Regional Nature Park. A wooded, 342-acre park on Seal Bay is a fifteen-minute drive north of Courtenay and Comox. It has one-hour loop trail hikes, one adapted to wheelchair use. You'll see wildflowers, seabirds, and seals.

Wesley Ridge Trail. Energetic hikers can walk this route in five hours. Starting in Little Qualicum Falls Park, west of Parksville, it leads to broad views of Mount Arrowsmith, the Strait of Georgia, and the coastal mountain range.

Strathcona Provincial Park, the oldest provincial park in British Columbia, is laced with rivers, lakes, and streams and dominated by snow-cloaked peaks with glistening glaciers. **Golden Hinde,** at 7,260 feet (2,200 m), is the highest point on Vancouver Island. **Della Falls,** at the south end of the park and accessible only by walking trail, is the highest waterfall in North America.

SPECIAL EVENTS

April. Brant Festival, Parksville and Qualicum Beach. Thousands of tiny brant geese stop on their way between Mexico and Alaska. Month-long celebrations.

Early May. Fire and Ice. Chili-making and ice-sculpture festival on the streets of Qualicum Beach.

Mid-May. Canadian Nature & Federation of British Columbia Naturalists Conference, Qualicum Beach. Visitors are invited to participate in seminars on British Columbia's natural history and attend related fieldtrips and receptions.

Early July. Canada Day Celebration, Qualicum Beach. Celebrate Canada's birthday with a parade, entertainment, displays, and fireworks.

Mid-July. International Sandcastle Competition, Parksville Beach. Popular sand-sculpture contest draws thousands of visitors a year. (250) 248–3613.

July and early August. Courtenay Youth Music Centre, Courtenay. Classes, concerts, musical theater productions by students from all over Canada.

Early August. Summer Festival, Campbell River. Parade, arts-and-crafts displays, fishing derby, fireworks, dancing, music, children's games, armwrestling contests.

Early August. Filberg Festival, Comox. Juried crafts show, entertainment, music, children's programs, food stands. On the grounds of Filberg Heritage Lodge and Park.

Late November through early December. Festival of Trees, Qualicum Beach. Magical gingerbread houses and artistically crafted Christmas trees.

OTHER RECOMMENDED RESTAURANTS AND LODGINGS

Campbell River

The Dolphins Resort, 4125 Discovery Drive. (250) 287–3066. Shoreside cedar cabins and luxury bungalows with wood stoves and stone fireplaces, equipped kitchens. Fishing gear and guided charters supplied. Your catch frozen, canned, or smoked and shipped.

Painter's Lodge, 1625 MacDonald Road, Campbell River. (250) 286–1102. Modern fishing resort overlooking Discovery Passage. Restaurant, lounge, outdoor heated pool. Accommodation rates include eight hours of fishing.

Courtenay

La Cremaillere Restaurant, 975 Como Road. (250) 338–8131. Tudor-style dining house with river view. Outstanding French cuisine and wines.

Mama Mia's, 932 Fitzgerald Avenue. (250) 338–6612. Bungalow converted to an intimate eatery, open for lunch, dinner. Fresh ingredients, lots of garlic. Closed Sunday.

Parksville

Island Hall Beach Resort, Island Highway. (250) 248–3225. One-hundred-room beachside motel with restaurant, lounge, lawns, flowers. Lovely blue-tiled indoor pool and whirlpool/sauna.

Tigh-na-Mara Resort, 1095 East Island Highway, Parksville, B.C. V9P 2E5. (250) 248–2072. Beachfront lodge and cabins, some with fireplaces and kitchens. Restaurant, pool, tennis courts.

Qualicum Beach

Qualicum College Inn, 427 College Road, Qualicum Beach, B.C. V9K 2G4. (250) 752–9262 or (800) 663–7306. Former boys' school, historic landmark overlooking Georgia Strait. Resort hotel with Old English atmosphere, indoor pool, restaurant.

Quathiaski Cove

Tsa-Kwa-Luten Lodge, P.O. Box 460. (250) 285–2042 or (800) 665–7745. Resort on Quadra Island based on Pacific coast native traditions. Fir lodge with thirty-five rooms and restaurant.

FOR MORE INFORMATION

BC Ferries, 1112 Fort Street, Victoria, B.C. V8V 4V2. Vancouver (604) 669–1211, Victoria (250) 386–3431.

British Columbia Travel Information. (800) 663–6000.

Campbell River Tourism, P.O. Box 482, 1235 Island Highway, Campbell River, B.C. V9W 5C1. (250) 286–2616 or (800) 463–1616.

Parksville and District Visitor Information Centre, 1275 East Island Highway, Parksville, B.C. V9P 2G3. (250) 248–3613.

Qualicum Beach Chamber of Commerce, 2711 West Island Highway, Qualicum Beach, B.C. V9K 2C4. (250) 752–9532.

INDEX

A

Active Pass Light Station, 249
Admiralty Inlet, 133
Aerie, The, 292
Agassiz, 209
Ainsworth State Park, 66, 83
airplane excursions, 128, 259, 303
Alder Bay Boat Company, 116
Alder House, 18
Alexandra Bridge, 221
Alfie's Wayside Country Inn, 75
Alley Way Cafe, 230
Aloha, 78
Alsea Bay Bridge Interpretive Center, 28
American Camp, 126
Amphitrite Point, 232
Anacortes, 121
Anglican Church of St. John and Divine, 222
Ann Starrett Mansion, 134
Anne Hathaway's Cottage, 238
Antelope, 86
Antique Market Place Mall, The, 168
antiques, 15, 18, 59, 75, 168, 193, 194
Ape Cave, 49
Aplets and Cotlets, 159
April Point Lodge, 302
Arch Cape, 15
Argyle, 76
Ark, The, 58
art galleries, 14, 15, 17, 193, 261, 270
Art Kinsman Park, 288
Arterberry Winery Cellars, 75
Arthur D. Feiro Marine Laboratory, 138
Arts Club Main Stage, 116
Arts Club Revue, 116
Asean Imports, 287
Ashcroft Manor and Teahouse, 219
Ashford, 181
Asotin, 5
Asotin County Historical Museum, 8
Astoria, Oregon, 52–61
Astoria Column, 54

Auberge La Cote d'Azur, 209
Auld Kirk Gallery, 291

B

British Columbia Falls, 280
British Columbia Orchard Industry Museum, 280
Backbone Ridge, 177
Bainbridge Island, 183
Bamberton Provincial Park, 292
Barlow Pass, 37, 169
Baston Square, 237
Bay City, 16
Bay Coffee Company and Espresso, 199
Bay House, 18
Beach Gardens Resort, 258
Beamer's Heller Bar Lodge, 5
Beamers Copper Creek Lodge, 7
Beamers Hell's Canyon Tours and Excursions, 2
Bear Creek Artichokes, 19
Bear Meadow, 47
Beaver, 147
Belknap Crater, 95
Bell Point Trail, 126
Bellingham, 114
Bend, 103, 108
Benham Falls, 105
Bennett Pass, 37
Benson's Restaurant, 185
Bentley's on the Bay, 238
bicycling, 128, 139, 162
Big Four Ice Caves, 169
Big Four Mountain, 169
Big Sky Golf and Country Club, 216
Bilknap Springs, 95
Billy Miner Pub, 206
Birth of a Lake Trail, 46
Bistro Car, 114
Black Butte, 105, 109
Black Crater Trail, 106
Blackman House Museum, 168
Blue Heron French Cheese Company, 17
Blue Heron Inn, 257

Blue Heron, The, 228
Blue River, 94
Bluenose Steak and Seafood House, 290
boating, 59, 77, 139, 173, 200, 250, 260, 292
Bob's Apple Barrel, 159
Boehm's Candies, 153, 162
Bonneville Dam, 66
Boulder River Wilderness, 168
Boundary Bay, 114
Box Canyon, 177
Bralorne, 216
Breckinridge Mountains, 208
Brentwood Bay, 285
Brick, The, 161
Bridal Falls Provincial Park, 209
Bridal Veil, 69
Bridal Veil Falls, 64, 209
Bridal Veil Falls State Park, 64
Bridge of the 23 Camels, 218
Bridge of the Gods Park, 39
Bridges Restaurant and Pub, 116
Bright Angel Provincial Park, 291
Briscoe Lake, 57
Britannia Beach, 214
British Camp, 126
British Columbia Forest Museum, 289
British Columbia Museum of Mining, 214
Broken Group Islands, 227
Brownsville, 96
brusseau's, 142
Bubba's Pizza, 56
Buffalo Eddy, 5
Buffalo Run Restaurant, 170
Burgoyne Bay, 267
Bush House Country Inn, 157
Butchart Gardens, 287
Butchart Gardens Dining Room, The, 287
Butterfly World, 231, 285

C

Cabin Fever Rustics, 158
Cache Creek, 219
Cafe de la Mer, 14
Cafe Olga, 124
Cafe Roma, 17 .
Cafe Zenon, 25
Calona Wines, 276
Cameron, 76
Camp 18, 11
Camp Sherman, 105
Campbell Bay, 249

Campbell River, 301, 306
Campbell River Museum, 301
Campbell River Sportfishing Rentals, 301
Campbell Valley Regional Park, 210
camping, 50, 146
Campus Cottage, 25
Canada Place, 118
Cannon Beach, 13, 20
Cannon Beach Cookie Company, 14
canoeing, 30, 260
Canyon Way Restaurant and Bookstore, 29
Cape Disappointment Lighthouse, 56
Cape Falcon, 15
Cape Flattery, 137
Cape Mudge, 301
Cape Perpetua, 27
car museum, 85
Caribou Jade and Gifts, 219
Caribou Wagon Road, 219
Carnation, 154
Carpenter House, 161
Carver's Coffee House, 259
Casablanca, 25
Cascade Head, 17
Cascade Lake, 123
Cascade Lakes Highway, 106
Cascade Locks, 39, 68
Cascade Mountain Inn, 170
Cascade Salmon Hatchery, 68
Cascades Dining Room, 37
Cashmere, 159
Castle Rock, 45
Cathedral Grove, 227
Cathlamet, 59
Cayoosh Creek, 217
Cayuse Pass, 177
Cedars Bed and Breakfast, 217
Celilo Park, 84
Centennial Park, 293
Central Oregon, 100–10
Channel Lodge, The, 193
Charles W. Bingham Mount St. Helens Forest
     Learning Center, 46
Chateau Benoit Winery, 75
Chateau Ste. Michelle Winery, 155
Chelan County Historical Museum, 159
Chemainiac Shop, 289
Chemainus, 289, 294
Chemainus Theatre, 293
Chemainus Valley Museum, 289
Chestnut Cottage, 136
Chetzemoka Park, 135

Chief Lelooska Living History Presentation, 50
Chief Looking Glass Park, 8
Chief Seattle, 183
Chief Timothy State Park, 8
Chilliwack, 209
Chimposium, 162
China Beach, 240
Chinese Tree of Heaven, 134
Chinook Pass, 177
Chuckanut Mountains, 114
Circle H Holiday Ranch, 160
City Pier, Port Angeles, 139
Clallam Bay, 136
Clallam County Historical Museum, 135
Clarion Lakeside Resort at Penticton, The, 275
Clarkston, 4, 9
Clarno Formation, 85
Clarno Palisades, 85
Clatsop County Heritage Museum, 55
Clay Sculpture Studio, 116
Clayoquot Sound, 228
Cle Elum, 163
Cle Elum Bakery, 161
Cle Elum Historical Telephone Museum, 161
Clear Lake, 96
Clear Lake Resort, 96
Clearwater Casino, 188
Cliffside Inn On-the-Sea, 246
climbing, 50, 107, 180
Cloud Cap Inn, 38
Cloverdale, 20
Clymer Gallery, 160
Coast Range, 114
Coaster Theater, 15
Cobble Hill, 291, 294
Coldwater Ridge Deck Talk, 46
Coldwater Ridge Visitor Center, 46
Coles Corner, 158
Columbia Gorge, 39
Columbia Gorge Hotel, 67
Columbia River, 81
Columbia River Gorge, 37, 39, 62–70
Columbia River Maritime Museum, 54
Columbia View Park, 54
Columbian Cafe, 54
Colvos Passage, 199
Combers Beach, 230
Comet Cafe and Rose's Bakery, 123
Common Loaf Bake Shop, 229
Comox Air Force Museum, 300
Comox Harbour, 299
Comox Marina Park, 300

Comox Valley, 299
Condon, 84
Cooper Spur, 38
Cougar, 49, 51
Cougar Ceramics, 49
Cougar Dam and Reservoir, 94
Country Flowers, 85
Country Flowers Soda Fountain, 85
Courtenay, 299, 306
Courtenay and District Museum and
    Archives, 299
Cove Palisades State Park, 102
covered bridges, 26, 29, 58, 93, 281
Cowichan Bay, 294
Cowichan Lake, 293
Cowichan Valley museum, 290
CP Rail Caboose, 206
Crab Bar, The, 230
Crafthouse, 116
Crafts Association of B.C., 116
Craig Heritage Museum Park, 297
Craigdorrach Castle, 237
Cranberry Pottery, 259
Creamery, The, 287
Crooked River Railroad Company, 107
Crown, 218
Crown Point, 64
cruises, 30, 39, 128, 195
Crystal Mountain, 181
Cuckoo Clock Shop, 158

D

D'Arcy, 216
Dalles, The, 83
Darlingtonia Wayside, 27
Darvill's, 123
Davison Orchards, 280
Dayton, 78
Deception Falls, 157
Dee's Country Accents, 158
Deep Creek, 7
Deer Harbor Road, 125
Deer Head Rapids, 6
Della Falls, 305
Demitasse, The, 238
Denney's, 34
Deschutes Brewery and Public House, 102
Deschutes Historical Center, 103
Deschutes River Canyon, 87, 102
Deschutes River Recreation Area, 84
Desolation Sound, 259

Detroit Lake, 106
Diable Lake Overlook, 171
Die Musik Box, 158
Dinner Bay Community Park, 248
Dinotown, 209
Discovery Passage, 301
Discovery Pier, 301
diving, 232, 251, 260
Dr. John C. Brougher Museum, 77
Doe Bay Village Resort, 124
Doe Island Marine Park, 124
Dolphin Bay Bicycles, 125
Dooger's, 13
Dorris Ranch, 30
Dower Cottage, 300
Drake Park, 105
Drift Creek Covered Bridge, 18
Drift Creek Wilderness, 30
Driftwood Inn, 257
Duck Brand Cantina, 173
Duck Pond Cellars, 76
Duck Soup Inn, 127
Duffy Lake, 217
Duffy Lake Road, 217
Dug Bar, 7
Duncan, 290, 295
Dundee, 78
Dungeness Spit, 139

E

Eagle's Nest Pub, 231
Eagle Aerie Gallery, 230
Eagle Creek Trail, 66
Earl's Cove, 258
Early Winter Spires, 171
East Point Seafood Company, 58
Eastsound, 123
Eaton's Department Store, 237
Echo Island, 208
Edinburgh Tartan Shop, 115
Elaine's Coffee Garden, 218
Elevated Ice Cream, 134
Eliot Hiking Trail, 58
Elizabeth Park and Bloedel Conservatory, 119
Elk Cove, 74
Ellensburg, 155–65
Elmira, 31
Elochoman Slough Marina, 59
Elphinstone Pioneer Museum, 256
Emily Carr College of Art and Design, 116
Emmons Glacier, 177

Emory's Bar, 222
Emory Creek Provincial Park, 222
Empress Hotel, 235
Englishman Falls, 227
Englishman River Falls, 299
Englishman River Falls Provincial Park, 227
Erath, 76
Errington, 225
Esquimault, 238
Eugene, 23–33, 91, 98
Eureka Bar, 6
Ewings, 87
Excellent Framing Gallery and Handcrafts, 287
Eyrie, 75

F

Factory Stores at Lincoln City, 18
Fall City, 148–54
False Creek, 115
Fat Rascal, The, 267
Father Pandosy's Mission, 277
Fenn Lodge, 207
Fern Ridge Lake, 26
Fifth Street Public Market, 25, 91
Finn's Waterfront Restaurant, 117
First Bank Antiques, 168
First Beach, 218
Fisgard Lighthouse, 238
fishing, 19, 40, 59, 89, 97, 129, 139, 173, 222, 232, 251, 260, 270, 280, 293, 303
Flamingo Jim's, 16
Florence, 23–33
Flying Pig, The, 287
Fogg 'n' Suds, 206
Forest Grove, 74, 79
Forks, 144, 147
Forks Timber Museum, 146
Fort Astoria log stockade, 54
Fort Canby State Park, 56
Fort Clatsop National Memorial, 55
Fort Langley, 210, 212
Fort Langley National Historic Site, 210
Fort Rodd Hill National Historic Park, 238
Fort Stevens State Park, 55
Fort Worden State Park, 134
Fort Yamhill blockhouse, 77
Fossil, 85
Fountain Cafe, 135
Fraser Canyon, 220
Fraser River, 206, 218
Fraser River Heritage Regional Park, 206

Fraser Valley, 204–13
French Beach Provincial Park, 239
Friday Harbor, 125, 130
Front Street Cafe, 127
Fulford Harbor, 267

G

Gaches Mansion, 193
Galiano Island, 246, 252
Gallery of B.C. Ceramics, 116
Gallery Players of Oregon, 77
Gallery Tantalus, 258
Galloping Goose Regional Park, 238
Ganges, 267
Garden Bay Lake, 258
Garibaldi, 16
Garibaldi Provincial Park, 214
Gassy Jack, 115
Gastown, 114
General Motors Place, 117
Geneva Bar, 6
Georgina Point, 249
Gibsons, 254, 263
Gig Harbor, 197–202
Gig Harbor Peninsula Historical Society and
    Museum, 201
Gilman Antique Gallery, 153
Gilman Village, 153
Ginkgo Petrified Forest State Park, 161
gliding, 222
Glondo's Sausage Company, 161
Goat Island, 259
Gold Bridge, 216
Golden Ears Provincial Park, 211
Golden Hinde, 305
golf, 19, 30, 59, 68, 77, 139, 153, 162, 201, 232,
    240, 251, 261, 280, 293, 303
Goodpasture Covered Bridge, 93
Gordon Wales Pottery, 269
Gorilla Rock, 124
Government Camp, 41
Governor Tom McCall Preserve at Rowena
    Plateau, 83
Granary, The, 192
Grand Ronde River, 5
Granite Falls, 169
Granny's Country Store, 28
Granville Island, 115
Granville Island Ferries, 115
Greater Vancouver Zoological Centre, 209
Green River, 216

Greystone Manor Bed and Breakfast, 300
Grove Hall Estate, 288
Grove of the Patriarchs, 177
Gulf Islands, 243–53, 267, 285
Gus Backstrom Park, 47
Gwyinn Creek Trail, 30

H

Half Moon Bay, 257, 263
Hall of Mosses, 145
Haller Fountain, The, 133
Hancock Field Station, 86
Haney House, 206
Hanging Tree, 218
Harbour Cafe, 256
Harrison's Bakery, 13
Harrison Hot Springs, 207, 212
Harrison Hot Springs Hotel, 207
Harrison Lake, 208
Harrison Mills, 207, 211
Hat Creek House, 219
Hat Creek Ranch, 218
Hatheume Lake, 282
Hayes Oysters, 16
Haystack Rock, 13
He Devil Mountain, 7
He Tin Kush Park, 232
Hebo, 21
Hecate Park, 288
Heceta Head lighthouse, 27
Hedges, 152
Hell's Canyon, 2–10
Hell's Gate, 221
Hell's Gate Airtram, 221
Heller Bar, 5
Hell's Canyon, 2–10
Hell's Canyon Adventures, 8
Hell's Canyon National Recreation Area, 6
Hendricks Park, 25
Henry M. Jackson Visitors' Center, 177
Henry M. Jackson Wilderness, 169
Herbfarm, 152
Heritage Pottery and Gallery, 299
Heritage River Walk, 206
Herons, 299
Hideway, The, 18
High Desert Museum, 104
High Mountain Sheep Rapids, 6
hiking, 30, 97, 139, 180, 270, 293, 304
Hill's Indian Crafts, 115, 290, 301
Hillside House Bed and Breakfast, 127

Hinman Vineyards, 26
Historic Fort Langley, 210
Hoffstadt Bluffs Visitor Center, 45
Hoh Rain Forest Visitor Center, 145
Hoh River Trail, 145
Hoh River Valley, 142–47
Honey Bear Express, 36
Hood Canal, 144
Hood River, 39, 69
Hood River Brewing Company, 68
Hood River County Historical Museum, 67
Hood River Golf Course, 68
Hood River Hotel, 67
Hood River Meadows, 38
Hood River Valley, 38, 66
Hood River Vineyards, 67
Hoover-Minthorn House, 77
Hope, 208, 222
Hope Bay, 246
Hope Slide, 209
Hopkins Hill, 51
horseback riding, 107, 161, 173, 251
Horsetail Falls, 66, 83
Hot Springs Cove, 232
Hotel Eldorado, 277
House of Himwitsa, 230
House of McLaren, 115
House Piccolo, 268
Hudson's Bay Company, 126
Hult Center for the Performing Arts, 23
Hummingbird, 247
Hunter Gallery, 261
Hurricane Ridge, 139
Hy'emass House, 299

I

Icicle Valley, 158
Ilwaco, 61
Ilwaco Heritage Museum, 55
Images for a Canadian Heritage, 115
Images of the Circle, 289
Imax Theatre, 118
Independence Pass, 48
Index, 157
Inland Lake, 261
Inn at Cooper Spur, The, 38
Inner Harbour, 235
Inspiration Point, 38
Inuit Gallery, 115
Iron Goat Trail, 157
Isadora's, 150

Island Bicycles, 129
Issaquah, 153, 162

J

Jack's, 50
Jack's Sporting Goods and Restaurant, 49
Jackson House, 46
Jakle's Lagoon, 126
James House, 135
Jefferson County Courthouse, 134
Jefferson County Historical Museum, 133
Jesse M. Honeyman State Park, 26
Joffre Glacier, 217
Joffre Lake, 217
John Day Fossil Beds, 81–90
John Day Fossil Beds National Monument, 85
John Day River, 84, 89
Johnson Street Bridge, 238
Johnston Ridge Observatory, 46
Johnstone Strait, 302
Judy Hill Gallery, 290

K

Kachess Lake, 161
Kalamalka Lookout, 280
Kaledan, 283
Kalvas Restaurant, 303
Kamloops, 279
Kamloops Wildlife Park, 280
kayaking, 124, 232, 260, 270
Kelowna, 276, 283
Kelowna Waterfront Park, 277
Kelsey Bay, 302
Kettle Valley Railway, 281
Kids Only Market, 116
Kilby Historic Store and Farm, 207
Kin Beach Provincial Park, 300
King Street Station, 112
Kirkwood Ranch, 7
Kites on Clouds, 115
Kitsap Peninsula, 183
Kitsap State Memorial Park, 187
Kittitas County Historic Museum, 160
Knox Heritage Church, 297
Koosah Falls, 95
Kopachuck State Park, 200
Kramer, 74
Kremeos, 275
Kremeos Grist Mill, 275
Kris Kringl, 158
Kwaguilth Museum and Cultural Centre, 301

L

L.T. Murray Wildlife Recreation Area, 161
La Conner, 192, 196
La Conner Flats, 192
La Serre, 28
Ladder Creek Rock Garden, 170
Lafayette, 75
Lafayette Schoolhouse Antique Mall, 75
Lahar Viewpoint, 49
Lake Billy Chinook, 102
Lake Crescent, 137, 144
Lake Crescent Lodge, 137
Lake Merwin, 50
Lake Okanagan, 275
Lake Ozette, 136
Lake Sammamish, 153
Lake Stevens, 168
Lake Wenatchee, 158
Lake Wenatchee State Park, 158
Lakeview Restaurant, 209
Lamplighter Gallery Cafe, 210
Landfall, The, 133
Landing, The, 115
Lane County Ice, 30
Langdale, 254–64
Lange, 76
Lara House, 104
Larry Aguilar Pottery Studio, 299
Latourell Falls, 64
Laurel Ridge Winery, 73
Lava Butte, 104
Lava Cast Forest, 107
Lava Lands Visitor Center, 104
Lava River Cave, 107
LaVelle Vineyards, 26
Lazy Susan Cafe, 15
Leaburg, 98
Leaburg Dam, 93
Leadbetter Point State Park, 58
Leavenworth, 155–65
Leavenworth Nutcracker Museum, 158
Leeward Pub, 300
Legends, 194
Lewis and Clark Interpretive Center, 56
Lewis and Clark State Park, 47
Lewis River, 49
Lewiston, 4, 9
Liberty Bay Park, 186
Liberty Bell Mountain, 171
Lillooet, 218
Lillooet Museum, 218

Lime Kiln Lighthouse, 126
Lime Kiln Point State Park, 126
Lime Point, 5
Lincoln City, 11–22
Linfield College, 75
Linn County Museum, 96
Little Log Church, 28
Little Mount Si, 152
Little Qualicum Falls, 231, 299
Lively Park Swim Center, 30
Living Rock Studios, The, 97
Lloyd Gallery, The, 281
Locomotive Park, 289
Loft, The, 230
Log Cabin Inn, 95
Log Cabin Museum, 199
Log Cabin Resort restaurant, 137
Log Cabin Restaurant, 95
Lolo Pass, 36
Long Beach, 52–61, 228
Long Harbour, 267
Longhouse Interpretive Centre, 207
Longmire, 178, 182
Lonsdale Quay, 117
Lopez Island, 128
Lorraine's Edel Haus, 158
Lover's Lane, 144
Lowe's Resort, 257
Lund, 254–64
Lytton, 220, 224

M

M.V. Lady Rose, 233
MacMillan Provincial Park, 227
MacMillan-Bloedel pulp-and-paper mill, 261
Madeira Park, 257, 263
Magnus Andersoin Cabin, 193
Mahle House, The, 232
Main Street, 188
Makah Cultural and Research Center, 136
Makah Indian Reservation, 136
Manning Provincial Park, 275
Manor Farm Inn, 186
Manzanita, 15, 21
Maple Bay, 295
Maple Ridge, 206
Maple Ridge Museum, 206
Marble Canyon Park, 218
Marblemount, 170
Marine Ecology Station, 288
Marine Park, 39
Mariners Museum, 200

Maritime Centre, The, 287
Maritime Market, 116
Maritime Museum of British Columbia, 237
Mark O. Hatfield Marine Science Center, 29
Marten Rapids, 93
Mary's Corner, 46
Marymere Falls, 137
Maupin, 87, 89
Mayne Island, 245, 248, 252
Mayne Street Mall, 249
Mazama, 172
Mazama Country Inn, 172
McCall Point, 83
McCullough Station, 276
McKenzie's Restaurant, 103
McKenzie Bridge, 95
McKenzie River, 93
McKenzie River Highway, 91–99
McMinnville, 79
Meager Creek Hot Springs, 216
Meare's Landing, 229
Meares Island, 230
Mechanical Music Museum, 289
Mekala's, 25, 93
Meeker Mansion, 179
Memorial Park, 222
Merritt, 279
Meta Lake, 48
Meta Lake Trail 48, 210
Methow River, 172
Methow Valley, 172
Mile 0 Cairn, 218
Mill Bay, 287, 295
Mill Hill Park, 238
Miller Tree Inn, 145
Miner's Bay Trading Post, 248
Miner's Car, 48
Miners Bay, 248
Mink Lake Trail, 144
Minter Gardens, 209
Miracle Beach Provincial Park, 301
Mission, 206
Miyazaki Residence, 218
Molly's Lane, 256
Molly's Reach, 256
Molly Ward Gardens, 187
Mom's Pies, 93
Monroe, 165
Montague Harbour Provincial Marine Park, 247
Montinore Vineyards, 74
Moran State Park, 123, 124
Morning Star II, 19

Morton, 47, 51
Mossy Creek, 18
Mossyrock, 47
Mossyrock Dam, 47
Mouat's Mall, 270
Mouht Pilchuck Lookout, 169
Mount Adams, 65
Mount Arrowsmith, 299
Mount Baker, 114, 123, 192
Mount Baker International, 112
Mount Baker–Snoqualmie National Forest, 169
Mount Constitution, 123
Mount Currie, 217
Mount Daniel, 257
Mount Finlayson, 126
Mount H'kusam, 302
Mount Hood Country Store, 39
Mount Hood Information Center, 36
Mount Hood, 34–42
Mount Hood Meadows Ski Area, 37
Mount Hood National Forest, 88
Mount Hood Railroad, 41, 68
Mount Index, 157
Mount Jefferson, 102
Mount Loop Highway, 168
Mount Maxwell, 267
Mount Pilchuck, 169
Mount Pilchuck Lookout, 169
Mount Rainier, 123, 175–82
Mount Rainier National Park, 177
Mount Rainier Scenic Railroad, 179
Mount Si, 150
Mount St. Helens, 43–51, 65
Mount St. Helens Visitors' Center, 45
Mount Storm King Trail, 138
Mountain Cimbing, 180
Mountain/Canyon Circle, 214–24
Moyer House, 96
Muddy River, 49
Multnomah Falls, 64, 81
Multnomah Falls Creek, 65
Multnomah Falls Lodge, 65
Multnomah Lodge, 81
Munson Creek Falls, 19
Munson Mountain, 281
museums, 8, 17, 18, 25, 27, 47, 54, 55, 59, 67,
        73, 75, 77, 84, 85, 96, 102, 104, 123, 125,
        127, 133, 135, 136, 146, 152, 159, 160,
        161, 168, 172, 185, 188, 193, 199, 200,
        201, 206, 214, 216, 218, 237, 238, 256,
        277, 280, 281, 289, 290, 297, 299, 300,
        301

Museum at Warm Springs, 102
Museum of Northwest Art, 193
mushroom collecting, 41

N

Nahcotta, 58
Nairn Falls Provincial Park, 216
National Historic Landmark, 36
Native Heritage Centre, 290
Native Interpretive Site, 219
Native Sons Hall, 299
National Scenic Area, 39
Nature Centre, 301
Naval Air Museum, 18
Neah Bay, 136
Neahkahnie Mountain, 15
Nehalem, 15
Nehalem River, 15
Neskowin, 17
Netarts Bay, 21
New Day Seafood, 185
New Morning Coffeehouse, 28
New Westminster, 117, 120, 210
Newberg, 79
Newberry Crater Obsidian Trail, 105
Newhalem, 170
Newport, 23–33
Nez Perce Crossing, 7
Nick's Italian Cafe, 74
Nisqually Glacier, 177
Nisqually River, 179
Norma Kenney House, 206
North Bend, 152, 154
North Cascades, 166–74
North Cascades Inn, 170
North Central Washington Museum, 159
North Fork of the Toutle River, 45
North Head Lighthouse, 56
North Kitsap Peninsula, 183–89
North Pender, 245
North Vancouver, 117
Northwest Trek, 179
Norway Pass Trail, 48
Nussknacker Haus, 158

O

O'Keefe Ranch, 278
Oak Bay, 237
Oak Bay Beach Hotel, 238
observatories, 107
Obsidian flows, 105

Oceanwood Country Inn, 248
Of Sea and Shore Museum, 188
Officers' Quarters, 126
Ohme Gardens, 159
Okanagan, 273–84
Okanagan Butterfly World, 276
Okanagan Game Farm, 281
Old Bay Front, 29
Old Bel Tower, 134
Old College Hall, 74
Old Country Market, 232
Old House Restaurant, 300
Old Man House State Park, 185
Old Mill Community Park, 291
Old School House Gallery and Art Centre, 299
Old Schoolhouse, 188
Old Scotch Church, 73
Old Settlers Museum, 47
Old St. Peter's Church, 84
Old Town, 26
old-growth forest, 47
Olde England Inn, 238
Olga, 124
Olmstead Place State Park, 160
Olympic Mountains, 114
Olympic Peninsula, 114, 131, 142–47
Olympic West Arttrek, 146
Omnimax Theatre, 119
Ona Beach State Park, 29
One-Mile Lake, 216
Oneonta Gorge Botanical Area, 66, 83
Operation Santa Claus, 107
Orcas Hotel, 125
Orcas Island, 121–30
Orcas Island Artworks, 124
Orcas Island Eclipse Charters, 125
Orcas Island Historical Museum, 123
Oregon Coast Aquarium, 29
Oregon Dunes National Recreation Area, 26
Oregon Dunes Overlook, 27
Oregon Trail Historic Marker, 84
Oswald West State Park, 15
Othello Quintette, 208
Othello Tunnels, 222
Otis, 18
Otis Cafe, 18
Otter Bay, 245
Oxbow Salmon Hatchery, 39
Oyster Bay, 249
Oysterville, 57

P

Pacific Central Station, 114
Pacific Coastal Air, 259
Pacific Crest National Scenic Trail, 37
Pacific Rim Art, 115
Pacific Rim National Park, 228
Pacific Sands Beach Resort, 228
Pacific University, 74
Packwood, 182
Padilla Bay, 190
Padilla Bay National Estuarine Research
    Reserve, 190
Palmer Glacier, 36
Palmers, 193
Panorama Point, 39, 68, 178
Panther Creek, 75
Paperworks Gallery, 258
Paradise, 177
Paradise Inn, 178
Paradise Park, 37, 178
Parksville, 231, 297, 306
Parliament Buildings, 235
Pasayten Wilderness, 172
Pavilion, 218
Peace Lutheran Church, 195
Peaches and Cream, 276
Peachland, 276
Pebbles Restaurant, 256
Pelton Dam, 102
Pemberton, 223
Pemberton Adventure Ranch, 216
Pemberton Airport, 216
Pemberton Museum, 216
Pemberton Valley, 216
Pemberton Valley Golf and Country Club, 216
Pemberton Village, 216
Pender Harbour, 257
Pender Islands, 245, 252
Pendleton, 4
Penticton, 275, 283
Penticton Museum, 281
Perdition Trail, 65
Performance Circle Theater, 201
Peter Iredale, 55
Peter Skeen Ogden Trail, 105
Petersen Rock Garden, 107
petroglyphs, 5
Pie in the Sky, 158
Pig War, 125
Pillars Bed and Breakfast, The, 200
Pillars of Hercules, 64

Pilot Butte, 102
Pine Mountain Observatory, 107
Pine Tavern Restaurant, 105
Pioneer Country Market and Museum, 277
Pioneer Hall, 75
Pioneer Museum, 17
Pioneer Village Museum, 168
Pipers Lagoon, 297
Pitt Meadows, 206
Plumper Pass Lockup, 250
Point Defiance, 200
Point No Point, 240
Point No Point Lighthouse, 188
Porpoise Bay, 257
Port Alberni, 227
Port Angeles, 135, 140
Port Angeles Fine Art Center, 135
Port Angeles Harbor, 136
Port Browning, 245
Port Browning Cafe or Pub, 245
Port Gamble, 187
Port Gamble Cemetery, 188
Port Gamble Historical Museum, 188
Port Haney Wharf, 206
Port Ludlow, 140
Port Madison Indian Reservation, 185
Port Marina Park, 67
Port Moody, 206
Port Orchard, 197
Port Townsend, 133, 141
Port Townsend Marine Science Center, 134
Potters' Guild of B.C., 116
Poulsbo, 185
Poulsbo Marine Science Center, 186
Powell Lake, 259
Powell River, 258, 263
Powell River Recreation and Cultural
    Centre, 261
Prime Air, 216
Princess Louisa Inlet, 261
Punchbowl Falls, 66
Puyallup, 179, 182

Q

Quadra Island, 301
Qualicum Beach, 299, 307
Qualicum River, 231
Quality Inn, Clarkston, 4
Quamichan Inn, 288
Quarry Wilderness Park, 291
Quathiaski Cove, 301, 307

Queen Elizabeth Park and Bloedel Cinservatory, 119
Queen Elizabeth Theatre, 117
Quilchena, 279
Quilchena Hotel, 279

R

Raab Park, 186
Rachael Griffin Historic Exhibition Center, 36
Radar Hill, 230
rafting, 87, 98, 161, 162, 223
Raintree Restaurant at the Landing, 117
Rainy Lake, 171
Rainy Lake National Recreation Trail, 171
Rainy Pass, 171
Ram's Head Bar, 37
Ramona Creek, 36
Ramona Falls, 36
Randle, 47
Raspberry Kitchen, 207
Raven's Coast Expeditions, 262
Raven's Cry Theatre, 256
Red Door, The, 288
Redmen Hall, 58
Remote Passages, 229
Rex Hill Vineyards, 76
Rhododendron, 41
Rialto Beach, 146
Ridge Winery, 73
Riffe Lake, 47
Rim Road, 102
River Bend Farm and Country Store, 68
River Life Interpretive Center, 58
river-rafting, 87
Riverside Park, 279
Roadhouse Inn, 47
Roberts Creek Provincial Park, 256
Robson Bight Charters, 302
Robson Bight Ecological Reserve, 303
Roche Harbor, 126
Rock Gems of Canada, 115
Rockaway Beach, 16
Rockport, 169
Rockport State Park, 169, 170
Rocky Reach Dam, 160
Romona Falls, 36
RoozenGaarde, 195
Rosario Resort, 124
Rose Garden, 275
Rosebriar Hotel, 55
Rosedale Gardens, 200

Roslyn, 161
Ross Lake, 171
Rothschild House, 134
Round Butte Dam, 102
Rowena's Inn on the River, 207
Rowena Crest View Point, 83
Rowena Dell, 83
Royal British Columbia Museum, 237
Ruby Creek, 171
Ruckle Provincial Park, 267
Run of the River, 159
Ryan House, 180

S

Sa-Cinn Native Enterprises, Ltd., 289
Sahalie Falls, 37, 96
Salish Lodge, 151
Salmon House, 221
Salmon Point Marine Pub and Restaurant, 301
Salmon River, 6
Salmon River Valley, 302
Salt Cairn, Seaside, 19
Salt Creek Recreation Area, 136
Salt Spring, 267
Salt Spring Island, 265–72
Saltery Bay Provincial Park, 262
Saltery Bay, 258
San Juan Island, 121–30
San Juan Island Historical Museum, 125
San Juan Island National Historic Park, 125
San Juan Islands, 114
San Juan Kayak Expeditions, 129
San Juan Transit, 126
Sandcut Beach, 240
Sandy, 42
Sandy River, 36
Sankey Park, 96
Santa Fe Station, 217
Santiam Pass, 106
Santiam River, 96, 106
Saturday Market, 30, 91
Sauk Mountain Trail, 169
Savary Island, 259
Sayward, 302
Scandia Bakery, 194
Scenic Highway, 64, 81
Science World, 119
Sea Lion Caves, 27
Seaback, 189
Seal Rock, 33
Sealand of the Pacific, 237

Seaside, 11–22
Seaside Guild of Artists, 13
Seattle National Historic District, 133
Seaview, 56, 61
Seaview Antiques and Collectibles Mall, 59
Sechelt, 256
Sechelt Indian Band's House of Hewhiwus, 256
Sechelt Inlet, 257
Second Beach, 218
Secret Cove, 257
Secwepemc Cultural and Education Society, 281
Sekiu, 136
Seton Lake, 217
Shafer Museum, 172
Shafer Vineyard Cellars, 73
Shamrock Lodgettes, 28
Shaniko Wedding Chapel, 86
Shaniko, 81–90
Shaniko Cafe, 86
Shaniko Hotel, 86
Shannon Falls Provincial Park, 214
Shawnigan Lake, 295
Shawnigan Lake Marina, 293
Shawnigan Lake Village, 291
Shearwater Sea Kayak Tours, 124
Shelburne Inn, The, 57
Shepherd's Dell, 64
Sherar Falls, 87
Shinglemill Restaurant Pub and Bistro, 259
Ship Inn, 55
Shoalwater Restaurant, 57
shopping, 128
Shop-Rite, 145
Shorepine Bog Trail, 228
Shorline Steak & Seafood, 199, 200
Silver Lake, 45
Silver Star Mountain, 171
Sisters, 105, 109
Siuslaw River cruises, 30
Skagit County, 190–96
Skagit County Museum, 193
Skagit Gardens, 195
Skagit River, 169, 190
Skagit Valley, 114, 192
Skagit Valley Bulb Farms, 195
Skagit Wildlife Recreation Area, 194
Skamokawa, 58
Skihist Provincial Park, 220
Skiing, 36, 162, 174, 180, 281
Skinner Butte Park, 23
Skookumchuk Narrows, 257, 262
Skykomish, 157

Skykomish River, 157
Skyline Trail, 178
Skytrain, 114
Sleighbells, 76
Slip Point, 136
Smith Rocks, 106
Snake River, 4
Snohomish, 166
Snoqualmie, 148, 154
Snoqualmie Falls, 148–54, 162
Snoqualmie Falls Forest Theatre and Family
    Park, 153
Snoqualmie River, 152
Snoqualmie Valley Historical Museum, 152
Snow Goose Produce, 194
Soames Hill, 256
Sokol Blosser Vinery, 75
Sol Duc Falls, 144
Sol Duc Hot Springs Resort, 144
Sol Duc River, 137
Somenos Marsh Wildlife Refuge, 289
Sooke, 238, 241
Sooke Charter Boat Association, 239
Sooke Harbour, 239
Sooke Harbour House, 239
Sooke Potholes Provincial Park, 240
Sooke Region Museum, 238
South Beach, 126
South Fork of the Sauk River, 169
South Fork of the Stillaguamish River, 168
South North Garden, 145
South Pender, 245
Southworth, 197
Spectacle Lake Provincial Park, 292
Spirit Circle, 217
Spirit Lake, 48
Spring Lake Park, 16
Springwater Lodge, 250
Spruce Nature Trail, 145
Spruce Railroad Trail, 138
Spuzzum, 222
St. Helens, 52
St. Helens Manorhouse, 47
St. Mary's Mission, 206
St. Mary Lake, 268
St. Mary Magdalene Church, 249
St. Michael and All Angels Church, 289
Stadium Station, 117
Stanley Park, 118
Stanwood, 194
Star Center Mall, 168
Steamboat Jean, 5

Steamwords Pub and Brewery, 115
Steelhead Inn, 220
Steiger Haus, 74
Stevens Canyon, 177
Stevens Pass, 157
Stevens Pass Ski Area, 157
Stonehedge Inn, 67
Storm King Information Station, 144
Strait of Georgia, 235, 285
Strait of Juan de Fuca, 131–41, 144
Strathcona Provincial Park, 305
Strawberry Island, 230
Streamliner Diner, 183
Summerland Research Station, 276
Sumner, 182
Sunrise Point, 177
Sunriver, 104, 109
Sunriver Lodge, 104
Sunriver Nature Center, 104
Suquamish Museum, 185
Surgeon's Quarters, 84
Susie's Moped, 126
Swanson Channel, 268
Swartz Bay, 235
Sweet Home, 96
Swift Reservoir, 48
Swinomish Channel, 192

Tacoma, 200
Talking Bear Totem, 299
Tamanawas Falls, 88
Tamanawas Falls Trail, 38
Tatoosh Island, 137
Tatoosh Peaks, 177
Teahouse Restaurant, 118
Terry's Diner, 25
Terwillinger Hot Springs, 94
Theo's, 275
Third Addition, 287
Thompson River, 220
Thorp Grist Mill, 160
Three Capes Scenic Drive, 19
3-D Laser Theatre, 119
Three Fingered Jack, 102
Three Sisters, 102
Thunderbird Park, 237
Tides Inn, 270
Tides Tavern, The, 201
Tillamook, 16, 22
Tillamook Bay, 16
Tillamook Cheese Factory, 17

Tillinghast Seed Company, 193
Timberline Lodge, 36, 37
Tofino, 228, 233
Toledo, 29
totem poles, 118, 290
Townsend's Deli and Espresso, 168
Trade Bead Gallery, 28
Trail of the Cedars, 170
Trail of Two Forests, 49
Trans-Canada Water Slides, 209
Traveler's Cove Restaurant and Imports, 27
Trout House, 104
Troutdale, 70
True Value Hardware, 16
Tualitin Mountains, 76
Tualatin Valley, 71–80
Tualatin Vineyards, 73
Tugboat Annie's, 68
Tumwater Canyon, 158
Tunnel Falls, 66
Turquoise, 218
Turtleback Farm Inn, 124
Tutt Street, 277
Tyee Plaza, 301
Tygh Valley, 88
Tygh Valley Wayside, 88

Ucluelet, 234
Umbrella Falls, 37
University of British Columbia, 119
University of Oregon, 25
University of Oregon Museum of Art, 25

V

Valentino Lounge, 67
Valley Art Association, 77
Valley Cafe, 160
Van Lierop Bulb Farm, 181
Vancouver, 112–20
Vancouver Aquatic Centre, 115
Vancouver Art Gallery, 119
Vancouver Island, 225–42, 285–307
Vancouver Public Aquarium, 118
Vashon Island, 199
Verksted, 185
Vernon, 278, 283
Vesuvius Bay, 269
Vesuvius Inn, 269
ViaRail Canada, 114
Victoria, 235, 241

Vida, 99
Vigneti Zanatta, 293
Village Bay, 248
Vista House, 64
Vista Park, 58
Volume One Bookstore, 287

W

Wahkeena Falls, 64
Wahkeenah Falls, 81
Wahkiakum County Historical Museum, 59
Wahtum Lake, 66
Waikiki Beach, 56
Waldport, 28
Walla Walla, 4
Wallace Falls, 157
Wallace Falls State Park, 157
Wallalute Falls, 38
Wanapum Lake, 161
Warm Springs, 109
Warm Springs Indian Reservation, 100
Wasco, 84
Wasco County Courthouse, 83
Washington Apple Commission Visitor
    Center, 159
Washington County Museum, 73
Washington Pass Overlook, 171
Water Board Park, 98
Water Street Cafe, 115
Waterfront Centre Hotel, 116, 117
Waterfront Park, 158
Waterfront Station, 114
Waterway, The, 16
Waterwheel Park, 289
Waves, The, 15
Wayfarer, The, 14
Weddle Bridge, 96
Weeping Cedar Woman, 230
Welches, 36, 42
Wenatchee, 159
Wenatchee River, 158
West Coast Express, 211
West Coast Trail, 228, 233, 240
West End, 115
Westbank, 276
Westminster Abbey, 207
Westminster Quay, 117, 210
Weston Lake Inn, 268
Westport, 59
Westshore Acres Bulb Farm and Display
    Garden, 195
Westsound Store and Deli, 125

Whale Museum, 127
Whale watching, 20, 29, 128
Whalewatch Park, 126
Wheeler, 22
Wheeler County Courthouse, 85
Whidbey Island, 127
Whiffen Spit, 240
Whistler Basin Viewpoint, 171
White Cap Pub, 68
White River, 37
White River Falls, 88
white-water rafting, 30, 107
Wickaninnish Centre, 228
Wiegardt Brothers' Jolly Roger Oysters, 58
Wild Goose Rapids, 6
Willamette Valley, 71–80, 106
Willingdon Beach, 258
Wilson Glacier, 177
Winds of Change Interpretive Trail, 46
Windsurfing, 69
Windy Ridge Viewpoint, 48
Wine Shack, The, 14
wineries, 14, 26, 68, 71–80, 73, 71, 75, 76, 102,
    106, 155, 276, 282, 293
Winslow, 146, 183
Winslow Way Cafe, 146
Winthrop, 172, 174
Wolf Rock, 94
Woodcarver Gallery, 158
Woodland, 50
Woodstone Country Inn, 248
Workshop, The, 299

X

XA:YTEM, 207

Y

Yachats, 27, 33
Yale, 222
Yale Reservoir, 49
Yamhill, 79
Yamhill County Historical Society Museum,
    75
Yamhill Locks, 75

Z

Zigzag, 36
Zigzag Canyon, 37

ABOUT THE AUTHOR

MARILYN MCFARLANE is the author of *Best Places to Stay in the Pacific Northwest* and *Best Places to Stay in California*. Her extensive writings on travel include a weekly column, "Northwest Discoveries," for *This Week,* an Oregon newspaper. McFarlane has lived on the West Coast all her life and has explored almost every corner. She now resides in Portland, Oregon, with her attorney husband, John M. Parkhurst, and their three cats.

ABOUT THE EDITOR

CHRISTINE CUNNINGHAM is a freelance writer who has lived in Eugene, Oregon, for twenty-five years and has explored all corners of the Pacific Northwest by car and on foot.